THE SCHOOLS HISTORY PROJECT

S·H·P

OFFICIAL TEXT

DISCOVERING THE PAST FOR GCSE

GERMANY 1918–1945

a study in depth

GREG
LACEY

KEITH
SHEPHARD

Series Editor:
Colin Shephard

HODDER
EDUCATION
AN HACHETTE UK COMPANY

The Schools History Project

Set up in 1972 to bring new life to history for students aged 13-16, the Schools History Project continues to play an innovatory role in secondary history education. From the start, SHP aimed to show how good history has an important contribution to make to the education of a young person. It does this by creating courses and materials which both respect the importance of up-to-date, well -researched history and provide enjoyable learning experiences for students.

Since 1978 the project has been based at Trinity and All Saints' University College Leeds. It continues to support, inspire and challenge teachers through the annual conferance, regional courses and website: http://www.schoolshistoryproject.org.uk. The Project is also closely involved with government bodies andawarding bodies in the planning of couses for Key Stage3, GCSE and A level.

Enquiries about the *Discovering the Past* series should be addressed to the publishers, John Murray.

Series consultants
Terry Fiehn
Tim Lomas
Martin and Jenny Tucker

Note: The wording and sentence structure of some written sources have been adapted and simplified to make them accessible to all pupils, while faithfully preserving the sense of the original.

Words printed in SMALL CAPITALS are defined in the Glossary on page 163.

© Greg Lacey and Keith Shephard 1997

First published in 1997
by Hodder Education, an Hachette UK Company
338 Euston Road
London NW1 3BH

Reprinted 1997, 1998, 1999, 2000, 2001, 2002 (three times), 2003, 2004, 2005, 2006 (twice), 2008 (twice), 2009, 2010, 2011

Layouts by Amanda Hawkes
Artwork by Tom Cross, Mike Humphries and Linden Artists

Colour separations by Colourscript, Mildenhall, Suffolk

Typeset in 10^1/₂ /12pt Walbaum Book by Wearset, Boldon, Tyne and Wear
Printed and bound in Dubai

A catalogue entry for this title is available from the British Library

ISBN 978 0 719 570 59 9
Teachers' Resource Book ISBN 978 0 7195 7220 3
Dynamic Learning ISBN 978 0 340 945 834

Contents

INTRODUCTION

In this book you will be investigating German history through one of its most troubled periods – from the end of the First World War in 1918 to the end of the Second World War in 1945. It is an extraordinary period, in which Germany went through political revolution and economic chaos, and then voted into power one of the most infamous leaders in history – Adolf Hitler. In this book you will consider why these events happened and how they affected the lives of ordinary Germans.

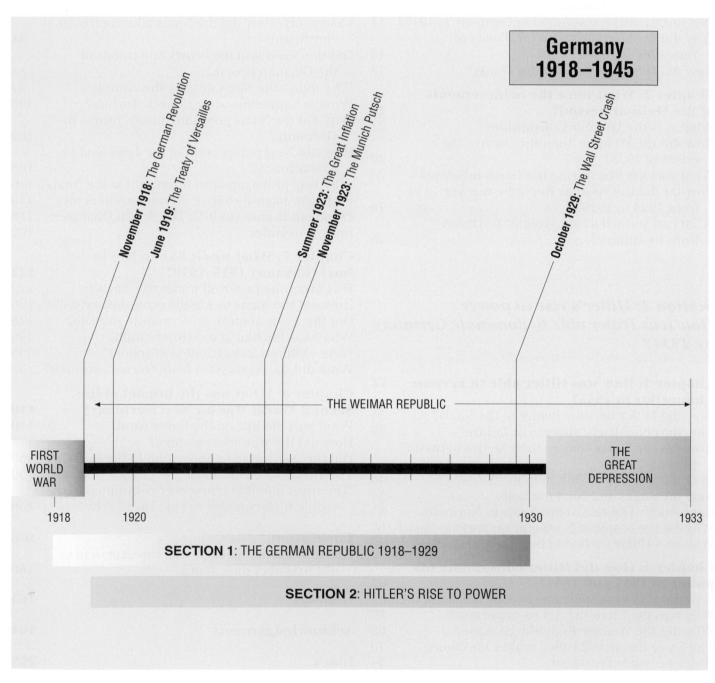

Germany 1918–1945

November 1918: The German Revolution

June 1919: The Treaty of Versailles

Summer 1923: The Great Inflation

November 1923: The Munich Putsch

October 1929: The Wall Street Crash

THE WEIMAR REPUBLIC

FIRST WORLD WAR

THE GREAT DEPRESSION

1918   1920   1930   1933

SECTION 1: THE GERMAN REPUBLIC 1918–1929

SECTION 2: HITLER'S RISE TO POWER

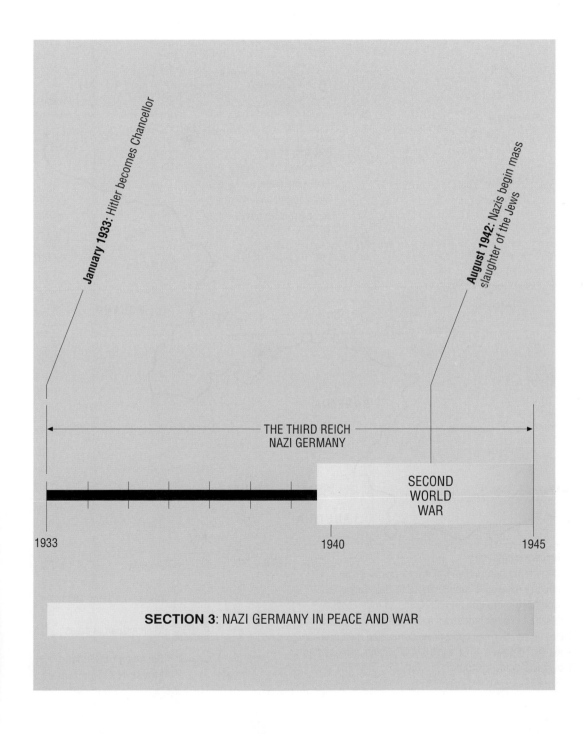

January 1933: Hitler becomes Chancellor

August 1942: Nazis begin mass slaughter of the Jews

THE THIRD REICH
NAZI GERMANY

SECOND
WORLD
WAR

1933

1940

1945

SECTION 3: NAZI GERMANY IN PEACE AND WAR

Why was Germany such an important country?

THE FOCUS OF this book is Germany from 1918 to 1945, but to see these years in context you will need to understand some of what had been going on in Germany in the previous fifty years.

SOURCE 1B The German states before 1871

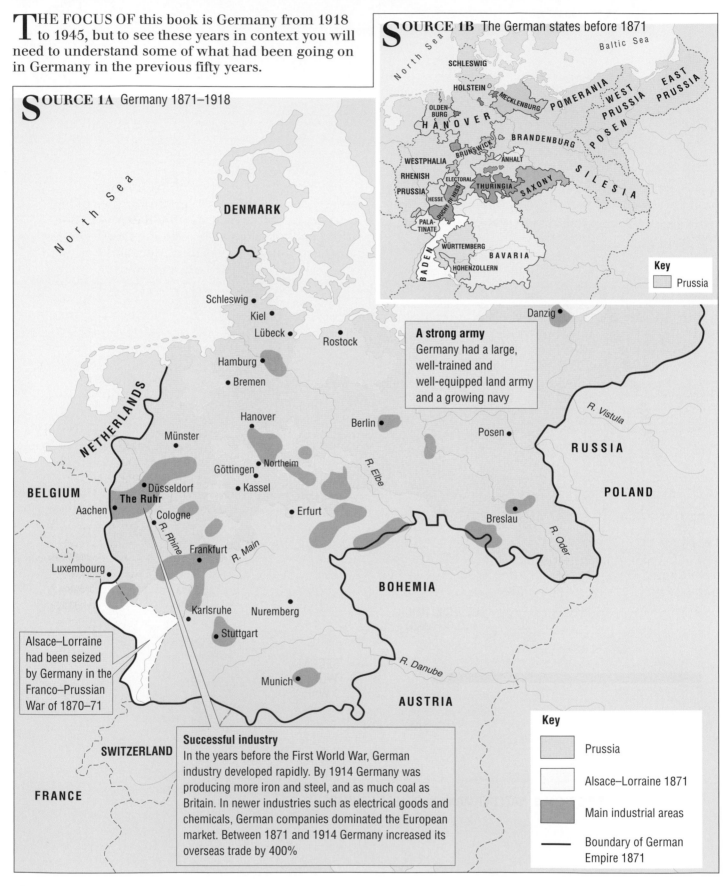

Key
Prussia

SOURCE 1A Germany 1871–1918

A strong army
Germany had a large, well-trained and well-equipped land army and a growing navy

Alsace–Lorraine had been seized by Germany in the Franco–Prussian War of 1870–71

Successful industry
In the years before the First World War, German industry developed rapidly. By 1914 Germany was producing more iron and steel, and as much coal as Britain. In newer industries such as electrical goods and chemicals, German companies dominated the European market. Between 1871 and 1914 Germany increased its overseas trade by 400%

Key

Prussia

Alsace–Lorraine 1871

Main industrial areas

Boundary of German Empire 1871

The creation of Germany

Before 1871 the area we call Germany had been made up of many separate states (see Source 1B). Prussia was the largest and strongest of these German states. In 1870–71 it defeated France in a short war. Prussia then united all these German states into the German REICH (empire).

This brought into being a new super-state which soon dominated Europe with its industrial and military power. As you can see from Source 1A, the new state covered a vast area. It had fertile farming land and rich natural resources. It had – after Russia – the second largest population of any country in Europe.

An overseas empire

All the other major European powers had an overseas empire. In the 1880s Germany started building one too. By 1914 it had colonies in Africa and the Pacific.

The German ruler

Because Prussia was the strongest state it controlled Germany, and the King of Prussia was the KAISER (emperor) of Germany. The Kaiser's chief minister was called the CHANCELLOR. Germany also had a parliament called the REICHSTAG. However, from the 1890s onwards neither the Reichstag nor the Chancellor was very powerful. Most power was in the hands of the Kaiser. He could appoint or dismiss the Chancellor. He could dissolve the Reichstag.

From 1888 the Kaiser was Wilhelm II. He was an ambitious ruler who worried other countries by his plans to build up the German armed forces. You can find out more about the Kaiser on pages 7–8.

The German people

Although Germany was made one country in 1871, regional differences remained very strong. In some areas there were big cities and flourishing industry. In the mountainous south there were many small farms. In the vast plains of north Germany you would find large farms run by rich landowners. In the north of the country almost everyone belonged to the Protestant churches. In the south there were many more Catholics.

In a country of such contrasts it is dangerous to generalise, but there are certain features of the German people which you could expect to find wherever you looked. As a result of their country's great economic success most Germans had good jobs. They could afford a healthy diet and lived in comfortable houses. By 1890 the Germans had one of the best welfare systems in Europe, including help for the unemployed and the sick. The British Prime Minister was very impressed by this when he visited Germany.

Germany had a young population – one-third of all Germans were under fifteen in 1890. The government provided good schools and by 1914 most Germans received a good education.

People in Germany were proud of their country's achievements. They were proud of all the great German writers and composers of the past. They were happy that Germany was so economically successful and had such a strong army. They wanted Germany to be seen as a leading power in Europe and in the world. In fact, some Germans were so obsessed with this that historians believe this prevented them doing enough to sort out problems at home. Anything that might cause conflict or division in Germany was swept under the carpet. Criticism of the government was not allowed, and obedience to authority – whether it be a parent, a teacher, an employer or the Kaiser – was considered to be a very good quality.

SOURCE 2 From a late nineteenth-century travel guide to Germany

❝ Some peculiarities of German manners ... A fondness for titles ... One habit of German society which occasions a smile is the need to address everybody, whether male or female, not by their own name but by the titles of the office which they hold ... even absent persons, when spoken of, are generally designated by their official titles ... All over Germany a wife insists on taking the title of her husband with a feminine termination. There is Madame General-ess, Madame privy-councillor-ess, Madame daybook-keeper-ess.

The outskirts of every German town abound in gardens and houses of public recreation, where the inhabitants, not merely of the lower orders, but of the most respectable classes also, go on summer afternoons and especially on Sunday to breathe the fresh air and forget the cares of business in the enjoyment of coffee, ices, beer and the never-absent pipe ... ❞

1. Choose words from this list which you think describe German people in around 1900: proud; humble; hard-working; lazy; well-educated; well-off; poor; wanting Germany to change; conservative.

SOURCE 3 Potsdamer Platz, Berlin, in 1898

SOURCE 4 Women preparing cucumbers for pickling in a German village, 1903

■ ACTIVITY

You have been asked to prepare further entries for the travel guide in Source 2 for a British traveller visiting Germany in the early 1900s. Write three entries giving information and advice on

- the recent history of Germany
- the German people
- another subject of your own choice.

Finally, add a description of Sources 3 and 4, including what aspects of German life they show.

Use the information on these two pages to help you.

What was Kaiser Wilhelm really like?

GERMANY WAS A powerful and influential country in the years before the First World War, so the person who ruled the country naturally excited a lot of interest. Let's see what kind of man Kaiser Wilhelm really was.

Background

Wilhelm was born in 1859. His mother was an English princess and Queen Victoria was his grandmother. He had a cold and unloving relationship with both his parents. When he became Kaiser he even had the palace surrounded by troops, not allowing his mother to leave because he suspected she would try to smuggle out his father's will and other important papers.

He was born with a badly withered left arm, but despite this he was put through rigorous physical training at a military school, and throughout his life he was obsessed with physical exercise and proving his strength.

When his grandfather died in 1888, his father became Kaiser – but only for ninety days. He died of throat cancer after three months as ruler. Suddenly and unexpectedly, at the age of 29, Wilhelm became Kaiser of Germany.

Personal qualities

He brought mixed qualities to the job. He was intelligent and well-informed, yet he would not concentrate on any idea or project for long. He wanted to make all the decisions, yet he did not want to look at the detailed information on which the decisions ought to have been based. Some psychologists have suggested he had suffered brain damage at birth which made him unable to concentrate on detail.

On the other hand, the Kaiser had a dazzling personality and he fascinated the people he met.

SOURCE 1 Written by members of the Kaiser's court

66 The last thing the Kaiser did last night was to read to us from an English magazine an article on a new theory of the origin of the world. It lasted until twelve o'clock. His interest in these things is astonishing, and while he was reading it out and when he was making his own commentaries on it, it seemed that he lived for nothing but this new idea. 99

66 In the evenings we talked – or rather the Kaiser did. I have never met a man who can remember such millions of things at the same time. 99

SOURCE 2 A portrait of the Kaiser painted in 1900. He was awarded an honorary degree by Oxford University in 1907. The Oxford University Magazine said about him in November 1907: 'He is one of the two or three most interesting personalities, perhaps the most interesting, now living'

Wilhelm liked grand display. He loved military parades. Some of his happiest times were when he was riding at the head of his regiment impressing the crowds. His court was grand and he entertained spectacularly, sometimes throwing bizarre fancy-dress parties.

He was fond of practical jokes – and could sometimes be quite cruel. He would turn the studded rings on his fingers inward, so that when he shook a visitor's hand, with his vicelike grip, he could deliver an excruciating handshake. He could also be rude. He shocked a visiting British ambassador by calling the King of Italy 'the Dwarf' and his Queen a 'peasant girl' and 'daughter of a cattle thief'.

How did he run Germany?

The Kaiser felt that his grandfather (who had been the first Kaiser) had given too much power to his ministers. The German CONSTITUTION gave the Kaiser great power, and he intended to use that power.

He did not like people to disagree with him. He soon quarrelled with his Chancellor, Bismarck, who resigned in 1890. From then on Wilhelm largely appointed ministers who would do what he wanted. If they did not, he sacked them.

SOURCE 3 The Kaiser in a speech in 1891

66 There is only one person who is master in this Empire and I am not going to tolerate any other. 99

SOURCE 4 The Kaiser in a speech to army recruits, 1891

66 You have sworn loyalty to me. You have only one enemy and that is my enemy. It may come about that I order you to shoot down your own relatives, brothers or parents, but even then you must follow my ideas without murmur. 99

He was ambitious for Germany. He was particularly keen that Germany build up a strong army and he took great pride in leading the army. He nearly always wore military dress and took an interest in all aspects of military tactics.

SOURCE 5 The Kaiser, quoted in A.N. Davis's book, *The Kaiser I Knew*

" The only nations which have progressed and become great are warring nations. Those which have not been ambitious and gone to war have been nothing. "

SOURCE 6 The opinion of a German politician of the time

" He is less of a soldier than his grandfather because he lacks the steadiness of view which only down-to-earth hard work can give. But he is convinced that he is a born leader. "

Leaders of other countries were alarmed by Wilhelm's obsession with the army and with war, particularly as it was combined with unpredictability. To many people the Kaiser was both puzzling and unreliable, as you can see from Sources 7–9.

SOURCE 7 The Crown Prince Rudolf of Austria–Hungary, writing about Wilhelm becoming Kaiser in 1888

" The Kaiser is likely to cause great confusion in Europe before long. He is just the man for it: energetic and unpredictable. He is convinced he is a genius. "

SOURCE 8 An assessment by Chancellor Bismarck, who resigned in 1890 after disagreements with Wilhelm

" The Kaiser is like a balloon ... if you don't keep hold of the string, you'll never know where he will be off to next. "

SOURCE 9 Wilhelm's friend and adviser Eulenberg, writing in the early 1900s after the Kaiser had just gone into one of his frequent tempers

" He is no longer in control of himself when he is seized by rage. I regard the situation as highly dangerous and am at a loss to know what to do ... [being with the Kaiser] is like sitting on a powder keg. "

SOURCE 10 An Italian cartoon depicting the Kaiser in the early 1900s. The caption reads 'Getting fatter – but it's too hard'

L'INGORDO
TROP DUR

1. Write down five words you could use to describe the Kaiser. Use Sources 1 and 2 and the information above.
2. What impression would it give to people that the Kaiser always wore army uniform in public?
3. Why do you think people thought the Kaiser was unreliable?
4. Compare Sources 2 and 10. Why do they give such different impressions of the Kaiser?
5. Choose the two sources from 1–9 which best support the view of the Kaiser in Source 2, and the two which best support the view in Source 10. Explain your choice.

■ TASK

Here are some qualities you might expect to find in a good leader. Give the Kaiser a score on a scale of 1–5 according to how far he had each quality.

■ Takes advice from ministers
■ Provides strong leadership
■ Is a good decision-maker
■ Is popular
■ Is reliable.

For each of your answers use evidence from these two pages to back up your score.

Write your own account of the Kaiser's strengths and weaknesses as a leader, using the information and sources on these two pages to support your judgement.

THE GERMAN REPUBLIC 1918–1929: WAS THE WEIMAR REPUBLIC DOOMED FROM THE START?

chapter 1

WHAT EFFECT DID THE FIRST WORLD WAR HAVE ON GERMANY?

IN EARLY 1918 the German people were celebrating. After years of stalemate the First World War was going their way. On the Eastern Front Russia had been defeated. The Bolshevik government had been forced to sign a humiliating peace treaty giving Germany a quarter of its best land and three-quarters of its iron ore.

A breakthrough!

German divisions were now transferred from the Eastern Front to the Western Front. They made a massive breakthrough all along the Western Front in the Ludendorff Offensive. German divisions were now, at last, advancing quickly through Belgium and northern France. Their leaders encouraged the German people to believe that victory would soon be theirs.

Reversal!

However, the Allies were stronger, and Germany weaker, than it seemed. The USA had entered the war in 1917. Every month it was sending fresh soldiers and equipment to build up the Allied forces. The German army had lost many of its best officers in earlier battles, and its soldiers were poorly supplied after years of the British naval blockade of its ports.

In **June 1918** the Ludendorff Offensive slowed, then ground to a halt.

Disaster!

In **August 1918** the Allies counter-attacked. The German army had little strength left to resist. Within a few weeks the Allies had recaptured all the land that the Germans had gained in the past three months. German territory itself was threatened.

Their army's fortunes had changed so quickly that it was difficult for most Germans to accept they were losing the war, but by **September 1918** it was clear that Germany had to make peace. All enthusiasm for the war had long since gone. Over a million German soldiers were dead and civilians faced starvation. Germany was in a desperate state, as you can see from Source 1. It could not and did not want to fight on. The Allies offered peace but on the condition that the Germans got rid of the Kaiser whom they blamed for starting the war. What would happen next?

Political effects
Germany had had political problems before the war. The Reichstag was weak. Working-class and even middle-class people had little say in the way Germany was run. There was no effective opposition to the Kaiser.

During the war this situation got worse. Opposition leaders were imprisoned. Germany was ruled as a miliary DICTATORSHIP by the Kaiser and his army leaders Ludendorff and Hindenburg. This weakened the Reichstag further.

Anarchy
Germany was extremely unstable. Armed DEMOBILISED soldiers were returning home, and joining in violent demonstrations against the war and the Kaiser.

Physical effects
Farming was disrupted because farm workers were drafted into the armed forces. By 1918 Germany was producing only 50% of the milk, and 60% of the butter and meat, which had been produced before the war. It could not make up for this by importing food because in the last two years of the war the British navy blockaded German ports, successfully preventing any food getting in. Many German people faced starvation. In the winter of 1916–17 the supply of potatoes ran out and there were only turnips left. In their weak condition civilians were vulnerable to disease. Probably three-quarters of a million German citizens died from the combined effects of hunger and disease.

Psychological effects
Before the war the Germans had been proud and ambitious for their country. They were prepared to work hard for its success. The experiences of war made many Germans bitter and angry. All the hopes of the pre-war years had been dashed. They looked around for someone to blame for defeat in the war. A society that had been famous for its unity and the obedience of its people now became famous for its squabbling and conflict.

SOURCE 1 How Germany emerged from the First World War

Was there really a revolution in Germany in 1918?

Stage 1: Getting rid of the Kaiser

It was a condition for peace that the Germans got rid of the Kaiser, but he refused to abdicate. This is how events moved during October and November 1918.

25 October 1918

Naval commanders at Kiel decided to send their ships out to fight the British fleet in one last suicidal bid for glory. Sailors mutinied.

26 October–5 November

The Kaiser and his government did not try to send the army to crush this mutiny and it was quickly followed by strikes and demonstrations against the war and the Kaiser all over Germany. Soldiers mutinied and joined the protests.

6 November 1918

By now soldiers' and workers' councils had taken control in many cities. Their main aim was to end the war, but to the politicians looking on there seemed a real danger of a total revolution, like the one which had taken place in Russia the previous year.

The Social Democrats were the leading party in the Reichstag. They were the party that the workers traditionally voted for. In theory they were socialists, committed to social change. In practice they were cautious and conservative. Their leader, Friedrich Ebert, even wanted to save the Kaiser, but his colleagues knew that if they did then more extreme left-wing revolutionaries would take over.

7 November

Social Democrat leaders sent an ultimatum to the Kaiser that unless he abdicated they would join the revolution.

9 November

There was a general strike in Berlin. Armed workers and soldiers roamed the streets.

The Social Democrats were afraid that the extremists would gain control of the revolution, so one of Ebert's colleagues announced the abdication of the Kaiser and the setting up of a German Republic which they would run in coalition with other socialist parties.

Ebert took over as Chancellor.

10 November

Kaiser Wilhelm fled into exile in Holland.

11 November 1918

An armistice was agreed between Germany and the Allies.

■ TASK

Look at Source 3. Imagine one of the people in this picture has asked you, 'Why has this happened?' Write out your answer, explaining the events that led to the abdication of the Kaiser and the setting up of the German Republic in November 1918.

SOURCE 3 After the Kaiser's abdication, some of his servants, no longer needed, leave his palace in Berlin

Stage 2: Who would control Germany?

With the Kaiser gone, the Social Democrats were in charge, but they were not in control. Germany was extremely unstable. As we have seen, armed demobilised soldiers were returning home from the front and joining in the demonstrations and violence on the streets. And there was still the threat from the extreme left-wing revolutionaries.

The left-wing revolutionaries

For left-wing revolutionaries, getting rid of the Kaiser was just the beginning. Now they wanted a real social revolution like the Russian Revolution of the previous year. They did not trust Ebert and the Social Democrats to look after the interests of working people.

The main group of revolutionaries was known as the Spartacus League, named after a famous Roman gladiator who had led a revolt in ancient Rome. The Spartacists disagreed among themselves about how to achieve the next stage of the revolution. Their leader, Rosa Luxemburg, thought that they would need to wait until workers in Germany were disillusioned with Ebert's government. But many members of the League wanted to try to seize power from the Social Democrats straight away while Berlin was still in turmoil.

SOURCE 4 A poster made by the Spartacists, entitled 'What does Spartacus want?' It shows how they intended to deal with rising militarism *(Neuer Militarismus)*, capitalism *(Kapitalismus)*, and the landowners *(Junkertum)*

Rosa Luxemburg was a revolutionary who had fled from Poland. She came to Germany in 1898. So that the police would not deport her she married a German socialist colleague, but parted from him straight after the ceremony.

She was a brilliant speaker and writer, and by the time of the First World War she was a leading socialist in Germany and had an international reputation as 'Red Rosa'.

In 1914 she split with the moderate German socialists when they expressed support for the war. She was soon imprisoned for spreading anti-war propaganda. In November 1918 she was released from prison and returned to Berlin to lead the Spartacists.

SOURCE 5 Rosa Luxemburg, Spartacist leader, speaking in 1918

❝ *The Revolution will be great and strong as long as the Social Democrats don't smash it up.* ❞

SOURCE 6 Rosa Luxemburg speaking at a socialist meeting in 1907

The Social Democrats

For the Social Democrats, getting rid of the Kaiser was the end of the revolution. Even that step had been too extreme for many of them. Their speeches were full of Marxist ideas, and they called each other 'comrade' as the Bolsheviks did. But they were actually very moderate and certainly did not want a Communist-style revolution. They were too afraid of losing the support of the rich ELITE – the landowners and industrialists who had been so important to Germany's success before the war. Their problem now was how to keep control of Germany and prevent the more extreme left-wing revolutionaries from taking over.

In a famous telephone call an army leader, General Groener, promised Ebert the support of the army in maintaining order inside Germany, and in suppressing left-wing revolutionaries. Ebert willingly accepted this offer. He also organised ex-soldiers into 'Freikorps' (volunteer corps) to help keep control. Many left-wing Independents who had supported the Social Democrats left them in protest at this.

SOURCE 7 Members of the Freikorps. These were mostly unemployed ex-soldiers with extreme right-wing views

SOURCE 8 Friedrich Ebert (right), leader of the Social Democrats and first President of the Weimar Republic from 1919 to 1923. Born in 1871, Ebert was a tailor's son and himself became a saddler. He later became a Social Democrat journalist, and then a member of the Reichstag in 1912

■ TASK

Work in pairs. One choose Ebert, the other Luxemburg. Write out how your character might have answered the following questions:

- Are you glad that the war is over?
- Was it a good idea to get rid of the Kaiser?
- What do you think of the Bolshevik Revolution in Russia?
- What is the best thing that can happen in Germany now?

Compare your answers with those of your partner:
a) Do they agree about anything?
b) What is the most serious disagreement?

The Spartacist rising: January 1919

Through December 1918 there were regular clashes between the government and the revolutionaries. Then in January 1919 some Spartacist members staged an attempted revolution in Berlin against Ebert's government.

On the night of 5 January the Spartacists captured the headquarters of the government's newspaper and the telegraph bureau, but they did not capture any other buildings. In fact, the whole uprising was badly prepared and had no hope of success. They did not get the support of the other left-wing groups. The Spartacist leaders only supported the action when it had already started.

The rising was easily crushed by the Freikorps. On 10 January they took over the Spartacist headquarters. By 15 January the Spartacists were crushed. A hundred Spartacists were killed compared to only thirteen Freikorps.

Most importantly, the Spartacist leaders, Rosa Luxemburg and Karl Liebknecht, were murdered. These murders robbed the Communists of their leaders and the movement did not recover.

Over the next four months the Freikorps crushed left-wing uprisings in many cities. They killed thousands more Communist supporters.

Ebert had succeeded in dealing with the threat to the Republic from left-wing revolutionaries, but at a high price. He had put his government into the hands of the army and the Freikorps, neither of which could be trusted to be loyal, and he had fatally undermined the position of the Social Democrats as the representatives of the working classes.

SOURCE 9 Spartacists defend the captured newspaper offices behind barricades of rolls of paper

■ TASK

Write an essay to explain whether you agree or disagree with Source 10. Use the information on pages 11–14. In your answer you should refer to the following:

■ change of governments
■ 'revolutionary noises'
■ the return to the status quo.

SOURCE 10 Imanuel Geiss, a German historian, writing in 1968

❝ According to many textbooks, a revolution is said to have taken place in Germany in November 1918.

Indeed there was turbulent change of governments in that period, there were revolutionary noises all over the place, but once the dust had settled, it soon emerged that precious little had changed in Germany. ❞

Who was to blame for the murder of Rosa Luxemburg?

After they were arrested, Luxemburg and Liebknecht were interrogated at the Freikorps' Berlin headquarters at the Eden Hotel and then taken away, supposedly to prison. As they left the hotel, they were hit on the head by a rifle butt wielded by a soldier named Runge and then dragged into separate cars.

Liebknecht was forced out of the car as it passed through the Tiergarten (a park), and was shot for 'trying to escape'. His body was then delivered to a mortuary without any information to identify it.

Luxemburg was shot by a Lieutenant Vogel and her body thrown into a canal, where it remained undiscovered until May.

When Ebert heard of the murders he was, according to eye-witnesses, sincerely horrified and angry. He had not even been informed of the arrest of Liebknecht and Luxemburg. Only that day he had issued instructions for Liebknecht's wife – another revolutionary – to be released.

Ebert ordered an investigation into the murders.

■ TASK

You have been asked to investigate the murders of Luxemburg and Liebknecht. You know who actually killed them, but your task is to decide if anyone else should share the blame. Use Sources 11–16 and the information on the past three pages to answer the following questions:

1. Were the Freikorps acting on orders from the government?
2. Did the government in any way encourage the Freikorps to murder Rosa Luxemburg?
3. Were the Spartacists themselves to blame for the murders?

SOURCE 11 A declaration by the government's Minister of Defence, early January 1919

&& Workers! The government has entrusted me with the leadership of the republican soldiers. You know me and my history in the Party . . . I promise that no unnecessary blood will be spilt. I am to cleanse, not destroy. With the new republican army I want to bring you freedom and peace. The working class must stand united against the Spartacists if democracy and socialism are not to be lost. 99

SOURCE 12 Rosa Luxemburg's instructions to the Spartacists, January 1919. Luxemburg was actually not in favour of a revolution at this stage. However, at meetings the Spartacists gave revolutionary speeches which worried the government greatly

&& Act! Act! Courageously, decisively and constantly . . . disarm the counter-revolution, arm the masses, occupy all positions of power. Act quickly! 99

SOURCE 13 From an article in a government newspaper, early January 1919

&& The despicable actions of Liebknecht and Rosa Luxemburg soil the revolution and endanger all its achievements. The masses must not sit quiet for one minute longer while these brutal beasts and their followers paralyse the activities of the republican government and incite the people more and more to civil war. 99

SOURCE 14 The opinion of German historian H. Heiber in his book *The Weimar Republic*, 1993

&& The government had not only given its approval to the forming of the Freikorps, but had participated actively in forming them. Those troops who were available for the purpose were for the most part men who had no homes and no jobs to go to, or who were reluctant to return to civilian life. All these Freikorps pursued their own policies, and very soon ceased to take any notice of the military leadership. They certainly took not the slightest notice of the despised democratic ministers. 99

SOURCE 15 Members of the Freikorps at the Eden Hotel on the day after Luxemburg's murder. One of her murderers, Runge, is sitting at the table (centre), with the dark moustache

SOURCE 16 Spartacist demonstrators carrying placards showing their murdered leaders, January 1919

Lieutenant Vogel was convicted of failing to report a death and of illegally disposing of a corpse. He had no difficulty in obtaining a false passport and crossing the Dutch border. After waiting in Holland for a few months he returned to Germany. He was never imprisoned. Private Runge served a sentence of several months for 'attempted manslaughter'.

Why did the Germans hate the Treaty of Versailles so much?

JUST FOUR DAYS after the Spartacist Uprising was crushed Germany held a general election. In the new National Assembly the Social Democrats were the largest party, and Ebert was the first President of the new Weimar Republic. It was called this because the government met in the town of Weimar – the capital Berlin was considered too unstable a place for it to meet.

As you have already seen, the Social Democrats had their work cut out just keeping control of Germany. But they also had another big problem – negotiating a peace treaty to end the First World War.

What kind of treaty were the Germans expecting?

After the First World War the Germans knew they would have to pay a price for peace. However, they had several reasons for hoping that the peace treaty would not be a harsh one.

The Kaiser had gone: Germany had a new democratic government
One of the Allies' conditions for peace was that the Kaiser be removed and democratic government be brought in. By January 1919 the Germans had already fulfilled that requirement. The revolution had overthrown the Kaiser. The new government was democratically elected. It could not be blamed for the war.

The new republic needed support
The Social Democrat leaders expected they would have great problems settling Germany down after the chaos of war and revolution. They assumed that the Allies would want to help them and give their new government a good chance to establish itself. A harsh treaty would make it far more difficult for them to create a stable government.

President Wilson believed in a fair treaty
President Wilson of the USA was to be the main force in the treaty negotiations. He believed that the treaty should not be too harsh on Germany. He said that if the treaty punished Germany too greatly it might one day recover and want revenge. He had declared 'Fourteen Points' that he believed should be features of a just and fair treaty.

Germany was not to blame for the war
Most Germans felt that all countries should bear equal blame for the First World War. In their view, Germany had been forced into war by the way it was treated by other countries. They did not expect to be punished as if they were the guilty party.

What kind of treaty did the Germans get?

When the Allies assembled at Versailles in 1919 to draw up the treaty, it soon became clear that the Germans were not going to get what they hoped for. Despite Wilson's hopes the emphasis seemed to be on punishing Germany. The French, in particular, wanted a peace which would weaken Germany so much that there would be no chance of it attacking France in the future.

Germany was not invited to the negotiations. The treaty was agreed by the Allies and then presented to Germany for signing. When the Germans refused to sign it they were told that if they did not sign, war would start again.

Finally, Germany had no choice but to accept. On 28 June 1919 the German representatives reluctantly signed the Treaty. But they called it 'the shameful diktat of Versailles'. Source 1 shows the terms of the Treaty.

■ ACTIVITY

To most Germans, these terms were humiliating and unfair. It is 29 June 1919. Plan out a full-page feature for a German newspaper, summarising the main points and explaining why these terms are unfair to Germany.

SOURCE 1 The terms of the Treaty of Versailles

War guilt

Article 231 of the Treaty said that Germany was to blame for causing the war. This was the term that the Germans most resented. To them the war had been one of self-defence.

Reparations

As Germany was held to be responsible for the war, the Allies could claim REPARATIONS (compensation) for damage caused by the war. In 1921 a special commission fixed a sum of £6600 million to be paid in annual instalments. Given that the Treaty also took away from Germany around 10% of its industry and 15% of its agricultural land, there was great doubt as to whether Germany could actually afford this.

Military restrictions

The French desire for security meant that the German armed forces had to be drastically reduced.

- The air force had to be disbanded
- The army was limited to 100,000 soldiers
- The navy was limited to 15,000 sailors, only six battleships and no submarines
- The Rhineland would be occupied by the Allies for fifteen years, and no German troops allowed in the area.

For a great power like Germany, these changes would reduce its armed forces to a humiliatingly low level.

Territorial losses

Germany lost 13% of its land, which contained about six million of its people.

- Alsace–Lorraine was returned to France
- West Prussia and Posen (the Polish Corridor) were lost to Poland
- After PLEBISCITES (votes) in 1920–21 by the people who lived there, the following areas were also lost:
  - Eupen and Malmedy to Belgium
  - Northern Schleswig to Denmark
  - Part of Upper Silesia to Poland
  - Danzig was taken over by the League of Nations as a free city
  - Memel was taken over by the League but was eventually taken by Lithuania in 1923
  - The Saarland was taken over by the League of Nations for fifteen years. There would then be a plebiscite to determine its future.

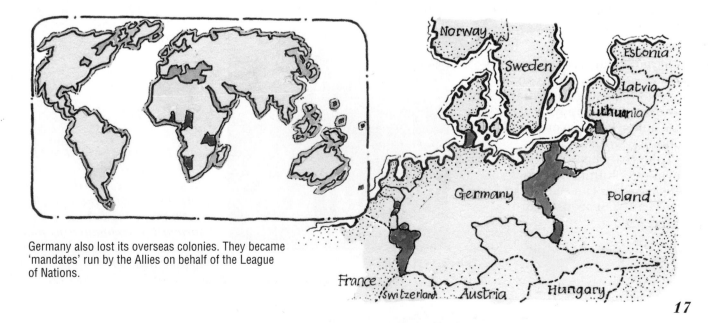

Germany also lost its overseas colonies. They became 'mandates' run by the Allies on behalf of the League of Nations.

WHEN THE TERMS of the Treaty first became known, the German government refused to sign it, and resigned. It was a hopeless gesture. The Allies made it clear that if the Germans did not sign, they would resume the war.

A new government was formed which did agree to sign the Treaty. It did not believe that the Treaty was fair any more than the previous government did, but knew it had no choice. As responsible politicians they had to sign. To allow war to restart would be suicidal for Germany.

But from the moment the Treaty was signed, many promised to do all they could to overthrow it.

The 'Stab in the Back' myth

The Treaty of Versailles greatly weakened the new government of Germany. It suited many Germans to believe that Germany had never really lost the war. Army leaders like Ludendorff encouraged this view. He said the army would have fought on to preserve Germany's honour, if only weak politicians and Communist revolutionaries had not demanded peace.

A powerful myth developed which said that the army had been 'stabbed in the back' by weak politicians. Right-wingers who looked back fondly to the pre-war days when Germany was powerful were happy to blame the new democratic government for making peace.

The Treaty became a symbol of Germany's humiliation and defeat. As you can see from Sources 1–8, it aroused strong feelings.

SOURCE 1

SOURCE 2

The Tiger: "Curious! I seem to hear a child weeping!"

SOURCE 3

OURCE 5

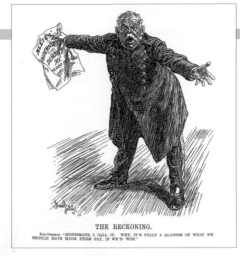

THE RECKONING.

Pan-German. "MONSTROUS, I CALL IT. WHY, IT'S FULLY A QUARTER OF WHAT WE SHOULD HAVE MADE THEM PAY, IF WE'D WON."

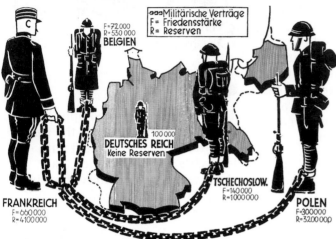

SOURCE 6

A From the newspaper *Deutsche Zeitung* (German News) on the day the Treaty was signed

B A French poster showing the French Prime Minister Clemenceau washing away Germany's crimes

C A cartoon from a German magazine attacking the Treaty of Versailles. It shows the leaders of Britain, France and the USA preparing to punish Germany

D A Nazi propaganda cartoon showing Germany, its army limited by the Versailles Treaty, surrounded by hostile neighbours

E A German cartoon protesting against the REPARATIONS payments. The caption read 'Germany, work! The liars blamed us for the war. Now they also burden us with reparations'

F A British cartoon printed at the time of the Treaty. It shows the leaders of Britain, France (Clemenceau was nicknamed 'The Tiger'), the USA and Italy leaving the peace discussions. The '1940 class' was those who would be called up into the armed forces in 1940

G A cartoon which appeared in the British magazine, *Punch*, after the reparations payments had been announced

H A protest march in Berlin, May 1919, by Germans living in areas to be lost by Germany in the Treaty of Versailles

SOURCE 7

SOURCE 8

■ **TASK**

1. Look at Sources 1–8. They are all reactions to the Treaty of Versailles. Work with a partner to match each source to one of the captions.

2. Look at the German sources. List their criticisms of the Treaty.

3. Using the information on pages 16–19 explain why the Germans found it so hard to accept the terms of the Treaty.

4. 'The Treaty of Versailles was unfair.' Write an essay to explain whether you agree or disagree. If you think it was fair, support your answer by referring to at least three terms from the Treaty. If you think it was unfair, suggest three aspects of the Treaty which you would change.

The aftermath of the Treaty – the Kapp Putsch

From the start, many Germans resented the Treaty. This resentment posed a great threat to the stability of the Weimar Republic. Of all the groups in Germany who were unhappy with the Treaty, the army was the most important. It hated the restrictions placed on it, and blamed the government for having agreed to them. The army was reduced, but many of the demobbed soldiers simply joined the Freikorps.

By early 1920 the Allies were getting worried by the size of these unofficial forces. They put pressure on Germany to disband them, so as to obey the limit of 100,000 men required by the Treaty. In March 1920, when the government tried to do this, Freikorps units led by Wolfgang Kapp marched into Berlin and declared a new national government. The army did not stop them.

Ebert's government had returned to Berlin after its success in the first elections following the founding of the Republic. Now it was forced to flee to Dresden. Realising that they would not be saved by the army, politicians appealed to the workers to help them.

SOURCE 11 Transport chaos caused by the general strike in Berlin, 1920

SOURCE 9 An appeal by the Social Democrats, March 1920

66 *We refuse to buckle under to this military pressure. We did not bring about the revolution to make this bloody Freikorps regiment legal.*

Workers! Comrades! . . . Go on strike, put down your work and stop the military dictatorship. There is only one way to prevent the return of Kaiser Wilhelm II: shut down the economy! **99**

■ TASK

The government faced opposition from extremists on both the right and the left wing. To deal with left-wing extremists they used right-wingers, to deal with right-wing extremists they used left-wingers.

1. Find an example of each of these approaches on pages 13–20.
2. Do you think this was a good policy? Explain your answer.

This general strike was so successful that Kapp's PUTSCH collapsed within days as public services ground to a halt. However, those who had participated in the putsch were never punished for their actions. Without the support of the army, the government could do little against them.

SOURCE 10 The Kapp Putsch. Putsch troops on the Potsdamer Platz in Berlin wearing helmets with swastikas

chapter 2

WHAT WERE THE ACHIEVEMENTS OF THE WEIMAR PERIOD?

What was the Weimar Constitution?

ALL COUNTRIES HAVE rules for how they are to be governed. These rules are called a constitution. Sometimes the rules are written down, sometimes not. In a country like Germany in 1919, which had just got rid of one system of government – the Kaiser's – and was trying to establish a new one, deciding on a new constitution was very important.

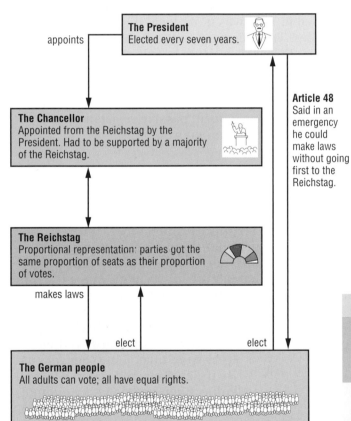

The President
Elected every seven years.

appoints

Article 48
Said in an emergency he could make laws without going first to the Reichstag.

The Chancellor
Appointed from the Reichstag by the President. Had to be supported by a majority of the Reichstag.

The Reichstag
Proportional representation: parties got the same proportion of seats as their proportion of votes.

makes laws

elect   elect

The German people
All adults can vote; all have equal rights.

The states kept their own governments, but with reduced powers. National laws could overrule state laws.

■ TASK

The chart on the right shows the strengths and weaknesses of the Constitution. Add another two rows explaining the strengths and weaknesses of the plans for

■ the Chancellor's role
■ Article 48.

Did the Constitution make the Republic weak?

The Constitution was a brave attempt to set up a genuinely democratic government. However, some historians have argued that weaknesses in the Constitution made it harder for the Republic to cope with all the difficulties it had to face.

In 1919 Germany was clearly a very divided country. The careful balance of power had dangers in a country so split in political opinion, and quite unaccustomed to the 'give and take' of democratic politics. Never in German history had one party taken over from another peacefully after an election. Politicians had no experience of making democracy work, and many influential Germans had very little commitment to democracy.

◄**SOURCE 1** The main features of the Weimar Constitution which was agreed by the National Assembly, July 1919

Strengths	Weaknesses
All Germans had equal rights, including the right to vote.	In 1919 the Republic had many enemies. It was not sensible to give equal rights to those who wished to destroy it.
Proportional representation made sure that political parties were allocated seats in Parliament in proportion to the number of votes they got. This was fair.	Proportional representation encouraged lots of small parties which each got a small number of MPs. No one party could get a majority, so governments had to be coalitions. There could never be a strong government.
A strong president was necessary to keep control over the government and to protect the country in a crisis.	The president had too much power. It was possible he could turn himself into a dictator.
Each state had its own traditions. It was right they should keep some control over their own affairs.	The states could be hostile to the national government, and even try to overthrow it.

DURING ITS FIRST few years the new German government faced many crises. It was working in very tough conditions: trying to stabilise Germany; rebuilding the country after the ravages of the First World War and, to cap it all, having to cope with the problems caused by the Treaty of Versailles. The new government's problems came to a head in 1923.

Crisis 1: The occupation of the Ruhr

Germany did not keep up with its reparations payments, and the French were determined to make the Germans pay, if necessary by seizing raw materials like coal for themselves. In January French and Belgian troops marched into the Ruhr, Germany's most important industrial region, and occupied it. This was quite legal under the Treaty of Versailles. The Germans in the Ruhr responded with a policy of passive resistance, which meant refusing to have anything to do with the French and, in particular, refusing to work. The problem was that Germany was now losing all that the Ruhr would normally have produced; passive resistance was making Germany even poorer.

Crisis 2: Inflation

The German government did not have enough money to pay for the costs of the passive resistance in the Ruhr, so it simply printed more. When a government prints money which it does not have, the value of money goes down and prices go up. This had been happening in Germany since the time of the Kaiser, but in 1923 it got much worse.

This was HYPERINFLATION. The effects were disastrous as you can see from pages 24–25. People who had worked hard all their lives were turned into beggars as their pensions and savings lost all value. Even people lucky enough to have a job found that wages could not keep up with the helter-skelter rise in prices.

People did not blame the Kaiser's war government which had started the inflation by its borrowing; instead they blamed the Weimar government, which had agreed to pay reparations under the Versailles Treaty.

Hände weg vom Ruhrgebiet!

SOURCE 1 A German poster from 1923. The text means 'Hands off the Ruhr!'

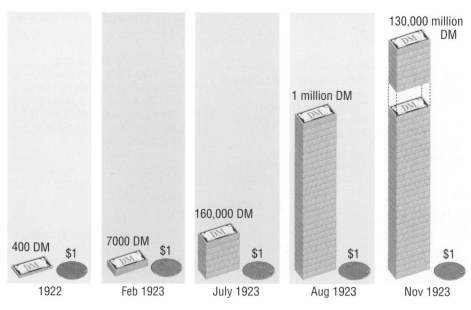

400 DM — $1 — 1922
7000 DM — $1 — Feb 1923
160,000 DM — $1 — July 1923
1 million DM — $1 — Aug 1923
130,000 million DM — $1 — Nov 1923

SOURCE 2 The value of the German mark against the dollar from 1922 to November 1923

Crisis 3: The Munich (Beer Hall) Putsch

In September 1923 the Chancellor, Stresemann, decided that Germany would have to give in to France. He ended the policy of passive resistance in the Ruhr. To those who hated the Republic, and particularly to the gangs of right-wing extremists who had made the southern state of Bavaria their base, Stresemann's decision was a betrayal. Encouraged by the government of Bavaria, they plotted a putsch against the Reich government. On 8–9 November Adolf Hitler's National Socialist (Nazi) Party launched an attempted revolution in Munich, the capital city of Bavaria. It was easily crushed by the army and the police, but it was yet another example of the violent political extremism which lay just beneath the surface of the Weimar Republic. You can find out more about the putsch on pages 38–43.

You can find out more about the putsch on pages 38–43.

■ TASK

Source 3 shows how the Weimar government dealt with the crises of 1923.

1. For each action, explain how it helped the government survive.
2. Draw a diagram to show how the actions are connected to each other.
3. Is one action more important than others in helping the government survive?
4. Now write your own balanced explanation of how the government survived the crises of 1923.

SOURCE 3 How the Weimar Republic dealt with the crises of 1923

In August 1923 Stresemann became Chancellor. He was willing to call off the policy of passive resistance. The policy was bankrupting Germany, but it took courage to abandon it as many felt he was giving in to France.

In October the government scrapped the old, worthless money, and introduced a new, temporary currency, the Rentenmark. By strictly limiting the amount of this currency in circulation the value of German money was stabilised, and in the next year a new permanent currency, the Reichsmark, was brought in.

To keep the support of the army, who were strongly right-wing, the government gave orders that left-wing state governments in Saxony and Thuringia should be deposed. Once this was done it was much easier for the government to get the army to act against the much more dangerous right-wing nationalists in Bavaria.

In November the German government agreed to resume payment of reparations. The Allies then set up a committee under an American banker, Charles Dawes, to resolve the problems of how Germany was going to pay. The Dawes Plan of April 1924 made a huge loan available to Germany. The idea was that the money would help rebuild German trade and industry. Money would then flow into the German government and they could pay regular reparations.

What was life like during the Great Inflation?

THE INFLATION AFFECTED people in different ways.

- Old people living on fixed pensions, or people who lived on their savings, found that these were now worthless.
- Workers, as long as they had a job, were to some extent protected, because they were simply paid higher and higher wages. Even unemployment benefit increased weekly.
- Those who had debts, or had taken out loans, actually benefited. They could pay the money back at a fraction of the real cost.
- The rich, who had not just money but land, possessions and foreign currency, were also protected.
- Many rich businessmen were able to take advantage of the situation by taking over smaller companies which were going bankrupt. In the end, though, inflation was so rapid that normal business and trade became impossible, which caused much unemployment.

The real losers of the Great Inflation were not the poor who had little to lose anyway, or the rich who found ways to protect their wealth. The real losers were the middle classes who saw their savings and businesses destroyed.

Sources 1–9 are recollections by people who lived in Germany in 1923.

SOURCE 1 A woman who ran a Quaker relief centre, which offered help to the poor

66 [There was] the widow of a policeman who was left with four children. She had been awarded three months of her late husband's salary. The papers were sent on, as required, to Wiesbaden. There they were again checked, rubber-stamped and sent back to Frankfurt. By the time all this was done, and the money finally paid out to the widow, the amount would only have paid for three boxes of matches. 99

SOURCE 2 A writer remembering the effects of the inflation on his father

66 My father had sold his business during the war, together with all the real-estate property he owned, and retired from business. He was, by middle-class standards, a rich man, and intended to live on the income from his investments. These were mainly life-insurance policies, fixed-value securities and a mortgage on a large agricultural estate, whose yield of 15,000 marks per annum would have provided a very good income. All this depreciated, of course, to zero – my father only managed to keep his head above water by resuming work. 99

SOURCE 3 A worker in a transport firm in Berlin

66 I vividly remember pay-days at that time. I used to have to accompany the manager to the bank in an open six-seater Benz which we filled to the brim with bundles and bundles of million and milliard mark notes. We then drove back through the narrow streets quite unmolested. And when they got their wages, the workmen did not even bother to count the number of notes in each bundle. 99

SOURCE 4 The memories of a German writer

66 A German landowner bought, on credit, a whole herd of valuable cattle. After a certain time he sold one cow from the herd. Because of the depreciation of the mark, the price he got for it was enough to pay off the whole cost of the herd. 99

SOURCE 5 A man whose father owned a small business

66 My father began to pay wages largely in goods, mostly foodstuffs. My mother stacked these in the flat where we lived. Livestock, such as chickens, was kept in the bathroom and on the balcony. Flour, fats etc. were bought in bulk as soon as money became available. My mother had to parcel all this food out in rough proportion to the employee's entitlement. Come pay-day the workforce assembled in the flat in groups for their handouts. 99

SOURCE 6 The memories of a German writer

66 One fine day I dropped into a café to have a coffee. As I went in I noticed the price was 5000 marks – just about what I had in my pocket. I sat down, read my paper, drank my coffee, and spent altogether about one hour in the café, and then asked for the bill. The waiter duly presented me with a bill for 8000 marks. 'Why 8000 marks?' I asked. The mark had dropped in the meantime, I was told. So I gave the waiter all the money I had, and he was generous enough to leave it at that. 99

SOURCE 7 The memories of a German writer

❝ Two women were carrying a laundry basket filled to the brim with banknotes. Seeing a crowd standing round a shop window, they put down the basket for a moment to see if there was anything they could buy. When they turned round a few moments later, they found the money there untouched. But the basket was gone. ❞

SOURCE 8 A German man who was a student at the time of the Great Inflation

❝ You very often bought things you did not need. But with those things in hand you could start to barter. You went round and exchanged a pair of shoes for a shirt, or a pair of socks for a sack of potatoes. And this process was repeated until you eventually ended up with the things you actually wanted. ❞

SOURCE 9 A currency dealer

❝ It was in many ways a cheerful time for the young. When I grew up we were taught to save money and not throw it away. But in the worst days of the inflation this principle was turned upside down. We knew that to hold on to money was the worst thing we could do. So this allowed us, with a good conscience, to spend whatever we had available. ❞

■ TASK

1. Look through Sources 1–11. Find at least three people who benefited from the Great Inflation and three who suffered.
2. Explain how the following people would have been affected by the inflation. Support your answer with reference to Sources 1–11.
   a) An old woman with a fixed pension, living alone
   b) A boy who had just left school and was looking for a job
   c) A businessman who employed a hundred people
   d) An American journalist living and working in Germany, but paid in dollars.
3. Choose one person from the sources who was badly affected by the Great Inflation and explain how their experiences might have changed their attitude towards the government.

SOURCE 10 Children playing with worthless banknotes

SOURCE 11 Two young women with a bag of flour they have just paid for using the family silver

How far did the Weimar Republic recover from 1924 to 1929?

STRESEMANN SAW THE Republic out of the crises of 1923, but his fragile coalition government could not keep the support of the Reichstag. Stresemann was too right-wing for the socialists and too moderate for the nationalists. However, he was very able and was a member of every government from 1923 until his death in 1929. Although he was only Chancellor for a few months, he remained the most influential politician in Germany as the government attempted to recover from the disasters of the early 1920s.

Foreign policy

Stresemann was Foreign Minister from 1924 to 1929.

> **SOURCE 1** A letter from Stresemann to the Kaiser's son, September 1925
>
> *In my opinion there are three great tasks that confront German foreign policy in the immediate future:*
>
> 1. *The solution of the reparations problem in a way that is tolerable for Germany.*
> 2. *The protection of those ten to twelve million Germans who now live under foreign control in foreign lands.*
> 3. *The readjustment of our eastern frontiers; the recovery of Danzig, the Polish Corridor, and a correction of the frontier in Upper Silesia.*

> **SOURCE 2** Chancellor Marx in a speech in the Reichstag, February 1927
>
> *The foreign policy which the government has pursued since the end of the war rejects the idea of revenge. Its purpose is rather the achievement of a mutual understanding.*

1. Why might Stresemann be writing to the Kaiser's son (Source 1)?
2. Do Sources 1 and 2 give the same impression of Weimar foreign policy? Explain any differences you notice.

Stresemann was responsible for a series of foreign policy successes. In 1925 Germany signed the Locarno Treaties with Britain, France and Italy. They guaranteed Germany's frontiers with France and Belgium. Stresemann avoided giving any guarantees over Germany's eastern frontiers.

In 1926 Stresemann took Germany into the League of Nations. Its status as a great power was recognised as it was given a permanent seat on the League's Council alongside Britain and France.

In 1929 the Young Plan produced a final agreement on the issue of reparations. As a result, Allied occupation forces were withdrawn from the Rhineland area of Germany.

SOURCE 3 A British cartoon showing the French, German and British foreign ministers joining hands in the Locarno Pact. The French politician, Briand, is wearing a boxing glove, prepared to deal Germany a knock-out blow

Political problems

During the years of the Weimar Republic no single party ever won a majority of seats in the Reichstag. Up to 1930 the Social Democrats always won the most votes, but never enough to govern on their own. So governments had to be formed from coalitions of parties working together. Sometimes these coalitions did not work well, and the governments were therefore unstable. There were twenty-five separate governments in fourteen years. Some governments lasted only a few weeks. Stresemann hoped that successes in foreign policy would make it easier for the political parties in Germany to work together. This did not happen.

Many nationalists opposed Stresemann's policies as being too cautious. They wanted to reject the Versailles Treaty completely, not just have it revised. All the centre and right-wing parties were suspicious of the Social Democrats. Parties such as the Communists and the Nazis made no secret of their wish to overthrow the Weimar Republic entirely.

In 1925 Hindenburg was elected President. He had been one of Germany's war leaders under the Kaiser and was a prominent critic of the Weimar Republic. This showed how weak support for the Republic was amongst the German people. Hindenburg represented old Germany. Before he took up the post of President, he actually asked the permission of the ex-Kaiser Wilhelm!

On the other hand, the period 1924–29 saw more stable governments. After the 1928 election the Social Democrats, for the first time since 1923, joined a government coalition with the other parties committed to the Republic. This showed that the middle-class parties were no longer so suspicious of the socialists.

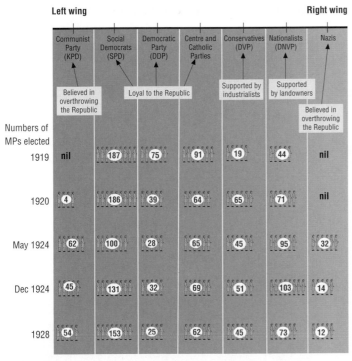

SOURCE 4 Political parties in the Weimar Republic

The economy

The inflation of 1923 had destroyed people's savings, so there was little money in Germany itself for investment. In 1924, through the Dawes Plan, Germany was lent 800 million marks by the USA to invest in industry and commerce. The economy began to recover. In 1928 industrial production finally surpassed pre-First World War levels. By 1930 Germany was one of the world's leading exporters of manufactured goods.

However, the German economy still had serious weaknesses.

- It depended on American loans which could be withdrawn at any time
- Unemployment was a serious problem. The economy might be growing, but it wasn't creating jobs fast enough for Germany's rising population
- Employers complained about the money the government spent on welfare benefits for the poor and unemployed. They said taxes were too high

- Some sectors of the economy were in trouble throughout the 1920s, farming in particular. Income from agriculture went down from 1925 to 1929. Farmworkers' earnings were, by 1929, little more than half the national average
- There were extremes of wealth and poverty in Germany
- There was still a concentration of power in the hands of just a few industrialists who ran more than half of Germany's industry.

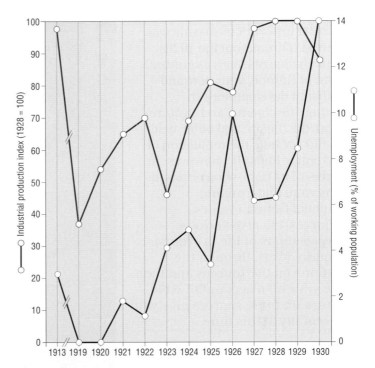

SOURCE 5 Graph showing changes in industrial output and unemployment

■ TASK

It is 1929. You have been asked to write a confidential report for the Chancellor on the current health of the Weimar Republic.

Using the following three headings, explain how far Germany's situation has improved since 1924.

- Relations with other countries
- Politics
- The economy.

Mention which problems have been solved and which remain unsolved by 1929.

Of the problems which have not been solved, which do you think is the most serious? Explain your answer.

What can you tell about Weimar Germany from its culture?

THE 1920S WERE a time of turmoil and anxiety for many Germans. As well as having to come to terms with defeat in the war and the losses imposed by the Treaty of Versailles, they had to cope with political and economic problems such as the rebellions of 1919 and 1920 and the inflation of 1923. Yet out of this time of tension came some of the most innovative and exciting art and culture in Europe. The strict pre-war CENSORSHIP was removed. Throughout the 1920s Berlin challenged Paris as cultural capital of Europe, with new and significant developments in painting, the cinema, architecture, design, the theatre and other fields. This did not help the reputation of the Weimar Republic, however; in the eyes of its right-wing critics, its artists were undermining traditional German values.

Sources 1–5 give various interpretations of life in Weimar Germany. Work through the questions on the sources and then write your own account of what impression these sources give you of Germany at this time.

Painting

Before the war most German art had been detached from everyday life. In contrast, most Weimar artists tried to show everyday life; they wanted to be understood by ordinary people, and they believed that art should comment on the society of the time. This new approach was given the name 'Neue Sachlichkeit' or 'new objectivity' because artists tried to portray society in an objective way. New objectivity was particularly associated with painters such as George Grosz and Otto Dix.

SOURCE 1 *Grey Day* by George Grosz, 1921. Grosz had been wounded in the war and often shows war disabled in his paintings, along with robot- or doll-like figures who seem to have no control over their lives. His characters are placed in hectic and depressing cities. He joined the Communist Party in 1918 but remained pessimistic about the chances of social improvement. In the same year as he completed this painting, he was taken to court on a charge of insulting the German army. The man with the moustache is wearing a badge which shows he supports the monarchy, not the Republic

1. This picture contains a number of symbolic characters. Who or what do you think each of them represents?

SOURCE 2 *Big City* by Otto Dix, 1927–28. Dix lived in the cities of Dresden, Düsseldorf and Berlin during the 1920s. He searched for personalities he could include in his paintings to show the uglier side of human nature. He said that it was his wartime experiences which had made him aware of this. The central panel shows a nightclub with a jazz band playing to fashionably dressed, middle-class urban people. The other two panels show the revellers on their way home, confronted by the other side of city life

2. What is Dix's attitude to the urban middle class? Explain your answer with reference to Source 2.
3. What do Sources 1 and 2 have in common?

Cinema

This was a golden age for German cinema with its best-known director Fritz Lang producing epic films such as *Metropolis*, which was the most technically advanced film of the decade.

German actress Marlene Dietrich became one of the most popular film stars in the world playing strong, mysterious and glamorous women.

4. Why do you think that the film shown in Source 3 would appeal to

■ men
■ women

in Weimar Germany?

SOURCE 3 A poster for the film *The Blue Angel*, starring Marlene Dietrich. The story is set before the war and concerns the obsession of a university professor with a cabaret singer called Lola

29

Architecture

A new group of architects and designers emerged called the Bauhaus. They designed anything from chairs, built-in cupboards and cigarette kiosks to town halls and enormous housing estates. Their slogan was 'Art and Technology – a new unity'. Their approach was very different from the elaborate and decorative style of pre-war Germany.

> **SOURCE 4** The aims of the Bauhaus, described by Walter Gropius, one of its leading figures
>
> *66 A welcoming attitude to vehicles and machines*
> *Avoiding all decoration*
> *Using only basic shapes and colours*
> *Economy in the use of space, materials, time and money*
> *Simplicity 99*

SOURCE 5 An apartment block designed by Bauhaus architects for a housing estate in Stuttgart

1. Look at Source 5. Which of the ideas in Source 4 have been realised?

Theatre

Theatre and opera had long attracted large audiences in Germany, but most performances were of classical works. In the 1920s these gave way to *Zeittheater* and *Zeitoper* – literally theatre and opera 'of the time'. These works were set in the society of the time and included greater realism – the heroine of one opera sings an aria in the bathtub! In Erwin Piscator's *The Salesman of Berlin* three street-sweepers sweep away the 'rubbish' of the early 1920s – a pile of paper money, a steel helmet (representing Germany's defeated army) and the body of the man who had worn it. In Piscator's adaptation of Jaroslav Hasek's novel *The Good Soldier Schweik*, the hero delivers his criticisms of Germany as he sits on the toilet.

Cabaret and nightlife

Berlin became famous for its nightlife. Alongside the theatres and cinemas was a vibrant nightclub scene with daring floor shows, risqué songs and naked dancing. To someone who had lived in Berlin before the war it would have seemed very experimental, but also very shocking.

Berlin was also famous for its transvestite balls. Hundreds of men in women's clothes and women in men's clothes danced together. Sex was discussed openly, and homosexuality, which had been treated as taboo before the war, was – at least in Berlin – no longer frowned upon.

The backlash

These sources might give the impression of a vibrant, creative society. However, as with so many other features of Weimar Germany, there was tension and conflict just below the surface. On the whole, the daring lifestyle and ideas which characterised 1920s Berlin were not to be found in other parts of Germany, where people were shocked by the liberal attitudes. Berlin was seen as sleazy, corrupt and sex-obsessed.

By the 1930s many of the artists featured on the last three pages had been forced to flee from Germany, despised or threatened by the Nazis. You will find out what kind of art the Nazis favoured and encouraged in Chapter 6.

■ TASK

- Weimar Germany was an exciting and creative place.
- The society of Weimar Germany was rotten and corrupt.

Explain whether you agree or disagree with each of these statements. Support your answer with reference to Sources 1-5 and the text on pages 28–30.

HITLER'S RISE TO POWER: HOW WAS HITLER ABLE TO DOMINATE GERMANY BY 1934?

3 HOW WAS HITLER ABLE TO BECOME CHANCELLOR IN 1933?

WHEN ADOLF HITLER joined the German Workers' Party in 1919 it had hardly any members, very little money and no real political programme. All its members knew was that they disliked the Weimar Republic and wanted to make Germany great again, as it had been before the war.

Over the next fourteen years under Hitler's leadership the Nazis moved from being an obscure minority party to being the most powerful party in Germany. In this section you will be investigating how Hitler and the Nazis achieved this transformation.

You will find that despite the problems facing Weimar Germany, through the 1920s the Nazis actually achieved very little success. It was not until the difficult Depression years of the 1930s that the Nazis made a real impact on Germany.

The timeline below summarises some of the key events in the rise of the Nazis. In Chapter 3 you will examine the most important of these events in greater detail. This timeline should also help you see the story of the Nazis against the wider background of the Weimar Republic which you have already studied in Section 1.

Hitler and the Nazis

1919
November: Hitler joins the German Workers' Party

1920
Hitler becomes leader of the Party
Renamed the National Socialist German Workers' Party (Nazi Party)

1921
Hitler founds the SA 'Sturm-Abteilung' or Stormtroopers) to intimidate opposition parties

1923
November: Hitler tries to seize power – the Munich or Beer Hall Putsch

1924
February: Hitler's trial and imprisonment for leading the Munich Putsch. In prison he writes Mein Kampf which puts across his views.
Hitler changes Nazi policy. They now try to win power by democratic means
The Nazis fight their first Reichstag elections. They win 32 seats

1929
October: The Wall Street Crash. Depression follows in Germany

1930
September: Nazis do well in elections. They win 107 seats

1932
July: Nazis become the biggest single party in the Reichstag with 230 seats

1933
January: Hitler becomes Chancellor

Other events

1919
January: Spartacist Uprising

1920
March: Kapp Putsch

1923
January: Occupation of the Ruhr
The Great Inflation
August: Stresemann becomes Chancellor

1924
April: The Dawes Plan is announced

1925
Hindenburg is elected President
The Locarno Treaties

1929
The Young Plan

How did Hitler become leader of the Nazis?

ADOLF HITLER WAS born in 1889 in Austria. His father was a customs official. He disliked his father but worshipped his mother. His father died when he was fourteen, his mother when he was eighteen.

There is little evidence from Hitler's early life that he possessed outstanding talent or ability. At school he was a failure. When his mother died he went to live in Vienna, and tried to earn a living as an artist. He was very poor and he lived in hostels. At one stage he worked as a builder's labourer, but lost his job when a Jewish trade-union official discovered he was not a member of the union.

During his time in Vienna he picked up many of the political ideas which later shaped the policies of the Nazi Party. In particular he developed his violent hatred of Jews (ANTI-SEMITISM).

SOURCE 1 Hitler (right) and army colleagues during the First World War

Hitler and the First World War

By the time the First World War broke out in 1914 Hitler had moved to Munich, and he immediately joined the German army. He was a good soldier, who won medals for bravery. His officers noticed how good a speaker he was. He was given the job of countering enemy propaganda whenever leaflets were showered on German trenches.

In 1918 he was badly gassed and was in hospital when the armistice and the German revolution took place in November 1918.

Germany's defeat in 1918 left him extremely bitter. Like many other soldiers he blamed defeat on the Communists and Jews who he felt had 'stabbed Germany in the back' (see page 18).

After the war he returned to Munich. He was still employed by the army. His job was to run evening classes in political education for the army. He had to check up on the various extremist groups which were flourishing in Munich at that time and if necessary to counter their propaganda.

Hitler joins the Nazis

In September 1919 Hitler was sent by the army to a meeting of a small, extreme nationalist group called the German Workers' Party. It had only six members and his first impression was not at all favourable.

However, Hitler also found that he agreed with many of the group's ideas. Only weeks later he himself became a member. The leader of the party soon spotted Hitler's talents as a propagandist. By February 1920 Hitler was helping to draft the party's programme (see Source 2).

SOURCE 2 The first four points of the German Workers' Party's programme, 1920. It changed its name to the Nazi Party later in the same year

> 1. *We demand the union of all Germans in a Greater Germany on the basis of national self-determination.*

Many Germans were living in Austria, Poland and Czechoslovakia – a new state created by the peace treaties after the First World War.

> 2. *We demand equality of rights for the German people in its dealings with other nations, and the revocation of the peace treaties of Versailles and Saint Germain.*

The Germans hated the Treaty of Versailles, which they thought humiliated Germany. See pages 16–17 for details. The Treaty of Saint Germain had forbidden the union of Austria and Germany, and moved borders so that 'Germans' in the former Austro-Hungarian Empire were now living in Italy and Poland.

> 3. *We demand land and territory to feed our people and settle our surplus population.*

The Nazis wanted to take over LEBENSRAUM, or living space, in eastern Europe for the growing German population.

> 4. *Only members of the nation may be citizens of the state. Only those of German blood, whatever their creed, may be members of the nation. Accordingly, no Jew may be a member of the nation.*

The Jews were very successful in business and commerce in Germany. The Nazis were jealous of their power. Hitler himself had an irrational hatred of the Jews. The Nazis thought only racially pure Germans, called ARYANS by the Nazis, could be citizens of the state.

In 1920 the party was renamed the National Socialist German Workers' Party (NSDAP or Nazis). In addition to the points in Source 2 the Nazis openly proclaimed their hatred of Communism. They saw the Social Democratic government as a Communist government and they made no secret of their plans to overthrow it when the time was right. They declared 25 Points, some of which are shown in Source 5.

Bavaria was a good base for such a right-wing party. It had a right-wing government, and many ordinary people in southern Germany were opposed to the Social Democrats. Even the Bavarian state government had plans to topple the Weimar government.

The SA

Hitler organised the Nazi Party along military lines. In 1921 he set up his own private army called the SA (*Sturm-Abteilung* or Stormtroopers). They were mostly young men. Some were former members of the Freikorps. They dressed in brown and were sometimes known as the Brownshirts. Supposedly the SA was formed to protect speakers at Nazi meetings from intimidation by left-wing opponents. In practice the SA often started the violence themselves by breaking up meetings of the Social Democratic Party which often ended in drunken brawls.

SOURCE 3 The pledge taken by members of the SA

66 As a member of the storm troop of the NSDAP I pledge myself to its storm flag:
to be always ready to stake life and limb in the struggle for the aims of the movement;
to give absolute military obedience to my military superiors and leaders;
to bear myself honourably in and out of service;
to be always companionable towards other comrades. 99

Rearm Germany

Abolish the Treaty of Versailles

Conquer Lebensraum

Nationalise important industries

What did the Nazis stand for in the 1920s?

Strong central government

Increase old-age pensions

SOURCE 5 Nazi ideas in the 1920s

The swastika

Hitler personally designed the Nazi flag, with its symbol, the swastika (see Source 4). The colours red, white and black had also been the colours of Germany's flag under the Kaiser. Very quickly the swastika became the best-known political symbol in Germany.

SOURCE 4 Hitler describing the Nazi flag in 1924

66 A symbol it really is!
In red we see the social idea of the movement, in white the nationalist idea, in the swastika the mission of the struggle for the victory of the Aryan man! 99

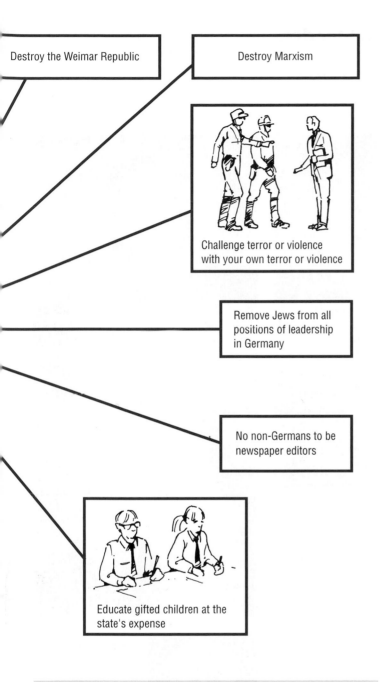

Destroy the Weimar Republic

Destroy Marxism

Challenge terror or violence with your own terror or violence

Remove Jews from all positions of leadership in Germany

No non-Germans to be newspaper editors

Educate gifted children at the state's expense

Hitler as leader

By 1922 Hitler was the undisputed leader of the party. He had a powerful, dominating personality.

He was intelligent and decisive. Although he was a small man he had great physical presence. He had piercing blue eyes which he would fix on his listeners and he was a charismatic public speaker.

When giving a speech he would often arrive late at a meeting, then stand silent for several minutes. He would start softly then gradually build up to a furious finish, driving the audience wild with enthusiasm. He rehearsed carefully for important speeches, even practising his hand gestures and his posture.

SOURCE 6 From a report written by an American diplomat, November 1922

66 Adolf Hitler has from the first been the dominating force in the Nazi movement, and the personality of this man has undoubtedly been one of the most important factors contributing to its success. His ability to influence an assembly is uncanny. In private conversation he is a forceful and logical speaker, which when tempered with a fanatical earnestness, made a very deep impression on a neutral observer. 99

SOURCE 7 Otto Strasser, one of Hitler's colleagues, remembering the early days of the Nazi Party

66 'Power!' screamed Adolf. 'We must have power!'
'Before we gain it,' I replied firmly, 'let us decide what we propose to do with it.'
Hitler, who even then could hardly bear contradiction, thumped the table and barked: 'Power first – afterwards we can act as circumstances dictate.' 99

1. Read Source 7. What do you think Hitler means by his final sentence?

■ TASK

Choose two events in Hitler's life so far that you would regard as turning points. Explain why each event you have chosen was so important.

■ ACTIVITY

Choose one idea from Source 2 or Source 5. Decide whom in Weimar Germany it might appeal to and design a poster to publicise it.

Hitler and his henchmen: the early Nazi leaders

The Nazi Party was dominated by Hitler but he was surrounded by skilled and committed 'henchmen'. The five below went on to play a prominent part in the Nazis' rise to power:

Josef Goebbels
Goebbels was the son of an office worker in a factory. He had not been able to fight in the First World War because he had a crippled foot which caused him to limp. Although small and physically weak, he was very intelligent, well educated and a brilliant public speaker. He joined the party in 1922. To start with he opposed Hitler's leadership, but then changed his mind and became one of Hitler's most influential supporters. He was appointed editor of the Nazi newspaper *Völkische Freiheit* ('People's Freedom').

Hermann Goering
Goering came from a middle-class background. He fought in the airforce in the First World War, shooting down twenty-two enemy aircraft and winning the highest medal for bravery under fire.

He was a loud, swaggering character who was intelligent, witty and charming, but also vain and greedy.

He joined the Nazi Party in 1922, and a year later was put in charge of the SA (Stormtroopers).

Rudolf Hess
Hess had been both a soldier and a pilot in the First World War. He joined the Nazi Party in 1920. He was a soft, sensitive and humourless man. Hess was not ambitious and did not crave power in the same way as other Nazis did. He worshipped Hitler. In the early days he was Hitler's private secretary and was later responsible for matters of party administration.

Heinrich Himmler

Himmler fought briefly in the First World War, and before the war had been an agricultural student. As a youth he was frail, timid and clumsy with short-cropped hair and an expressionless face. But he was hard-working and very precise. He even recorded in his diary each time he shaved or had a haircut. He joined the party in 1923. His early posts were as Gauleiter (regional party chief) for various regions.

Ernst Röhm

From childhood Röhm had wanted to be a soldier. He was a captain in the German army during the First World War. This was a great achievement for a working-class boy – most officers were from the upper classes. He was a tough, brutal, but efficient leader. He had a very violent temper. After the war he joined the Freikorps and helped crush the Spartacist rising. He was a founder member of the German Workers' Party in 1919. He supported Hitler when he took over as Nazi leader in 1920 and he set up and ran the SA for Hitler in 1921.

■ TASK

On five pages in the back of your exercise book write the names of each of these Nazi leaders. For each one summarise the important information about their

■ background
■ character
■ work for the Nazis.

As you work through this book add any further information you get about them. Try to find out what happened to each one between 1920 and 1945.

Nazi growth

The Nazi Party was based in Munich but its influence, and Hitler's reputation as a political leader, soon began to spread outside Bavaria to other parts of the country. The Nazis published their own newspaper to help spread their ideas.

In the tensc and strained period from 1920 to 1923 the Nazis gathered support among extreme nationalists and anti-Communists elsewhere in Germany. The Nazis were not the only extreme right-wing group in Germany, but in the eyes of their supporters they were the group which seemed most likely to do something about the crisis in Germany. Far away from Bavaria, in a small town in northern Germany, five young middle-class men – two shopkeepers, an accountant, a businessman and a bookseller – got together to form a local branch of the Nazi Party. You will find out what happened to them on page 56.

By 1922 the Nazi Party had 3000 members and the Prussian state government was worried enough to make it an illegal organisation. Hitler was privately warned against attempting a coup in Bavaria. He promised he had no such plans!

■ ACTIVITY

You are a British visitor in Munich and are writing a letter home to your family. Your family know nothing at all about the Nazis, so make sure you explain carefully:

■ who the Nazis are
■ what they stand for
■ what kind of people support them
■ why they support them
■ what you think of them.

The Munich Putsch: success or failure?

ON PAGE 23 you learned how the German government dealt with the Munich Putsch in 1923. There are two interpretations of this event:

■ It was a failure for the Nazis. Their putsch was a fiasco. It was easily crushed and showed how powerless they really were.
■ It was a success for the Nazis. The putsch itself may have failed but it launched the Nazis onto the national scene, made Hitler famous and was the main building block for the Nazis' later success.

In this investigation you can decide which of the interpretations you most agree with.

Why did Hitler attempt a putsch in 1923?

Although the Nazis had grown in strength from 1919 to 1923 this success must be seen in perspective. Their support was still mainly in Bavaria (see page 34). They only had 3000 members. That is hardly the basis on which to organise a revolution to take over the whole of the country. But all the same, in November 1923, Hitler and the Nazis attempted to seize power in Germany. What reasons did they have to think they might succeed?

Reason 1: The support of the army
You will remember from your study of the German revolution (pages 11–14) how important the support of the army was in keeping control of Germany. Many right-wing groups, the Nazis included, thought the German army could be persuaded to abandon the government and support them instead.

Hitler was developing an increasingly close relationship with the former army leader, Ludendorff, and he believed that if it came to a crisis, Ludendorff would be willing and able to persuade the German army to desert the government and side with the Nazis.

Reason 2: The support of the Bavarian state government
The Bavarian government was right-wing. Its leaders had themselves been plotting against the Reich government. Hitler was sure that they would support a Nazi putsch.

The trigger

In September Stresemann's government called off passive resistance in the Ruhr (see page 23) and began again to pay the hated reparations to France. Many right-wingers in Germany saw this as a humiliating climb-down – yet another illustration of the weakness of the Reich government. Hitler believed that the time was right for a putsch.

Gustav Kahr, head of the Bavarian government, was not so sure. He doubted whether the army would support it. Hitler was furious at Kahr's hesitation and decided to force him to act.

8 November: What happened in the beer hall?

■ SOURCE INVESTIGATION

On 8 November Kahr, the Bavarian Prime Minister, and his two most senior Bavarian officials were addressing a meeting of around 3000 businessmen at a beer hall (a drinking club) in Munich.

Hitler and Goering arrived with 600 Stormtroopers. Hitler stopped the meeting, and took Kahr and his ministers into a side room at gunpoint where he persuaded them to support him in overthrowing the Reich government.

This is how one of the eyewitnesses reported the events in the beer hall.

SOURCE 1 An account by Karl von Müller. He was an historian who was at the meeting. This account is based on evidence he gave at Hitler's trial

66 *Kahr had spoken for half an hour. Then there was movement at the entrance as if people wanted to push their way in. Despite several warnings, the disturbance did not die down so Kahr had to stop speaking.*

Eventually, steel helmets came into sight. From this moment on, the view from my seat was rather obscured. People stood on chairs so that I did not see Hitler until he had come fairly near along the main gangway.

Just before Hitler turned to the platform, I saw him emerge between two armed soldiers in steel helmets who carried pistols next to their heads, pointing at the ceiling. Hitler climbed onto a chair on my left.

The hall was still restless. Hitler made a sign to the man on his right, who fired a shot at the ceiling. Thereupon Hitler called out (I cannot recollect the exact order of his words):

'The national revolution has broken out. The hall is surrounded.' Maybe he mentioned the exact number of men surrounding it, I am not sure.

He asked Kahr and the other two gentlemen to come out [to a nearby room]. He guaranteed their personal freedom. The gentlemen did not move. Hitler went towards the platform. What happened I could not see exactly. I heard him talk to the gentlemen and I heard the words – everything would be over in ten minutes if the gentlemen would go out with him. To my surprise the three gentlemen went out with him immediately.

SOURCE 2
An artist's impression of the layout of the beer hall on 8 November 1923

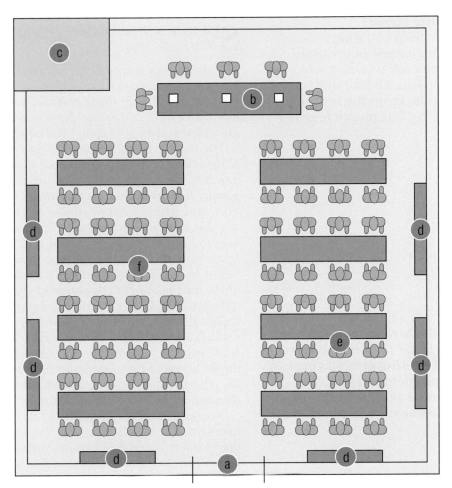

Key

(a) Where Nazis entered

(b) Stage

(c) Side room

(d) SA troops

(e) Eye-witness historian

(f) Hitler speaking

The general mood – I can of course judge only from my surroundings, but I think this represented the general feeling in the hall – was still against the whole business.

The change came only during Hitler's second speech when he came back about ten minutes later.

When he stepped onto the platform the disturbance was so great that he could not be heard, and he fired a shot. I can still see the gesture. He got the Browning out of his back pocket, and I think it was on this occasion that he shouted angrily at the audience: 'If you are not quiet, I shall have a machine-gun put up in the gallery.'

[When he spoke] it was a rhetorical masterpiece. In fact, in a few sentences he totally transformed the mood of the audience. I have rarely experienced anything like it.

He said that his prediction of everything being over in ten minutes had not come true. But he said it in such a way that when he finally went out it was if he had the support of the whole audience to say to Kahr that the whole assembly would be behind him if he were to join.

It was a complete reversal of mood. One could hear it being said that the whole thing had been arranged, that it was a phoney performance. I did not share this opinion because Kahr's attitude seemed to contradict it. Seeing Kahr at close quarters, one got the impression of confusion, of great dismay.

An hour after Hitler's first appearance, the three gentlemen came back into the hall with Hitler and Ludendorff. They were enthusiastically received. On the platform Kahr began to speak first without being requested to. Ludendorff too in my opinion spoke without being requested to. The other two gentlemen spoke only after repeated requests.

Throughout this time Hitler was radiant with joy. One had the feeling that he was delighted to have succeeded in persuading Kahr to collaborate. There was in his demeanour, I would say, a kind of childlike joy, a very frank expression which I shall never forget. Excellency Ludendorff by comparison was extremely grave; when he came in he was pale with suppressed emotion. His appearance as well as his words were those of a man who knew it was a matter of life or death, probably death rather than life. I shall never forget his expression. **99**

What happened in the side room?

The eyewitness in Source 1 gives you a very thorough account of what happened in the main beer hall. However, he cannot tell us about what happened in the adjoining room. To find that out we need to turn to other accounts. From the testimonies of those involved one historian has pieced together this account.

■ TASK 1

Both of these accounts tell you a lot about events in the beer hall on the night of 8 November 1923. Together they give a much fuller picture of the event than each on its own could do. However, having two such sources also poses a problem. When they describe the same thing – such as Hitler's second speech – there are contradictions.

1. What do the sources
a) disagree
b) agree
   about in their account of Hitler's second speech?
2. Where the accounts agree, can you be sure that they are both accurate?
3. Where the accounts disagree, which would you believe and why?
4. Which of these accounts is more useful to you as evidence of
a) Hitler's part in the events
b) the reactions of the crowd?
5. Explain why both of these statements are wrong.

   ■ 'Source 1 is more useful than Source 3 because it was written by an eyewitness, so he must know what happened.'
   ■ 'Source 3 is more useful than Source 1 because it was written by an historian who has had the chance of looking at all the evidence of what happened.'

■ TASK 2

Success or failure? On a scale of 1 (failure) to 10 (success), say how successful the Nazis were on 8 November.

SOURCE 3 William L. Shirer, *The Rise and Fall of the Third Reich*, 1959

❝ *[In the side room] Hitler told his prisoners: 'No one leaves this room alive without my permission.' He then informed them that he would give them all key jobs either in the Bavarian government or in the Reich government which he was forming with Ludendorff.*

The three prisoners at first refused even to speak to Hitler. He continued to harangue them. They did not answer. Their continued silence unnerved Hitler. Finally he waved his gun at them. 'I have four shots in my pistol. Three for my collaborators, if they abandon me. The last bullet for myself!' Pointing the weapon to his forehead, he cried, 'If I am not victorious by tomorrow afternoon, I shall be a dead man!'

But he was getting nowhere with his talk. Not one of the men who held the power of the Bavarian state agreed to join him, even at pistol point. The putsch wasn't going according to plan. Then Hitler acted on a sudden impulse. Without a further word, he dashed back into the hall. Mounting the platform, he faced the sullen crowd and announced that the members of the triumvirate in the next room had joined him in forming a new national government.

'I propose that the direction of national policy be taken over by me,' he shouted. 'Ludendorff will take over leadership of the German national army. Tomorrow will find either a national government in Germany or us dead!'

When the gathering heard that Kahr and the others had joined Hitler, its mood changed abruptly. Not for the first time and certainly not for the last, Hitler had told a masterful lie, and it had worked. There were loud cheers. The sound impressed the three men still locked up in the little side room.

General Ludendorff now appeared as if out of a hat. The war hero was furious with Hitler for pulling such a complete surprise on him. He spoke scarcely a word to the brash young man. But Hitler did not mind, so long as Ludendorff lent his famous name to the undertaking and won over the three Bavarian leaders.

This Ludendorff proceeded to do; it is now a question of a great national cause, he said, and he advised the three gentlemen to co-operate. Awed by the attention of the generalissimo, the trio appeared to give in. Ludendorff's timely arrival had saved Hitler.

Overjoyed at his lucky break, Hitler led the others back to the platform, where each made a brief speech and swore loyalty to each other and to the new regime. The crowd leaped on chairs and tables in a delirium of enthusiasm, and Hitler beamed with joy. The meeting began to break up. ❞

9 November: The march on Munich

The first part of Hitler's plan had succeeded. But now he made a big mistake. He let Kahr and his colleagues go, while he and Ludendorff planned how their supporters could seize Munich the following day. It was soon clear that Kahr's pledge of support, made at gunpoint, was worthless. When news of the putsch reached Berlin the government ordered the army in Bavaria to crush it. Kahr would not attempt to stop it. The Nazis could not backtrack now, however. They would march on Munich the next day as planned. They would challenge the army and the police not to fire on them, but to support them. With Ludendorff as their leader, Hitler hoped they might succeed.

So the next morning, in driving snow, Hitler, Ludendorff and 3000 Nazis marched into Munich. When they reached the city centre, they found the police and the army waiting for them. In a narrow street called the Residenzstrasse about 100 police blocked the path of the march.

The police used rubber truncheons and rifle butts to push back the crowd. One of the Nazis ran forward and shouted to the police: 'Don't shoot, Ludendorff and Hitler are coming.' Hitler cried out 'Surrender!' Then a shot rang out – no one knows who fired first – and a hail of bullets swept the street from either side.

Hitler fell, either pulled down or seeking cover. He had dislocated his shoulder. The shooting lasted only a minute, but sixteen Nazis and three policemen lay dead or dying in the street.

According to eyewitnesses Hitler now lost his nerve. He was the first to scramble to his feet. He struggled to a yellow motor-car which was waiting nearby. He was undoubtedly in great pain from his dislocated shoulder, and probably believed himself to have been wounded.

Ludendorff, on the other hand, marched onwards to the next square where he was arrested. Hitler himself was arrested two days later.

■ TASK 3

Success or failure? On the same scale of 1–10 (see Task 2) say how successful the Nazis were on 9 November.

■ ACTIVITY

Work in pairs. Each of you should write a newspaper report describing the events of 8 and 9 November 1923. One of you write as a supporter of the Nazis. The other write as a critic of the Nazis.

The pro-Nazi article should explain how the putsch showed the authority and leadership skills of Hitler and the strength of Nazi support. The anti-Nazi article should make it clear how Hitler only achieved support by violence and threats, and how he showed his cowardice in the end.

Choose one of Sources 4 and 5 to illustrate your article. Explain why you chose that picture.

SOURCE 4 Nazis marching into the centre of Munich on the morning of 9 November

SOURCE 5 A painting made later by one of the participants in the putsch. In the foreground the police are opening fire on the Nazis. Hitler stands with his arm raised with Ludendorff on his right

1924: The trial

In February 1924 the trial began of the leading members of the putsch. Hitler, Ludendorff and Röhm stood trial alongside other Nazi leaders.

SOURCE 6 The leading members of the putsch pose before their trial. Hitler and Ludendorff are in the centre, and Röhm is standing second from the right

It was at this point that Hitler seemed to snatch some kind of victory out of the jaws of defeat. The trial gave him a national platform on which to speak. He greatly impressed his audience by his eloquence and the strength of his nationalist feelings. Newspapers throughout Germany and around the world reported his claim that he had led the movement against the 'treasonable' Weimar system in Berlin. The trial established his reputation as the natural leader of extreme right-wing nationalist elements throughout Germany.

In the glare of publicity even the putsch itself seemed to confirm that Hitler was a man with immense and unusual political talent. By sheer bluff he had secured the support of the famed general Ludendorff who had publicly promised to serve under the dictatorship of ex-corporal Hitler. Anyone who could so transform a situation by powerful public speaking was certainly a force to be reckoned with.

Hitler's performance at the trial undoubtedly influenced the judges. He was treated leniently. He was sentenced to five years' imprisonment, but served less than nine months before he was released. His prison was Landsberg Castle. He had his own room, was allowed as many visitors as he wanted, and spent the time writing his book, *Mein Kampf* ('My Struggle'). Ludendorff was let off without a prison sentence. Other Nazi leaders were given short sentences. Röhm, for example, received fifteen months but was released immediately.

Although the years after the putsch were a difficult time for the Nazis, Hitler emerged from it a much stronger figure. Ten years later this was Hitler's own assessment on how the putsch affected the prospects of the Nazis.

SOURCE 7 Hitler and his fellow Nazis pose for a photograph in Landsberg prison. Rudolph Hess sits second from the right

SOURCE 8 Hitler's assessment of the putsch. He was speaking in 1933

66 *It was the greatest good fortune for us Nazis that the putsch collapsed because:*

1. *Co-operation with General Ludendorff would have been absolutely impossible.*
2. *The sudden takeover of power in the whole of Germany would have led to the greatest of difficulties in 1923 because the essential preparations had not even been begun by the National Socialist Party.*
3. *The events of 9 November 1923, with their blood sacrifice, have proven the most effective propaganda for National Socialism.* 99

■ TASK

Success or failure? Look back at your scores for Tasks 2 and 3 on pages 40 and 41. On the same scale indicate how successful the putsch was, viewed with hindsight. Finally, write a paragraph explaining your view as to whether the putsch was a success or failure.

How did the Nazis change their tactics between 1924 and 1929?

THE FAILURE OF the Munich Putsch convinced Hitler that the only sure way of getting power was by legal means.

SOURCE 1 Hitler speaking in the mid-1920s

66 *Instead of working to achieve power by armed coup, we shall have to hold our noses and enter the Reichstag against the opposition deputies. If outvoting them takes longer than outshooting them, at least the results will be guaranteed by their own constitution. Sooner or later we shall have a majority, and after that – Germany.* 99

The Nazi Party was banned in the immediate aftermath of the putsch. However, while Hitler was still in prison the Nazis – under another name – entered the Reichstag elections for the first time. In the afterglow of the trial, they won 32 seats in the May election. However, just seven months later there was another election. The Nazis did disastrously, their seats reduced to just fourteen.

Reorganising the party

Clearly electoral success would require a different kind of Nazi Party. Two weeks after his release from prison in December, the ban on the party was lifted and it was officially re-launched at a rally (in the Munich beer hall!) on 27 February 1925. Hitler began to reorganise the party to make it more effective in elections.

Winning over the working classes

Through the late 1920s the Nazis worked steadily. They ran many public meetings and tried harder to win the support of the working classes. They discovered that it was their anti-Jewish message which had most appeal among the working classes and they increased their anti-Jewish propaganda.

Mein Kampf

Hitler's *Mein Kampf* was published in 1925. His national fame was now such that it became a best-seller.

1. Why might each of the points in Source 2 appeal to people in Weimar Germany?
2. Critics said that *Mein Kampf* contained nothing new but just recapped all the old Nazi ideas. Do the extracts in Source 2 support this view? You may need to refer back to pages 33–35.

SOURCE 2 Extracts from *Mein Kampf*

66 *There must be no majority decisions. The decisions will be made by one man, only he alone may possess the authority and right to command.*

Blood mixture and the resultant drop in the racial level is the sole cause of the dying out of old cultures. All who are not of good race in the world are chaff.

The danger to which Russia has succumbed is always present for Germany. In Russian Bolshevism we must see the attempt undertaken by the Jews to achieve world domination.

History proves that the German people owes its existence solely to its determination to fight in the East and to obtain land by military conquest. 99

Increased membership

Gradually, year by year, the Nazis increased their membership.

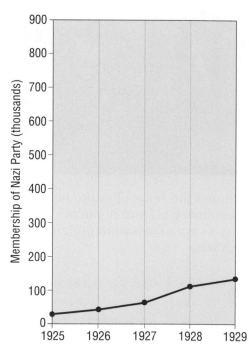

SOURCE 3 Nazi Party membership, 1925–29

Despite this rise in membership, the Nazis were actually losing ground in the only place it now really mattered – in the Reichstag. After four years of campaigning and reorganisation, in the 1928 Reichstag elections the Nazis were reduced to just twelve deputies. Their hated rivals the Social Democrats had 153 seats. Even the Communists had four times as many seats as the Nazis.

Winning over the middle classes

In 1928 the Nazis decided on another change of policy. They were increasingly convinced that they were getting nowhere in their appeals to the working classes. But they were doing well among the middle classes and among farmers, and this is where most of their new members were coming from. They began to focus on the parts of their message which would appeal to this section of society.

> **S**OURCE 4 From a resolution passed at a Nazi meeting for farmers, January 1928
>
> ❝ *We have recognised that the distress of agriculture is inseparably bound up with the political misery of the German people. Let us do away with this Marxist–capitalist extortion system that has made Germany, our homeland, powerless, without honour, defenceless, and has turned free German farmers into poor, misused slaves of the world stock exchange.* ❞

Public meetings

Whereas political parties today have television as their main way of communicating with the public, parties at that time depended mainly on public meetings. The Nazis were the only party in Germany to run evening classes for their members to train them in public-speaking skills. Nazi activists in villages and towns throughout Germany would put on meetings with visiting speakers. If a subject proved popular then they would repeat it. In this way the Nazis developed a very sensitive system of propaganda. They learnt the skill of focusing on the issues that people thought were important. If this also meant changing their policies to fit, then they seemed prepared to do so.

As you can see from Source 3, Nazi membership almost doubled between 1927 and 1928. Would this growth have continued? Maybe. But in 1929 other events over which the Nazis had no control brought about a change in their fortunes which launched them on the path to power.

■ TASK

One historian has said of Hitler in the summer of 1929 that he was 'no more than the leader of a small splinter party, scarcely known outside Bavaria and very likely doomed to remain forever on the fringe of political life'. Does the information on pages 44–45 support this viewpoint? Explain your answer carefully.

SOURCE 5 1924 election poster criticising Stresemann's policies – suggesting the Dawes Plan and Jewish bankers holding Germany to ransom

SOURCE 6 1928 election poster. The Nazis present their 'building blocks' for the reconstruction of Germany – work, freedom, bread – as opposed to the unemployment, social spending cuts, corruption and lying of the other parties

How did the Depression help the Nazis?

IN OCTOBER 1929 the WALL STREET CRASH was the beginning of a worldwide slide into the Great Depression. The effects were felt everywhere but Germany was hit particularly badly because American banks recalled the loans which were the lifeblood of German industry. Businesses had to close. As world trade declined, German exports slumped. Millions of people lost their jobs.

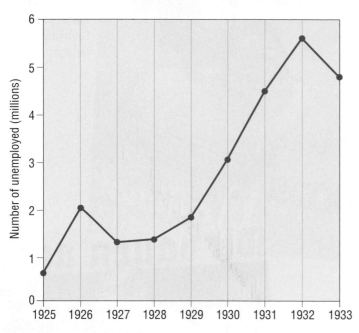

SOURCE 1 Unemployment in Germany 1925–33

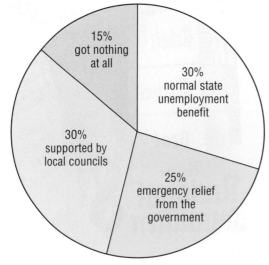

SOURCE 2 How the unemployed were supported in 1932. Those on emergency relief from the government received a payment lower than normal unemployment benefit, while the support from local councils was a lower payment still

What was life like in the Depression?

The Depression affected different people in different ways. For those who had lost their jobs there was poverty, hunger and homelessness. Of course not all Germans suffered equally, but even those who were protected from the worst of the Depression felt its impact in other ways.

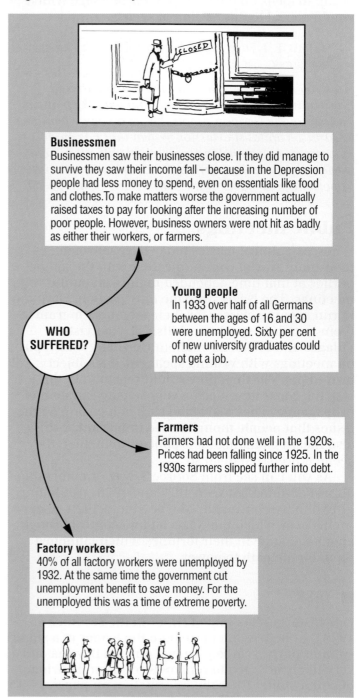

Businessmen
Businessmen saw their businesses close. If they did manage to survive they saw their income fall – because in the Depression people had less money to spend, even on essentials like food and clothes. To make matters worse the government actually raised taxes to pay for looking after the increasing number of poor people. However, business owners were not hit as badly as either their workers, or farmers.

WHO SUFFERED?

Young people
In 1933 over half of all Germans between the ages of 16 and 30 were unemployed. Sixty per cent of new university graduates could not get a job.

Farmers
Farmers had not done well in the 1920s. Prices had been falling since 1925. In the 1930s farmers slipped further into debt.

Factory workers
40% of all factory workers were unemployed by 1932. At the same time the government cut unemployment benefit to save money. For the unemployed this was a time of extreme poverty.

SOURCE 3 Who suffered in the Depression?

SOURCE 4 The writer Heinrich Hauser describes what he saw as he toured Germany in 1932

❝ An almost unbroken chain of homeless men extends the whole length of the great Hamburg–Berlin highway. It is the same scene for the entire two hundred miles, and all the highways in Germany over which I travelled this year.

They walked separately or in small groups with their eyes on the ground. And they had the queer, stumbling gait of barefoot people, for their shoes were slung over their shoulders. Some of them were guild members – carpenters with broad felt hats, milkmen with striped red shirts, and bricklayers with tall black hats – but they were in a minority. Far more numerous were those to whom one could assign no special profession or craft – unskilled young people for the most part who had been unable to find a place for themselves in any city or town in Germany, and who had never had a job and never expected to have one.

There was something else that had never been seen before – whole families who had piled all their goods into baby carriages and wheelbarrows that they were pushing along as they plodded forward in dumb despair. It was a whole nation on the march.

I saw them – and this was the strongest impression that the year 1932 left with me – I saw them, gathered into groups of fifty or a hundred men, attacking fields of potatoes. I saw them digging up the potatoes and throwing them into sacks while the farmer who owned the field watched them in despair and the local policeman looked on gloomily from the distance. I saw them staggering towards the lights of the city as night fell, with their sacks on their backs. What did it remind me of? Of the war, of the worst period of starvation in 1917 and 1918, but even then people paid for the potatoes. ❞

1. Why do you think the homeless men in Source 4 carried their shoes rather than wore them?
2. What would be the best way for the government to help the people in Source 4?

SOURCE 5 A camp for the homeless in a Berlin park. There were so many homeless that large camps of tents were set up. The tents were numbered and erected in neat rows which even had names as if they were streets. The camps had children's playgrounds and communal kitchens

SOURCE 6 A soup kitchen providing food for unemployed Germans. The government kept food prices high to protect the farmers from the worst of the Depression. The result was that many unemployed people could not afford to eat

SOURCE 7 Heinrich Hauser (see Source 4) describes the Berlin municipal lodging house where many young unemployed men had to stay

> *Long lines of men were leaning against the wooden walls, waiting in silence and staring. Heavy steam rose from the men's clothes. Some of them sat down on the floor, pulled off their shoes, and unwound the rags that bound their feet. More people were constantly pouring in the door, and we stood closely packed together. The municipal lodging house means waiting, waiting, standing around. We arrange ourselves in long lines, each leading up to an official. The man wants to know: When and where were you born, and where have you come from? Name of your parents? Ever been in a municipal lodging house before? Where have you spent the last three nights? Where did you work last? Have you begged? My impression is the helplessness of the men. Eight out of every ten men are young fellows and about a third of these are mere boys.*
>
> *I have been given a night's sleep and food in the lodging house. The bare walls of the room that we have entered are lined with iron bedsteads. There are no windows but a sloping roof with skylights that reminds me of a factory. They do not make it easy for you to get supper and a bed in a municipal lodging house.*

SOURCE 8 A woman textile worker describes her weekend in 1930. She worked six days a week, for a very low wage

> *I would be happy if I could properly provide for my household and children, but of the 25 marks a week one and a half marks goes for transport, six marks for childcare and what it otherwise costs to be out of the house all day.*
>
> *Saturdays and every night are spent washing. If I'm finished with the housework on Saturdays around 9.30, I'm usually too tired to give the child a bath so I have to start up again Sunday morning. Then there are things to mend, and everything else that didn't get done during the week. Those are the famous weekend joys of a working woman. I often wonder what I live for, and why everything is so unequal.*

SOURCE 9 Farmers ploughing by hand in East Prussia, 1933 – probably because they could not afford a horse

SOURCE 10 A shop forced to close because of the Depression and sell all its goods 'for any reasonable price', 1931

3. Why do you think the woman in Source 8 did the work she did if she was so dissatisfied with it?
4. Who would you rather have been of all the people in Sources 3–10? Explain your choice.

■ ACTIVITY

Imagine two of the people in Sources 3–10 meet each other. Either role-play or write out a conversation between them in which they talk about what life is like in the Depression.

How did the Depression weaken the Weimar government?

1. Unpopular economic policies

For half a century or more Germans had judged their country by its economic success. So if the economy was failing then the country must be going down the drain! The Weimar government seemed to have no idea what to do about the problems of rising unemployment and growing poverty.

The government did of course try to get Germany out of depression, but with little success. To be fair, no other country affected by the Depression did much better, but the Weimar government faced particular problems. For example, one way out of depression is to print money and increase government expenditure – but all Weimar leaders were aware that these were the policies which had led to disastrous inflation in 1923. What if the same happened again? The government was more scared of what would happen if there was another period of inflation than it was of unemployment. So instead the Chancellor raised taxes, cut wages and reduced unemployment benefit – hardly the policies to win support from the German people.

2. Presidential rule

These policies also caused the collapse of the government because the Social Democrats withdrew from the coalition. In order for his government to survive the Chancellor fell back on Article 48 of the Weimar Constitution (see page 21) which gave the President special powers in an emergency. Germany was now ruled by presidential decree. But who was the President? An 84-year-old war hero, apparently controlled by business and army leaders, and who seemed to be well past his prime.

3. The rise of extremism

To many Germans it seemed that the Weimar government was making a hopeless mess of handling the situation. Some people who had never bothered to vote in elections before – because they were not interested in politics – now became more involved. Politics did matter. Something had to be done!

From right and left they could hear the claims of extremist parties who said they could solve all these problems. The Communists said that the Depression showed that the capitalist system was doomed and that only communism had the answer. The Nazis blamed the Weimar Republic, the Treaty of Versailles, the Marxists and the Jews and promised to get rid of 'the enemy within' who was destroying Germany.

As extremism increased, so too did political violence. Nazi and Communist supporters fought regular battles. Five hundred were killed or seriously wounded in a seven-week frenzy of political fighting during the elections of 1932. Town halls were bombed by farmers.

SOURCE 11 Police in Berlin, 1932, on the way to deal with a demonstration

How did these problems help the Nazis?

The Depression was a gift to Hitler and the Nazis. For every problem the Nazis had an explanation or a promise:

- The Weimar government is weak: you need strong leadership. Hitler is your man.
- Unemployment? The Nazis will get people back to work on road-building and public works.
- Worried about the Communists? Look at the Nazis' SA – we are the only ones who really know how to deal with the Communists.

Most importantly, Hitler, standing before a crowd delivering his powerful and moving speeches, seemed to represent strong, decisive leadership in the great German tradition going back to the Kaiser and beyond. While the Weimar Republic appeared simply to be muddling through indecisively, Hitler's strong personality and powerful ideas seemed to be just what Germany needed.

As you can see from Source 12, in the Reichstag elections in 1930 the Nazis made their first great breakthrough, jumping from twelve to 107 seats. They were suddenly the second largest party and were well ahead of the Communists. In the July 1932 elections they advanced to 230 seats and were the biggest party. The Nazi Party was now *the* major force in German politics.

SOURCE 13 Hitler addressing an open-air meeting during the 1932 presidential election campaign

Summary: how did the Nazis do it?

The impact of the Depression can only partly explain the success of the Nazis. All parties claimed they had solutions. Why was it the Nazis and not the other parties who managed to convince Germans they could solve the country's problems?

	Left wing						Right wing	Unemployment
	Communist Party	Social Democrats	Democratic Party	Centre Party	Conservatives	Nationalists	Nazis	Unemployment figures
1928	54	153	25	61	45	73	12 (2.6%)	1,391,000
1930	77	143	20	68	30	41	107 (18.3%)	3,076,000
Jul 1932	89	133	4	75	7	37	230 (37.3%)	5,603,000
Nov 1932	100	121	2	70	11	52	196 (33.1%)	
1933	81	120	5	74	2	52	288 (43.9%)	4,804,000

SOURCE 12 Reichstag election results, 1928–33, and unemployment figures 1925–33

Organisation

They were very well organised. Many Nazis had been soldiers in the First World War. They brought to party work the same obedience, organisation and teamwork skills which they had needed in the trenches. The local workers were well trained and motivated. They had skilled leaders at almost every level.

Propaganda

Their national leaders were masters of propaganda, and they carefully trained their local groups in propaganda skills. They used every trick in the book to get their message home. They knew that their anti-Communist stance was very popular and their propaganda further whipped up fear and hatred of the Communists. They stirred up violence at election meetings so that the SA could crush it and be seen 'dealing with the Communist threat'. Hitler pointed to the Nazis' ten-year track record in leading the fight against Communism.

Support of the industrialists

One of their aims – which was partly successful – was to earn the support of the powerful industrialists. Traditionally they had voted for the Conservative Party, which lost much of its support after 1930. In 1931 Hitler made a deal with the other main right-wing party, the Nationalists, by which the two parties agreed to co-operate. The Nazi Party also received some financial backing from big business.

Use of technology

The Nazis could now redouble their propaganda. Radio was used for the first time. In the 1932 presidential election, while Hindenburg gave just one election speech, Goebbels chartered planes to fly Hitler all over Germany in order to speak to four or five massive rallies per day. Radio broadcasts, millions of election posters, rallies, parades and marches carried the Nazi message into every town and home in Germany.

Promises to voters

And every sector of German society seemed to hear something it wanted to hear.

Workers were promised jobs (Hitler could point to how the Nazis' SA had taken in the unemployed and fed and housed them). Employers were promised restored profits; farmers higher prices; shopkeepers protection against competition. There was something for everybody.

Flexibility

In fact, one reason for the Nazis' success was that they were flexible. If they found an idea was losing them support they would change it. In one election speech a leading Nazi spoke powerfully for the nationalisation of industry (which had always been one of the Nazis' beliefs). When they found out how alarmed the industrialists were they quickly dropped the idea. In their campaigns it was never mentioned again. In their all-out push for electoral success they realised that it doesn't really matter what you promise as long as people trust you. If all else failed the Nazis simply went for vague promises: they would 'make Germany great again'. In the end, despite the extreme beliefs expressed in the Nazis' 25 Points – of which they made no secret (see page 34) – Germans were actually very unsure as to what the Nazis really stood for.

Hitler the superman

Only one thing really stayed consistent throughout this barrage of electioneering: the unblinking focus on Hitler, the strong leader whom Germany needed and wanted. Posters and rallies built him up into a superman. His physical appearance was adapted (on posters at least). Hitler himself developed his speech-making skills still further. He wore spectacles to read but refused to be seen wearing them in public and so his speeches were typed in large – 12mm high – print. It no longer seemed to matter *what* he said, just *how* he said it. Hitler was the Nazis' trump card. The campaigns focused around his personality and his skills. The opposition had no one to match him.

Weaknesses of opposition

Other parties were very weak and they consistently underestimated the Nazis. The Social Democrats feared they would attempt a putsch, but they thought that the Nazis' electioneering was so absurd that ordinary Germans would see through it. And their own support was constant so they were not eager to change. They quarrelled among themselves rather than uniting to face the Nazis' challenge.

■ TASK

1. The text describes many factors which helped the Nazis. Explain *how* each one helped them.
2. Which of these factors were also present in the 1920s?
3. Why were the Nazis less successful in the 1920s?

Nazi messages and Nazi methods

What was the Nazis' message... and how did they get it across?

SOURCE 1 'Our last hope: Hitler': a 1932 election poster

SOURCE 2 A 1932 election poster. The text at the top reads: 'Women! Millions of men without work. Millions of children without a future'

1. Look at Sources 1–4. For each source explain whom you think it was designed to appeal to.
2. Which of Sources 1–4 best shows the following Nazis messages?
a) The Nazis will make Germany great again.
b) Hitler is a great leader.
c) The Nazis will deal with the Communists. Explain your choice.
3. What other messages are given by these sources?
4. Which do you think is the most effective piece of propaganda?

The Duties of German Communist Party volunteers

Unselfishly they help the farmers to dry the harvest.

Particular detachments are responsible for improving transport.

They work nights and overtime getting together useful equipment.

They increase their fitness for the fatherland with target practice.

SOURCE 3 A Nazi election poster (we have translated the text into English)

SOURCE 4 Nazi election poster from 1928. The text reads: 'Work, freedom and bread! Vote for the National Socialists!'

SOURCE 5 A Hamburg schoolteacher recalls a Nazi meeting in 1932

    It was nearly 3 p.m. 'The FÜHRER is coming!' A ripple went through the crowd. Around the speakers' platform one could see hands raised in the Hitler salute. There stood Hitler in a simple black coat and he looked over the crowd, waiting – a forest of swastika pennants swished up, the jubilation of this moment was given vent in a roaring salute.

    [Hitler's main theme was] out of parties shall grow a nation. 'Thirteen years ago I was a simple unknown soldier. I went my way. I never turned back. Nor shall I turn back now.'

    When the speech was over there was roaring enthusiasm and applause. Then he went. How many look up to him with touching faith, as their helper, their saviour, their deliverer from unbearable distress.

SOURCE 6 From a report by the British Ambassador to Berlin in 1932

    According to official statistics there were between 1 June and 20 July in Prussia alone, excluding Berlin, 322 serious clashes, involving 72 deaths and 497 injured. The most disgusting outrages were in East Prussia, now the stronghold of the Nazi Party. Prominent Socialists and Communists were surprised at night and murdered in their own beds or shot down at the doors of their houses. The windows of shops owned by Jews were smashed and the contents looted. There were attacks with high explosives on the offices of democratically owned newspapers. The assailants used firearms, hand grenades and acid.

SOURCE 7 From a description of Hitler written by a member of the British Foreign Office in the 1930s as information for the government

    As a speaker, Hitler exercises astonishing sway over a German audience, presumably because public speaking is an unknown art in Germany. His speeches are practically repetitions of a few simple main ideas, in the course of which platitudes [everyday ideas] are uttered with such extraordinary emphasis that an unsophisticated audience mistakes them for newly minted political theories. He has sized up the German audience with astonishing accuracy. This and an undeniable political instinct have brought him to the top of the tree.

5. Read Source 6. Explain how these tactics helped the Nazis to achieve success in elections.
6. How far do Sources 5 and 7 agree in their assessment of Hitler as a public speaker?
7. Explain why Goebbels was keen for Hitler to speak at as many meetings as possible.
8. Which of Sources 1–7 is the most helpful in explaining the Nazis' success in the 1932 elections?

Who supported the Nazis?

Source 8 shows Nazi support in 1932.

1. Study Source 8. Re-order the following list so that the largest segment of Nazi support is at the top and the smallest at the bottom:

   ■ office workers
   ■ industrial workers
   ■ peasants
   ■ the self-employed
   ■ government employees.

2. If the Nazis were doing equally well in all groups in society, then the bottom bar of Source 8 would look the same as the top bar. As you can see, they did **proportionately** better in some groups, and proportionately worse in others.
   a) Which groups did they do best in proportionately?
   b) Which worst?

The Nazis also did better in some areas than in others (see Source 9).

■ They were more successful in rural areas than in industrial or urban areas.
■ They were more successful in northern Germany than in south Germany.
■ They were more successful in Protestant areas than in Catholic areas.
■ They were more successful in middle-class areas than in working-class areas.

The big question is why they were so successful in these areas and among these groups. The previous pages will have given you some general ideas. You are now going to look in detail at one small town to see if you can answer the question as to why the Nazis were so successful among the middle classes in rural, Protestant, north Germany.

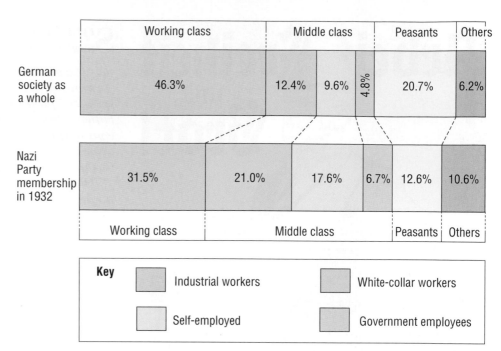

SOURCE 8 Who supported the Nazis?

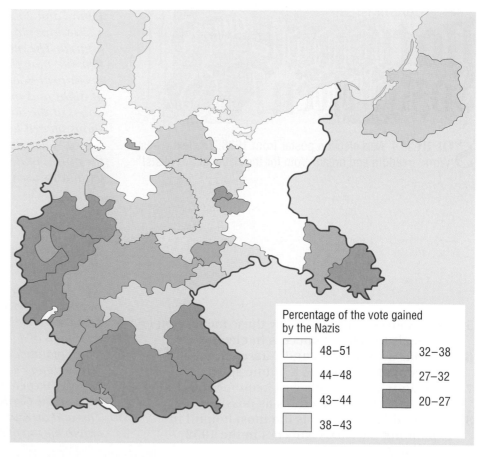

SOURCE 9 Map showing support for the Nazis in Germany, based on the July 1932 election figures. It may help you to refer back to the map on page 4

Case study: The rise of the Nazis in Northeim

OVER PAGES 44–54 you have gained a general picture of the success of the Nazis. You are now going to study the growth of the Nazis in one town. How far does this one place fit the general pattern?

The historian, W.S. Allen, has done a detailed study of Northeim in his book *The Nazi Seizure of Power*. Most of the sources and information on pages 55-59 come from this book.

What was Northeim like?

Northeim was a small but thriving country town in northern Germany (see Source 2 on page 4) with shops and businesses serving the local farming community. It nestled on a hillside, overlooking the River Leine. In 1930 it had a population of 10,000.

It was both a railway centre (more than a thousand Northeimers worked for the railways) and a centre of local government (which employed another 1300). However, it had little industry. In the 1920s the railways and the civil service were the biggest employers.

As you can see from Source 1, it was very clearly divided along class lines. The rich lived in one area of the town, the poor in another. Social life was also divided along class lines. There were dozens of societies and groups. There were even three different choirs – one for workers, one for the middle classes, and one for the elite.

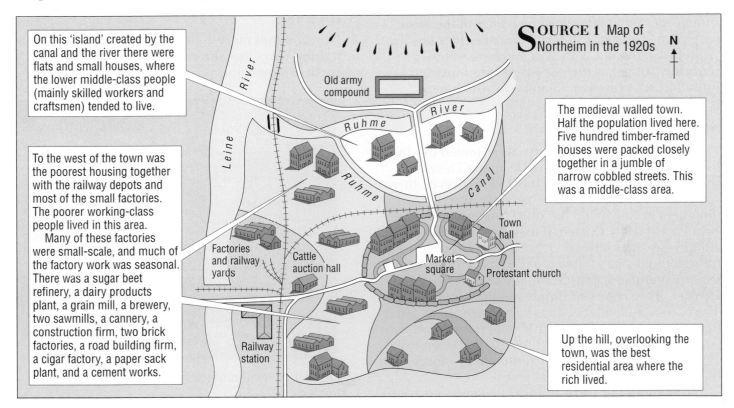

On this 'island' created by the canal and the river there were flats and small houses, where the lower middle-class people (mainly skilled workers and craftsmen) tended to live.

To the west of the town was the poorest housing together with the railway depots and most of the small factories. The poorer working-class people lived in this area.

Many of these factories were small-scale, and much of the factory work was seasonal. There was a sugar beet refinery, a dairy products plant, a grain mill, a brewery, two sawmills, a cannery, a construction firm, two brick factories, a road building firm, a cigar factory, a paper sack plant, and a cement works.

The medieval walled town. Half the population lived here. Five hundred timber-framed houses were packed closely together in a jumble of narrow cobbled streets. This was a middle-class area.

Up the hill, overlooking the town, was the best residential area where the rich lived.

SOURCE 1 Map of Northeim in the 1920s

Old army compound · River Ruhme · River Leine · Ruhme · Canal · Town hall · Factories and railway yards · Cattle auction hall · Market square · Protestant church · Railway station

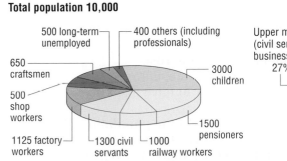

Total population 10,000

500 long-term unemployed · 400 others (including professionals) · 650 craftsmen · 500 shop workers · 3000 children · 1125 factory workers · 1300 civil servants · 1000 railway workers · 1500 pensioners

SOURCE 2 Employment in Northeim

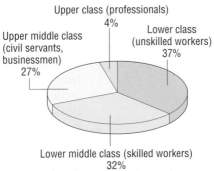

Upper class (professionals) 4% · Upper middle class (civil servants, businessmen) 27% · Lower class (unskilled workers) 37% · Lower middle class (skilled workers) 32%

SOURCE 3 Class structure in Northeim in 1930

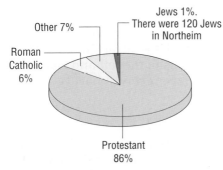

Jews 1%. There were 120 Jews in Northeim · Other 7% · Roman Catholic 6% · Protestant 86%

SOURCE 4 Religion in Northeim

Who were the first Nazis in Northeim?

Northeimers sacrificed a lot for Germany in the First World War; 253 were killed. Like other Germans, Northeimers were very alarmed at the revolution of 1918. In the turbulent years after the war many Northeimers sided with the right-wing nationalist parties. In 1922 there was a major pitched battle in the town centre between socialists and nationalists. Gangs fought hand-to-hand with beer bottles and cobble stones. Almost every shop window in Broad Street was broken before the police restored control.

In the wake of this battle five middle-class Northeimers decided to set up a local branch of the Nazi Party. They were: Ernst Girmann, a 26-year-old shopkeeper, who later became leader of the local party; Karl Girmann, aged 29 (Ernst's elder brother); Wilhelm Spannaus, a 35-year-old bookseller; Heinrich Böhme, a 19-year-old accountant; and Rudolf Ernst, who was 33 and a businessman.

Stagnation

The five men mentioned above were joined by other local businessmen, including Hermann Denzler, a shopkeeper, who set up the local SA. However, three years later in 1925 the party had only twelve members in Northeim. For most Northeimers the Nazi Party hardly existed. If they did know about it at all they saw it as a fringe organisation left over from the turbulent years following the war. Two of its leading members, Ernst Girmann and Hermann Denzler, were regarded simply as thugs or bully-boys. The Nazis' political meetings were attended by fewer than fifteen people. They could not even cover the costs of the speakers they drafted in. By December 1928 there were only five Nazi members – too few for them to count as a local Nazi group.

Throughout the 1920s the Social Democrats were the most successful party in Northeim. Most working people voted for them. Among the farmers in the area it was still the more conservative and nationalist parties which attracted support. However, the extremists of the left and right wing, the Communists and Nazis, received hardly any votes.

Recovery

As you saw on page 45, in 1928 the Nazis adjusted their policies nationally. Instead of focusing on the working classes and emphasising their anti-Jewish propaganda they decided to target the middle classes, and particularly to stress their anti-Communist

ideas and to concentrate their attacks on the economic policies of the Weimar Republic. In Northeim they latched onto the grievances of farmers and local businessmen, denouncing the ideas of the Social Democratic Party as Marxist.

These tactics had immediate effects in Northeim. Attendance at meetings went up from fifteen to forty, and then to eighty. In the Northeim area in the first nine months of 1929 the Nazis gained more than fifty new members – with only two exceptions, small businessmen or craftsmen. Thus many months before the stock market crash on Wall Street triggered off the Depression in Germany, Nazism was on the rise in Northeim.

Success

Building on that more solid foundation, over the next three years the Nazis went from strength to strength in Northeim.

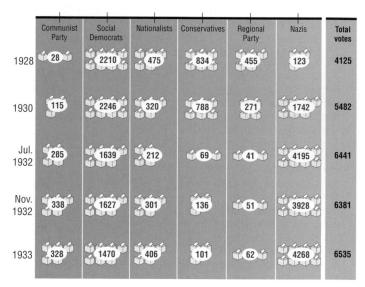

	Communist Party	Social Democrats	Nationalists	Conservatives	Regional Party	Nazis	Total votes
1928	28	2210	475	834	455	123	4125
1930	115	2246	320	788	271	1742	5482
Jul. 1932	285	1639	212	69	41	4195	6441
Nov. 1932	338	1627	301	136	51	3928	6381
1933	328	1470	406	101	62	4268	6535

SOURCE 5 Number of votes cast in national elections in Northeim, 1928–33

1. Write a detailed description of the changes shown in Source 5. Include:
   a) how much the Nazi vote rose
   b) how the Communist vote changed
   c) which parties appear to have lost most votes to the Nazis.
2. Between 1928 and 1933 the population of Northeim changed very little, yet the number of people voting increased greatly. Why do you think this happened?
3. What factors contributed to the growth of the Nazi Party in Northeim before the Wall Street Crash?

Why did the people of Northeim support the Nazis?

■ SOURCE INVESTIGATION

NAZISM WAS ON the rise before 1930 but it was the Depression years that saw its biggest breakthrough.

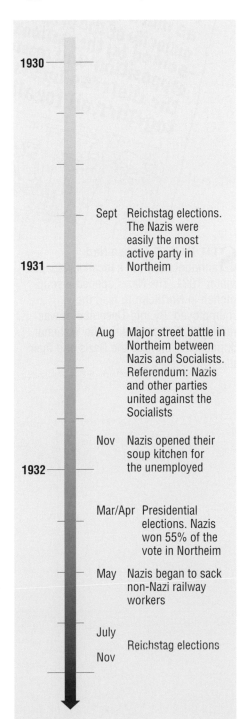

1930

1931

Sept Reichstag elections. The Nazis were easily the most active party in Northeim

Aug Major street battle in Northeim between Nazis and Socialists. Referendum: Nazis and other parties united against the Socialists

Nov Nazis opened their soup kitchen for the unemployed

1932

Mar/Apr Presidential elections. Nazis won 55% of the vote in Northeim

May Nazis began to sack non-Nazi railway workers

July

Reichstag elections

Nov

SOURCE 1 Summary of events in Northeim, 1930–32

■ TASK

Sources 2–11 are evidence gathered by W.S. Allen in his attempt to explain the success of the Nazis in Northeim. They are mostly extracts from interviews conducted in the 1960s with people who had lived in Northeim in the 1920s and 1930s.

Take two sheets of paper. On sheet A list actions taken by the Nazis in Northeim. On sheet B list the reasons people gave for supporting the Nazis. Some things may appear in both lists.

Then use the sheets to write your own answers to these questions. Write a paragraph for each question.

1. What different kinds of people supported the Nazis?
2. What methods did the Nazis use to gain support?
3. What do you think were the most important reasons for Nazi support increasing in Northeim?

SOURCE 2 W.S. Allen describes the attitude of Northeimers to the local Nazi leader, Wilhelm Spannaus, who was from an old Northeim family and ran the town bookshop

66 *Wilhelm Spannaus was exceedingly well liked in Northeim. He was gentle and kindly, friendly to everyone, yet thoughtful and reserved enough to hold people's respect. His bookstore was the intellectual centre of the town. He was chairman of the Northeim Lecture Society. He was a prominent member of the Lutheran Church.*

'Wilhelm Spannaus bears a heavy burden, for it was mainly his example which led many people to join the Nazis,' remarked one Northeimer to me. 'People said "If he's in it, it must be all right".'

Girmann (who effectively ran the party in Northeim) and Denzler (who ran the Northeim SA) were of the 'gutter' type that Northeimers thought belonged to the fringes of the Nazi movement. It was easiest to identify the movement with a serious or 'decent' person like Wilhelm Spannaus; everyone knew him. 99

SOURCE 3 A Northeim businessman

66 *It was the Depression and business was bad. The Nazis asked my father for contributions and he refused. As a consequence of this he lost business. So he joined the Nazi Party. He probably would not have joined of his own choice.* 99

SOURCE 4 A Northeim housewife

The ranks of the Nazi Party were filled with young people. Those serious people who joined did so because they were for social justice, or against unemployment. There was a feeling of restless energy about the Nazis. You constantly saw the swastika painted on the sidewalks or found them littered with pamphlets put out by the Nazis. I was drawn by the feeling of strength about the party, even though there was much in it that was highly questionable.

SOURCE 5 The principal of the Northeim Girls' School

I saw the Communist danger, their gangs breaking up bourgeois [middle-class] meetings, the bourgeois parties being utterly helpless, the Nazis being the only party that broke terror by anti-terror. I saw the complete failure of the bourgeois parties to deal with the economic crisis. Only National Socialism offered any hope.

Nazis mostly did not hate Jews individually, but they were concerned about the Jewish problem. Most Jews persisted in being loyal to their Jewish fellows, so that more and more Jews got positions in trade, banking, the newspapers, etc. Many people saw the danger of that problem. Nobody knew of any way to deal with it, but they hoped that the Nazis would know.

SOURCE 7 From a Nazi announcement in a local newspaper, winter 1931. The Nazis opened a soup-kitchen in Northeim to feed the unemployed. By mid-December it was serving 200 meals a day. The 'National Opposition' refers to the Nazis and their allies

SOURCE 6 A teenage boy who joined the Hitler Youth in Northeim in 1930

There was no pressure on me to join the Hitler Youth. I decided to join it independently simply because I wanted to be in a boys' club with a nationalistic aim. The Hitler Youth had camping, hikes and group meetings. There were boys from all kinds of families, though mainly middle-class and workers.

SOURCE 8 A Northeim railway worker describes events in the spring of 1932

66 *The Nazis made their first attempt to organise the railway workers. Nazism was already strong amongst the [office staff]. It started with the highest officials and worked downwards. From 1931 the officials saw to it that those who belonged to the Brownshirts [the SA] got privileged treatment. When I argued with workers against the Nazis I was told not to speak during working hours.* 99

In the late spring of 1932 all socialist workers were offered new contracts on inferior terms.

66 *The bulk of them signed rather than lose their jobs. The pressure began to be applied to the other workers and the final step was 'either join the Nazis or be fired'.* 99

CITIZENS OF NORTHEIM!

For fourteen years you were the playthings of the Marxist system. For fourteen years you had to look on while they governed Germany into the dirt! Tomorrow you must carry out your national duty in our town, Northeim. This is the last chance you will have to end Marxist armed rule. Tomorrow will see nationalist Northeim oppose the remains of Marxism in closed ranks.

For Northeim's recovery in a free Germany!

SOURCE 9 Reconstruction of a Nazi election advertisement, March 1933

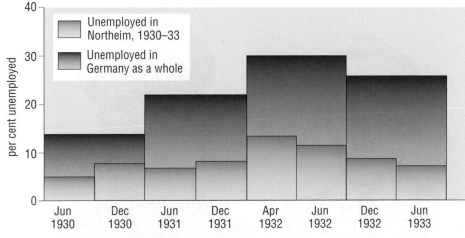

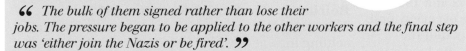

SOURCE 10 Unemployment in Northeim and Germany as a whole, 1930–33. Unemployment was always well below the national average. However, see also Source 11

SOURCE 11 W.S. Allen, writing about the unemployed who passed through Northeim every week on their way to the District Employment Office

66 *Every week in September 1930, about 6000 men came to Northeim. They came from four counties to look for jobs or to receive their dole ... The Employment Office was located in one of the barracks of the old army compound north of town. The barracks of the compound formed a quadrangle, and it was within this small area that the bitter unemployed milled about while waiting their turn ... Most of the jobless belonged to the SPD but there were enough Nazis and Communists to guarantee frequent fights. In the supercharged political atmosphere, the army compound, with its daily influx of hungry and worried men, was a concrete example to Northeimers of what the deepening depression could bring.*

The misery of the jobless evoked suspicion and disgust more often than compassion. One teacher recalled that 'Masses of young men stood idle on corners and made a lot of noise, often insulting people who were passing by'. A housewife had similar reactions: 'There were great numbers of unemployed who just stood around – the bulk of them were just lazy and didn't want to work – theirs was a sad case.' 99

■ TASK

Historians suggest that many people did not know what they were voting for when they voted for the Nazis.

1. On the evidence of Sources 2–11, what did Northeimers seem to think they were voting for?
2. How does this compare with the actual views of the Nazis (see pages 33–35)?

Why was Hitler invited to become Chancellor?

YOU HAVE ALREADY investigated the strengths and weaknesses of the Weimar Constitution (see page 21). In 1932 the weaknesses of the constitution were clear to all. Because of its careful balance of power and proportional representation, no political leader was strong enough to rule. During this period Germany was effectively being run by 84-year-old President Hindenburg. He was a relic from the past. Policy was being set by a tiny group of rich, conservative industrialists and army leaders. The Reichstag offered very little leadership.

Overview

You are going to study the events of 1932 and 1933 in some detail, so it is important to get the overview first. At the heart of the problem was the fact that the Nazis were the largest party. Normally the leader of such a party would become Chancellor, but the other parties in the Reichstag would not work with Hitler. The constitution gave President Hindenburg the right to appoint the Chancellor and he did not want Hitler as Chancellor.

So month after month there were arguments and back-room deals as different politicians struggled to assemble a workable government. The weakness of the Reichstag would have been a problem even if things had been going well in Germany. But when faced with the chronic problems of the Depression it was disastrous.

As you study the twists and turns of 1932–33, these are the main characters you will meet.

Reichstag elections: July 1932

In the July 1932 elections the Nazis won 37.3 per cent of the vote (230 seats) – their best result ever. They were now by far the largest party. Hitler demanded to be appointed Chancellor.

Hindenburg despised Hitler, but he could see the value of trying to use the Nazis for his own ends. Hindenburg appointed Franz von Papen as his Chancellor. Von Papen had no support in the Reichstag but he hoped he could create a right-wing coalition government with the support of the Nazis and other right-wing parties in the Reichstag.

Hitler refused to co-operate, so Hindenburg called another election.

Reichstag elections: November 1932

This was a bad election for the Nazis. Apathy was settling in.

In Northeim the Nazis were in financial trouble and made a public appeal for party funds. In an attempt to regain support, the SA and leading Nazis went to church *en masse* and got a Protestant minister to speak for them. They placed advertisements in the local newspapers and mobilised all sections of the party to distribute leaflets and tickets to meetings. All this activity was in vain, however – the Nazis lost 267 votes in the town.

In Germany as a whole, the thuggery and intimidation by the SA had begun to lose the Nazis support. Their vote fell to 33.1 per cent. They lost 34 seats. They were still the largest party but there was a real sense of gloom among the Nazis. After years of continuous campaigning they were running short of money. Goebbels wrote in his diary: 'the future looks dark and gloomy; all chances and hopes have quite disappeared.'

President Hindenburg
Former army leader. Hated Hitler. He called him 'the little Bohemian corporal'. His main advisers were rich, conservative industrialists and army leaders.

Franz von Papen
Rich Catholic nobleman. A favourite of Hindenburg. Distrusted Hitler.

General von Schleicher
Former army leader. The main adviser to Hindenburg. Supported von Papen to start with. Distrusted Hitler.

In fact, success was just around the corner. Hitler's help came from a surprising source. General von Schleicher stopped supporting von Papen and decided he himself should become Chancellor. This triggered off a power struggle between von Schleicher and von Papen, which ended with them handing power to Hitler. This is how it happened:

1932

3 December: Hindenburg (reluctantly) appoints von Schleicher Chancellor.

1933

4 January: Von Papen can see that von Schleicher is having difficulty keeping a Reichstag majority. He sees his chance to win back power. He privately agrees to work with Hitler. Hitler will be Chancellor. Von Papen will be in the Cabinet.

22 January: Von Papen asks Hindenburg to make Hitler Chancellor. Hindenburg refuses.

28 January: Von Schleicher finally has to admit defeat in raising support in the Reichstag. He has to resign.

30 January: Hindenburg wants von Papen back but is advised that reappointing such an unpopular Chancellor might trigger a movement against Hindenburg himself.

Von Papen persuades Hindenburg that as long as the number of Nazis in the Cabinet is limited, then even with Hitler as Chancellor the most extreme Nazi policies could be resisted. He also warns that the alternative is a Nazi revolt and civil war.

Hindenburg appoints Hitler as Chancellor and von Papen as Vice-Chancellor.

S OURCE 1 An American cartoon from early 1933 with the caption 'Not the most comfortable seat'

■ TASK

You are now going to write an essay on the subject 'Why did Hitler become Chancellor in January 1933?' Over pages 44-61 you have investigated different factors which contributed to this. They are summarised in the diagram opposite. Use each point in the diagram as the basis for one paragraph in your essay. In the final paragraph of your essay reach your own conclusions as to which factors were, in your opinion, most important.

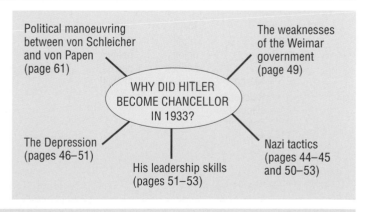

Political manoeuvring between von Schleicher and von Papen (page 61)

The weaknesses of the Weimar government (page 49)

WHY DID HITLER BECOME CHANCELLOR IN 1933?

The Depression (pages 46–51)

His leadership skills (pages 51–53)

Nazi tactics (pages 44–45 and 50–53)

chapter 4

HOW DID HITLER CONSOLIDATE HIS POWER IN 1933 AND 1934?

O N 30 JANUARY 1933 the Nazis celebrated Hitler's appointment as Chancellor with cheering parades through the streets of Berlin.

It seemed that the Nazis had achieved their ambitions. However, Hitler knew that his hold on power was fragile. He was Chancellor, but there were only two other Nazis in the Cabinet of twelve ministers. Hitler's opponents were confident that they could resist his extremist demands. They were soon to be proved very wrong. Over the next eighteen months Hitler eliminated all political opposition on his way to becoming absolute and undisputed ruler; Germany became a one-party state.

The timeline below summarises how he achieved this. On pages 63-74 you will examine the main steps he took in greater detail.

Nazi parade to celebrate Hitler's appointment as Chancellor

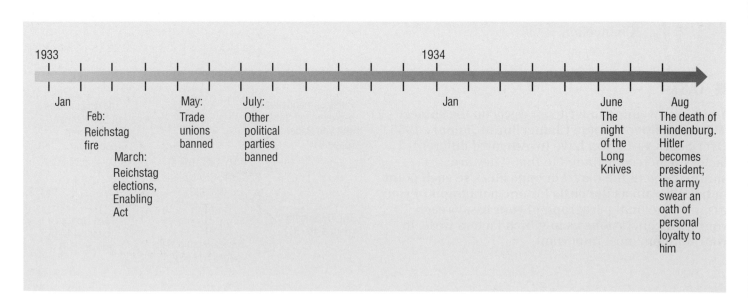

1933

Jan

Feb:
Reichstag
fire

March:
Reichstag
elections,
Enabling
Act

May:
Trade
unions
banned

July:
Other
political
parties
banned

1934

Jan

June
The
night
of the
Long
Knives

Aug
The death of
Hindenburg.
Hitler
becomes
president;
the army
swear an
oath of
personal
loyalty to
him

How did Hitler take advantage of the Reichstag fire?

ONCE HE WAS installed as Chancellor, Hitler insisted on new Reichstag elections. They were called for 5 March. He was determined to win an absolute majority for the Nazis, and as Chancellor he was now in a position to use all the powers of the state against his opponents.

On 4 February he got President Hindenburg to pass a decree supposedly to ensure free and peaceful elections. All election meetings had to be notified to police at least forty-eight hours in advance. In theory this was to ensure that meetings could be adequately policed. In fact it allowed Nazi-controlled police to come and break up the meetings themselves.

The decree gave the police the authority to prohibit any election meeting where a danger to public security was feared. It ordered that the police were to be given a prominent place at every meeting.

These powers were particularly useful in the important state of Prussia, where the Nazi, Hermann Goering, was Minister of the Interior and controlled the police.

On 17 February Goering told his police force that SA or nationalist meetings were not to be impeded by police restrictions but that those of Communists must be dealt with with all severity. He promised his officers: 'I shall cover for police officers who use firearms in the discharge of their duties, regardless of the consequences of the use of firearms.'

On 22 February Goering appointed members of the Nazis' own SA as auxiliary police officers, giving them the same free rein as the official police force. They disrupted opposition meetings, and beat up opponents.

Goering also planned control of other aspects of the election:

> **SOURCE 1** Goering writing in his diary in February 1933 about the March elections
>
> *66 Radio causes me some trouble. All the important positions are held by supporters of 'the old system'. They have to be got rid of as soon as possible, that is by 5 March, lest they endanger the election. 99*

The Reichstag fire

On the night of 27 February came the sensational news that the Reichstag building had been set on fire. Inside the burning building the police found a Dutch Communist, van der Lubbe, who was arrested and charged with starting the fire. Hitler used this as evidence that the Communists were plotting against his government. That night Goering's Prussian police arrested and imprisoned 4000 Communist leaders.

SOURCE 2 The Reichstag building on fire

The next day Hitler persuaded President Hindenburg to pass an emergency decree suspending all the articles in the constitution which guaranteed personal liberty, freedom of speech, freedom of the press, and freedom of assembly.

It thus gave the police emergency powers to search houses, confiscate property, and detain people indefinitely without trial. It decreed the death penalty for a wide range of crimes. The police could ban meetings, close newspapers, round up political opponents and drag them off to their hastily organised concentration camps and detention centres. True to his word, Goering's police seized the state radio station.

This might have been an emergency decree but in fact it stayed in place for twelve years, throughout the period of Nazi rule. It formed the rather fragile legal base for much of the Nazis' twelve-year terror against their opponents in Germany.

In the short term, however, the fire seemed like a windfall to the Nazis. It provided them with just the excuse they needed to tighten the screw on the opposition. So the question was naturally asked then – and has been asked repeatedly ever since – whether the Nazis actually organised the fire themselves. You can investigate this in detail in the Source Investigation starting on the next page.

1. Goering had promised in his diary that the March 1933 elections would be 'a masterpiece of propaganda'. Explain what you think he meant by this.

Who was to blame for the Reichstag fire?

■ SOURCE INVESTIGATION

Historians still cannot agree on who was to blame for the Reichstag fire. There is evidence to support three different verdicts:

a) **That van der Lubbe started the fire and that he was acting alone**, not as part of a Communist plot. Throughout his trial he claimed this was the case. This was accepted at the trial. Van der Lubbe was found guilty, and executed.

b) **That van der Lubbe was acting as part of a Communist plot.** The Nazis claimed they found incendiary devices at the homes of many Communists, along with plans for which public buildings would be targeted.

c) **That the Nazis started the fire themselves** as part of their terror tactics, and somehow used van der Lubbe in order to blame the Communists. There was direct, secret access from Goering's headquarters to the Reichstag building and his own SA chief claimed to have started the fire.

■ TASK

Read through Sources 3–9, answering the questions as you do so. Make sure you explain your answers.

Then write your own summary of the evidence for and against each of verdicts a), b) and c). You could do this as an essay or as a diagram or as a combination of both. Conclude with your own explanation of which verdict seems the most likely.

SOURCE 3 From an account written in 1950 by Rudolf Diels, head of the Prussian political police

66 *When I arrived a few officers of my department were already interrogating van der Lubbe. Naked from the waist upwards, smeared with dirt and sweating, he sat in front of them, breathing heavily. He panted as if he had completed a tremendous task.*

I sat opposite him in the police headquarters several times that night and listened to his confused stories. I read the Communist pamphlets he carried in his trouser pockets. [His] voluntary confessions prevented me from thinking that an arsonist who was such an expert needed any helpers ... This specialist had used a whole knapsack full of inflammable material. He had been so active that he had laid several dozen fires. With a firelighter, he had set the Chamber aflame. Then he had run through the big corridors with his burning shirt which he brandished in his right hand like a torch to lay more fires under the old leather sofas. During this hectic activity he was overpowered by Reichstag officials.

Shortly after my arrival at the burning Reichstag, Goering and Hitler arrived. Goering came towards me. His voice was heavy with the emotion of the dramatic moment: 'This is the beginning of the Communist revolt, they will start their attack now! Not a moment must be lost!' Hitler turned to the assembled company. He shouted uncontrollably: 'There will be no mercy now. Anyone who stands in our way will be cut down. Every Communist official will be shot where he is found. Everybody in league with the Communists must be arrested.'

I reported on the results of the first interrogations of van der Lubbe – that in my opinion he was a maniac. Hitler ridiculed my childish view: 'That is something really cunning, prepared a long time ago. The criminals have thought this out beautifully, but they've miscalculated, haven't they?'

I pulled Goering aside but he did not let me start. He said, 'Police on an emergency footing; shoot to kill; and any other emergency regulations which might be appropriate.'

When I returned to headquarters after midnight it was buzzing like a beehive. While squad vans arrived, and whole troops of detectives, with registers [of Communists] prepared years before, jumped on the ramps, the first cars were arriving back at the entrance of the building with dazed prisoners who had been woken from their sleep. 99

1. Read Source 3. Which theory is supported by
   a) Diels
   b) Goering and Hitler?
2. What evidence is there in Source 3 that the Nazis were taken by surprise by the fire?

SOURCE 4 An historian's account which is based on the testimony of Karl Ernst – the Berlin SA leader. Ernst's story was published by Communists in Paris in 1934. Ernst was killed in Hitler's purge of the SA a year after the fire

An underground passage, built to carry the central heating system, ran from Goering's palace to the Reichstag building. Through this tunnel Karl Ernst led a small detachment of Stormtroopers. They scattered gasoline and self-igniting chemicals and then made their way back to the palace.

At the same time a half-witted Dutch Communist with a passion for arson, Marinus van der Lubbe, had made his way into the huge, darkened, and to him, unfamiliar building, and set some fires of his own. This feeble-minded pyromaniac [person who has an inner compulsion to start fires] was a godsend to the Nazis. He had been picked up by the SA a few days before after having been heard in a bar boasting that he had attempted to set fire to several public buildings, and that he was going to try the Reichstag next.

The coincidence that the Nazis had found a demented Communist arsonist who was out to do exactly what they themselves had determined to do seems incredible, but it is nevertheless supported by the evidence.

3. Read Source 4. Does this support or contradict Source 3?
4. Do you think Dicls (Source 3) or Ernst (Source 4) is a more reliable witness?

SOURCE 5 From Goering's testimony at van der Lubbe's trial

It never occurred to me that the Reichstag might have been set on fire; I thought the fire had been caused by carelessness, or something of that sort.

Only when his car drew up at the Reichstag and he heard someone use the word 'arson' did it occur to him that incendiaries had been at work.

In this moment I knew that the Communist Party was the culprit;
I only wish that the rest of the world had seen this as clearly.

SOURCE 6 General Halder, Chief of the German General Staff, speaking at the Nuremberg War Crimes trial, 1945

At a luncheon on the birthday of the Führer in 1942 the conversation turned to the topic of the Reichstag building. I heard with my own ears when Goering interrupted the conversation and shouted: 'The only one who really knows about the Reichstag is I, because I set it on fire!'

5. Compare Sources 5 and 6. How can you explain the contradictions in these two sources?
6. Which of Sources 5 and 6 do you think is more reliable?

SOURCE 7 From a letter written by a British journalist who witnessed the Reichstag fire, published in a German newspaper in 1959

That evening Hitler himself was not absolutely certain that the fire was a Communist plot. As we walked side by side through the burning building [he said], 'God grant that this be the work of the Communists!'

7. Read Source 7. Does this source prove that the Nazis did not plan the fire?

SOURCE 8 A British cartoon from *Punch* magazine, 8 March 1933. It shows Hindenburg speaking to Hitler

THE RED PERIL.

THE OLD CONSUL (*to* HITLER). "THIS IS A HEAVEN-SENT OPPORTUNITY, MY LAD. IF YOU CAN'T BE A DICTATOR NOW, YOU NEVER WILL BE."

8. Explain what Source 8 is suggesting about the fire.

SOURCE 9 Van der Lubbe (standing) on trial for starting the Reichstag fire. The Dutch Communist – who had only been in Germany for a week before the fire – was described as 'half-witted'

9. Study Source 9. At his trial van der Lubbe knew he faced the death penalty yet he stuck to his story that he was acting alone. Does this mean he was telling the truth? Explain your answer.

Why was the Enabling Act so important?

NAZI TERROR TACTICS reached a peak in the days after the Reichstag fire. Thousands of political opponents were arrested. Only the Nazis were allowed to campaign for the forthcoming election – a flood of propaganda was unleashed, urging Germans to vote for them. On election day itself each polling station was policed by a mass of uniformed Nazis who watched each ballot paper being marked.

a) Workers were no longer allowed to join trade unions

b) Opposition politicians were arrested and imprisoned

c) Enemies of the Nazis, especially Communists, could be executed

d) The SA could search and ransack the homes of suspected opponents

e) Many opponents were driven into exile

f) The Nazis intimidated voters by watching over them as they crossed their ballot papers

The March 1933 election

In the election on 5 March the Nazis got their best-ever result. Yet despite that, the election still failed to give the Nazis an overall majority. The results are shown in Source 2. What Hitler wanted now was an 'Enabling Law' which would place all power in his hands, allow him to pass laws without consulting the Reichstag, and effectively allow him to establish a dictatorship. The Nationalists were prepared to support him in this, but even then Hitler would be well short of the two-thirds of Reichstag seats that he needed to pass a change to the constitution. How would he get the votes he needed?

Ban the Communists

The first step was to ban the Communists from serving in the Reichstag. That was relatively simple under his emergency powers. But he still needed to convince the members of the other parties.

Intimidate the Social Democrats

The newly elected Reichstag members met for the first time in the Kroll Opera House in Berlin on 23 March (see Source 3).

Despite this pressure many Social Democrats still voted against the Enabling Act – but to no effect. All the other parties gave in to Nazi pressure. The Enabling Act was passed by 444 votes to 94.

■ **ACTIVITY**

Read Source 3. Rewrite it as you think a Nazi supporter might report the same events.

SOURCE 2 The results of the election, 5 March 1933

Nazis	*288 seats*	
Nationalists	*52*	
Social Democrats (SPD)	*120*	*359 seats in*
Communists	*81*	*total*
Centre Party	*74*	
Others	*32*	

SOURCE 3 A Social Democrat MP recounts the passing of the Enabling Act

66 *The wide square in front of the Kroll Opera House was crowded with dark masses of people. We were received with wild choruses: 'We want an Enabling Act!' Youths with swastikas on their chests eyed us insolently, blocked our way, in fact made us run the gauntlet, calling us names like 'Centre [Catholic Party] pig', 'Marxist sow'. The Opera House was crawling with armed SA and SS men. The assembly hall was decorated with swastikas. When we Social Democrats had taken our seats on the extreme left, SA and SS men lined up at the exits and along the walls behind us in a semi-circle. Their expressions boded no good.*

Hitler read out his government declaration in a surprisingly calm voice. Only in a few places did he raise it to a fanatical frenzy: when he demanded the public execution of van der Lubbe, and when, at the end of his speech, he uttered dark threats of what would happen if the Reichstag did not vote for the Enabling Act.

Otto Wels read out our reply. It was a masterpiece in form and content, a farewell to the fading era of human rights and humanity. With his voice half-choking, he gave our good wishes to the persecuted and oppressed in the country who, though innocent, were already filling the prisons and concentration camps simply on account of their political creed.

Hitler jumped up furiously and launched into a passionate reply. 'You are over-sensitive, gentlemen, if you talk of persecution already. You, gentlemen, are no longer needed. I do not even want you to vote for the Enabling Act. Germany shall become free, but not through you!'

We tried to dam the flood of Hitler's accusations with interruptions of 'No!', 'An error!', 'False!' But that did us no good. The SA and the SS people hissed loudly and murmured, 'Shut up!', 'Traitors!', 'You'll be strung up today!' 99

The Enabling Act

The Act gave Hitler the power to make laws without the approval of either the Reichstag or the President. The Reichstag had in effect voted itself out of existence. It had voted to introduce a Nazi dictatorship. Through the next eleven years of Nazi rule the Reichstag met twelve times – but simply to listen to Hitler speaking. They never held a debate. They had no say on policies. The Weimar Republic was over.

The Enabling Act triggered a six-month period of rapid change throughout Germany, which is known as the Nazi revolution.

Why did the Weimar Republic collapse?

THE WEIMAR REPUBLIC lasted fourteen years (see the timeline
below). Right up to the present day historians have disagreed on
the reasons for its collapse.

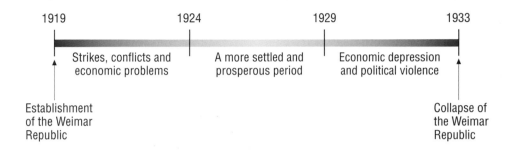

1919   1924   1929   1933

Strikes, conflicts and economic problems

A more settled and prosperous period

Economic depression and political violence

Establishment of the Weimar Republic

Collapse of the Weimar Republic

■ TASK

Sources 1–3 are historians' judgements on why the Weimar
Republic collapsed.

1. a) How much do they differ?
   b) What reasons can you think of for this?
2. Explain whether you agree or disagree with each of them.
   Support your answer with evidence from pages 21–68.
   If you disagree with all the judgements, then write your own
   analysis of why the Weimar Republic collapsed, supporting
   your answer with evidence from pages 21–68.

SOURCE 1 British historian
J.W. Hiden, 1974

❝ *No single problem 'caused'
the downfall of the Weimar
Republic. The interaction of
problems progressively
weakened the new German
state, and reached its climax in
the crisis of 1929–33.* ❞

SOURCE 2 German historian C.L.
Holtfrerich, 1990

❝ *Conflict was going on
throughout the lifetime of the
Weimar Republic. Yet Nazism
was not then successful. The Nazi
rise to power was essentially
linked to the Great Depression
which was a worldwide
phenomenon and had little to do
with the domestic conflict.* ❞

SOURCE 3 American historian
William L. Shirer, 1959

❝ *The weaknesses of the
Weimar regime were obvious.
There were too many political
parties, and they were unable
to form an enduring majority
in the Reichstag that could
back a stable government.*

*[By 1932] political power . . .
was concentrated in the hands
of a senile President and in
those of a few shallow,
ambitious men around him.
Hitler saw this clearly, and it
suited his purposes.* ❞

The SA or the army? Hitler makes his choice

BY MID-1934 a power struggle had developed in the Nazi leadership. It was clear that Hitler had to make a choice between the SA and the army.

The SA

Throughout the rise of the Nazis Hitler depended on the SA to put his policies into action. They had fought loyally for Hitler against the Communists and had helped him come to power. By 1934 the SA was an enormous organisation with more than two million members. It was also very powerful. In fact, its leader Ernst Röhm was a potential rival to Hitler.

Röhm wanted Hitler to continue the Nazi revolution by reducing the power of big business and carrying out the anti-capitalist parts of the Nazi programme – such as taking over major industries. Röhm also wanted the SA to take control of the army.

■ ACTIVITY

The advantages and disadvantages for Hitler in supporting the SA or the army are set out in the diagram below. Discuss them with a partner. Decide which Hitler should choose.

The army

The army was much smaller than the SA – it had only 100,000 soldiers. The army leadership were supported by big business. They wanted Hitler to expand the army and to buy new weapons. The army was totally opposed to being taken over by the SA and was very suspicious of Röhm.

Hitler had always known how important the army was in gaining effective control of Germany. The opposition of the army had been his main problem in 1923 when the Munich Putsch failed (see page 41). As soon as he became Chancellor on 3 February 1933 he went to the army leaders to explain his aims. He told them he intended to rearm Germany (thus overturning a central part of the Treaty of Versailles), and to take over Lebensraum in eastern Europe. He also told them that his plans would involve defeating France in a war.

While many army leaders might have welcomed such plans, others remained very suspicious of Hitler.

Many of the army chiefs were from upper-class families and rather looked down on Hitler. On the other hand they agreed with Hitler's nationalist aims and his belief that the army needed to be much larger.

Supporting the SA

Reasons for:

1. Röhm was an old friend of Hitler.

2. The SA had fought for Hitler in the 1923 Munich Putsch and in later fights against the Communists.

3. They were committed Nazis.

4. The SA had grown to over 2,500,000 men – it was much larger than the army if it came to a fight.

Reasons against:

1. The SA was beginning to get out of hand. It was interfering in the running of the country and the law courts.

2. It disapproved of some of the Nazi leaders.

3. If Hitler used the SA to control the army, then he would have to go along with their other demands.

4. Hitler did not agree with many of the SA's anti-capitalist policies and working-class aims.

Supporting the army

Reasons for:

1. The army was well trained, organised and disciplined.

2. It was the only organisation which had the power to remove Hitler.

3. It had the support of big business and conservatives.

4. An efficient army was needed for Hitler to retake the land lost in the Treaty of Versailles.

Reasons against:

1. The army was small – it had only 100,000 men.

2. How loyal the army would be to Hitler was unknown.

3. Some of the generals disliked Hitler and the Nazis.

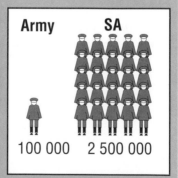

Army   SA

100 000   2 500 000

What did Hitler think of Röhm and the SA?

Röhm was a tough soldier who had fought both in the German army in the First World War and in the Freikorps after it. He was one of Hitler's earliest supporters. He had helped create the SA as a private army. In 1923 Röhm stood alongside Hitler in the Munich Putsch. He was not sent to prison and was appointed by Hitler to keep the party going whilst Hitler served his sentence.

Röhm had an unruly temper. He was on bad terms with some other Nazi leaders, particularly Goering whom he disliked for his aristocratic manner, and Himmler, commander of the SS.

The debate over the SA had been rumbling for ten years. In 1924 Röhm had quarrelled with Hitler about it. Röhm wanted to replace the German army when the Nazis won power. After the quarrel he had emigrated to Bolivia where as a military adviser he helped build an army and fought in a war.

By 1930 Hitler was having trouble controlling the SA – most of them were simply thugs – so he asked Röhm to return to take control of them. Röhm made them a more disciplined body but still wanted them to become the most powerful force in Germany.

However, Röhm was devoted to Hitler and was a very efficient organiser. He was also homosexual and a drunkard, but Hitler was not worried about this in the early years.

SOURCE 1 Hitler's description of the role of the SA in the Nazis' early years

66 Such men are unusable in times of peace, but in troubled times it's quite different ... With blind confidence they followed me! Fundamentally, they were just overgrown children ... During the war they had fought with bayonets and thrown hand grenades. They couldn't let the country be sold out to the scum who were the product of defeat ... These fine chaps, what sacrifices they were willing to make. All day at their jobs, and all night off on a mission for the Party. 99

SOURCE 2 The smiles of the SA leader, Röhm (on the left), and Himmler, commander of the SS (on the right), hide their rivalry

The Night of the Long Knives

On 29 June 1934 Hitler acted. He called a meeting of SA leaders for the following day at Wiessee in Bavaria. Source 3 tells you what happened on 30 June, which has become known as The Night of the Long Knives.

SOURCE 3 Written after the war by Hitler's chauffeur, Eric Kempka

Just before Wiessee, Hitler suddenly breaks his silence: 'Kempka,' he says, 'drive carefully when we come to the Hotel Hanselbauer. You must drive up without making any noise. If you see an SA guard in the front of the hotel, don't wait for them to report to me; drive on and stop at the hotel entrance.' Then, after a moment of deathly silence: 'Röhm wants to carry out a coup.'

An icy shiver runs down my back. I could have believed anything, but not a coup by Röhm!

I drive up carefully to the hotel entrance as Hitler had ordered. Hitler jumps out of the car, and after him Goebbels, Lutze and the adjutants. Right behind us another car stops with a squad of detectives which had been raised in Munich.

As soon as I have turned the car so that it is ready to leave in a moment, I rush into the hotel with my gun at the ready ... I run quickly up the stairs to the first floor where Hitler is just coming out of Röhm's bedroom ...

[A few seconds later] Röhm comes out of his room in a blue suit and with a cigar in the corner of his mouth. Hitler glares at him but says nothing. Two detectives take Röhm to the vestibule of the hotel where he throws himself into an armchair and orders coffee from the waiter.

I stay in the corridor a little to one side and a detective tells me about Röhm's arrest.

Hitler entered Röhm's bedroom alone with a whip in his hand. Behind him were two detectives with pistols at the ready. He spat out the words: 'Röhm, you are under arrest.' Röhm looked up sleepily from his pillow: 'Heil, my Führer.'

'You are under arrest,' bawled Hitler for the second time, turned on his heel and left the room.

Over the weekend Röhm and around 200 other SA leaders were executed. These also included other opponents of Hitler who were not part of the SA, for example the former Chancellor von Schleicher.

■ SOURCE INVESTIGATION

On 13 July 1934 Hitler told the Reichstag that Röhm had been arrested and shot because he was plotting to seize power. Was this true or was Hitler lying? Study Sources 4–11 and see if you can decide.

SOURCE 4 In a newspaper article in June 1933 Röhm made it clear that he was not happy with the way things were going

Already here and there philistines and grumblers are daring to ask in astonishment what the SA and the SS are still here for since Hitler is now in power. Anyone who believes he has taken part in the German Revolution can go home! He has confused the 'national uprising' with the German Revolution.

The SA and SS [which at the time was part of the SA] will not tolerate the German Revolution going to sleep or being betrayed at the half-way stage ... Whether they like it or not, we will continue our struggle with them; if they are unwilling – without them; and if necessary – against them!

SOURCE 5 Röhm speaking to Nazi friends during a drunken conversation. This report of the conversation is by Rauschning, who subsequently left the Nazi party and fled to England

Adolf is a swine. He is betraying all of us. He is ... getting matey with the Prussian generals. Adolf knows exactly what I want. I've told him often enough ... The generals are a lot of old fogeys ... I'm the nucleus of the new army, don't you see that? ... Hitler puts me off with fair words.

SOURCE 6 A description of Röhm by the British politician Anthony Eden, who met him in 1934

Röhm was a ... flamboyant figure, scarred and scented, with a jewelled dagger at his waist ... But he was not just a perverted swashbuckler, he had intelligence of a kind and, a rarity in the modern world, he was a man who boasted of his bravery, yet was brave.

SOURCE 7 Hitler in a speech to regional governors on 6 July 1933

66 *Revolution must not develop into a lasting state. We must look to gradual evolution through educating the people. A businessman must not be dismissed if he is a good businessman even if he is not yet a good National Socialist ... The carriers of intellectual poison now seeking to penetrate the economy are a menace to both the state and people. We must not act like fools and overturn everything.* 99

1. Using Sources 4–7 and your own background knowledge explain whether you think it was likely that Röhm and Hitler would come into conflict.

SOURCE 8 On 7 June 1934, following a long interview with Hitler, Röhm published this announcement

66 *I have decided to follow the advice of my doctors and take a cure [go to a health spa] to restore my energies which have been severely strained by a painful nervous complaint. 1934 will require all the energies of every SA fighter. I recommend, therefore, to all SA leaders to begin organising leave now in June. Therefore, for some SA leaders and men, June, and for the majority of the SA, July, will be a period of complete relaxation in which they can recover their strength. I expect the SA to return on 1 August completely rested and refreshed.* 99

2. Read Source 8. Does this source show that Röhm had agreed to what Hitler wanted in Source 7? Explain your answer.

SOURCE 9 Field-Marshal von Kleist's description of events in June 1934. He was commander of the army in Silesia. He was writing after the war

66 *About 24 June, I was warned that an attack by the SA on the army was imminent. On 28 June I asked the local SA leader to come to see me. I told him I knew of his plans. He replied that he had only put his men on alert to resist my attack.*

I told the government that I had the impression that the army and the SA were being egged on against each other by Himmler. 99

SOURCE 10 General Goering, a leading Nazi, quickly held a press conference which was reported in *The Times* newspaper on 2 July 1934

66 *General Goering explained that he and Herr Himmler, who were responsible for security, had been watching for weeks, even months, and had been aware that preparations for a 'second revolution' were being made by certain ambitious SA leaders, headed by Röhm. Hitler had decided to suppress the movement with a firm hand at a suitable moment.* 99

SOURCE 11 The historian Karl Bracher, in his book *The German Dictatorship*, 1971

66 *The smoothness with which the murders of 30 June were carried out is powerful proof that no Röhm plot was imminent. There was no resistance encountered anywhere ... many victims unsuspectingly surrendered voluntarily, believing it was all a big mistake. The only shots fired were those of the executioners ... the numbers of victims is estimated at between 150 and 200.* 99

SOURCE 12 A British cartoon about the Night of the Long Knives. Its caption was 'They salute with both hands now'

3. Which sources support Hitler's claim that Röhm was plotting against him and which do not? For each source pick the sentence or part of a sentence which best supports your decision.
4. Explain which sources you think are reliable and which unreliable as evidence of Röhm's plans in June 1934.
5. Is Röhm's grumbling about Hitler evidence of a plot?
6. Which source best supports the argument of the historian Karl Bracher in Source 11?
7. Use all the sources and your own background knowledge to decide whether you think the SA was plotting against Hitler. Explain your answer.

Hitler becomes President

ON 2 AUGUST 1934, just weeks after the Night of the Long Knives, President Hindenburg died. Within hours Hitler had declared himself President. He was now not only Chancellor, but Head of State and Commander of the Army. Every soldier swore an oath of personal loyalty to Hitler. The German army had a tradition of discipline and obedience and soldiers took this oath seriously. To break it would be the most serious crime.

SOURCE 1 The army's oath of loyalty

« I swear by God this sacred oath: that I will render unconditional obedience to the Führer of the German Reich and people, Adolf Hitler, the Supreme Commander of the Armed Forces, and will be ready as a brave soldier to risk my life at any time for this oath. »

1. Which two phrases in the oath are the most important?

■ TASK

1. Draw up a timeline from 1919 to 1934. Mark on it the important dates in the rise of the Nazis.
2. Make a copy of the diagram below and add your own notes to show how Hitler himself helped the Nazis in their rise to power.
3. What other factors contributed to their rise?
4. Is one factor more important than the others?
5. Could the Nazis have been successful without Hitler?

Beliefs

Actions
25 Points
Munich Putsch
Trial speeches
Decision to go democratic
Mein Kampf

Personal qualities
Charismatic speaker

Other

Leadership skills
Clever politician

chapter 5

WHAT WERE THE NAZIS TRYING TO ACHIEVE, AND HOW DID THEY TRY TO ACHIEVE IT?

What kind of Germany did the Nazis want to create?

Aim: A strong Germany

THE NAZIS BELIEVED that many of Germany's problems had been caused by the weak leadership of the Weimar period. They wanted Germany to be strong again. They wanted a government strong enough to overturn the Treaty of Versailles, a strong army to make Germany once again the great military power it had been before the war, and a strong thriving economy to restore the prosperity of the German people after the helplessness of the Depression.

How would they create it?

A strong Germany needed a forceful and decisive leader. Within days of his appointment as Chancellor, even before the Enabling Act had been passed, Hitler met with army leaders to tell them of his plans to rearm Germany and to beat France in a war if necessary. The humiliation of the Treaty of Versailles was to be laid aside.

As far as the economy was concerned, the Nazis wanted to make German industries as powerful as they had been before the First World War.

Aim: A racial Germany

Hitler believed that the so-called Aryan people (blond, blue-eyed Germans) were superior to other races. He believed that many of Germany's past problems had been created because Germany was not run by racially pure Aryans. From his earliest days Hitler had advanced racist policies. Now the Nazis wanted to create a racially pure Germany.

How would they create it?

They wanted to get rid of racial minorities such as the Jews, by removing them from positions of power, hounding them out of the country or isolating them from pure Aryans. They would also have to get rid of other people who had undesirable qualities.

To create a racially pure Germany required a particular contribution from German women. They must consider it their highest duty to have as many racially pure children as possible. They should be prevented from marrying men of other races.

The Nazis did not want women to work for a living but believed that it was their national duty to have children and look after their families.

Ein Volk, ein Reich, ein Führer

Aim: The Volk or the people's community

The Nazis wanted all (racially 'pure') Germans to feel they were part of the VOLK or 'the people's community'. In the Volk people would see their own lives as less important than their contribution to Germany itself. In the Volk individual liberties, such as the right to think differently from others, would be less valued than loyalty to the German people (the Volk), to Hitler (the Führer) and to Germany (the Fatherland). They summed this up in the phrase 'Volk, Führer und Vaterland'.

How would they create it?

To create this people's community all other claims on people's loyalties were to be removed. Organisations such as churches, political parties or even swimming clubs or choirs which might divert people's attention away from serving the Volk would have to be dissolved or taken over by the Nazis. Even family loyalties would take second place. The Führer wanted to win the hearts and minds of the German people.

There would be no room for free speech. Even everyday conversations between friends should be controlled because the Nazis wanted to ensure that ideas opposed to Nazism were banished.

1. Which of these aims do you think would be:
a) easiest
b) most difficult
   for the Nazis to achieve? Explain your choice.
2. From what you know about the rise of the Nazis, which of these aims would be most supported by:
a) ordinary Germans
b) loyal members of the Nazi Party?
   Explain your choice.

■ ACTIVITY

Design a poster directed at one of the following groups, indicating what their role will be in the new Germany:
a) mothers
b) businessmen
c) young people.

How would the Nazis run Germany?

The Nazis were well aware of the problems facing them in achieving their aims. In the elections of 1932 they were supported by only 37 per cent of Germans in July and 32 per cent in November. Even in the March 1933 elections, with the Communists banned and supporters of the Social Democrats intimidated by SA men as they cast their votes, the Nazis still polled only 44 per cent. Yet what they had in mind would require total obedience in every aspect of a person's life. How could they control Germany?

1. A dictatorship

Nazi Germany would be a dictatorship. The Nazis did not believe in democracy. They thought that the democratic system of the Weimar government had been a disaster for the country. What Germany needed was a dictator who knew what was best for Germany, who made decisions which everyone else obeyed because they were in the people's interest.

2. A one-party state

The Nazi Party would be the only political party. Every state, every committee, every organisation, every club would be led by members of the Party.

3. Economic success

They would make sure that the German people had jobs and food. They would help them save for their own cars. They would provide holidays and entertainments for loyal Germans.

4. A police state

If there was opposition, the SS and the police (see page 80) would have absolute power to arrest, punish and if necessary to execute the enemies of the state who did not follow the dictator or submit to his demands for total loyalty.

5. A propaganda state

Nazis believed that if they controlled what people in Germany heard, saw and read then they would be able to win their hearts and minds. Goebbels had already shown in the Nazi election campaigns of the early 1930s how successfully he could use propaganda. The Nazis believed this would be equally important now they were in power.

3. For each of points 1–5 explain how this is similar to or different from the system of government in Weimar Germany.
4. The Nazis' methods can be seen as a carrot and stick approach. Draw a diagram to summarise which of the methods are 'carrots' and which are 'sticks'.

Was Hitler really in control of Germany?

WHEN HITLER WAS declared President in 1934 his power was in theory unlimited. Nazi Germany was a one-party state. Hitler was the undisputed leader of that party and dictator of Germany. But was he really in control? This may sound like a silly question. Of course he was: he was the Führer, the dictator! Everybody waited for his orders and then they obeyed! Or so Nazi propaganda would have us believe. One of the greatest successes of Nazi propaganda was that it did manage to present the impression that Hitler was hardworking and in control, and that the Nazi regime was efficient and orderly. This image has remained popular even up to the present day. However, historians now question it.

Hitler the decision-maker

After his death Hitler's personal assistants were able to reveal more about his way of working.

To start with Hitler kept a reasonably ordered daily routine but gradually this routine broke down. He suffered from insomnia. He often stayed up until two or three o'clock in the morning talking to friends on his pet subjects. He rarely got up before late morning. When he did he quickly read the newspapers, and then went to lunch. Far from being the ever-present dictator, with this routine it became more and more difficult to get him to make decisions which he alone could make as Head of State.

It was worse at the weekends as he would often spend Friday to Monday at his retreat at the Berghof in the Bavarian mountains. When there he never left his room before 2 p.m., then he went to lunch. He spent most afternoons taking a walk. In the evenings there were films. It was difficult for government officials to get in touch with him, let alone get him to make a decision. In the summer he left Berlin for even longer periods.

One historian who has studied Hitler's approach to decision-making has concluded that 'he was unwilling to take decisions, frequently uncertain, exclusively concerned with upholding his personal prestige and personal authority, influenced in the strongest way by his closest advisers'.

Hitler distrusted argument and criticism and hated intellectuals. He disliked paperwork and increasingly opted out of the day-to-day running of the government so that he could concentrate on what most interested him – military questions, foreign policy and his favourite architectural projects.

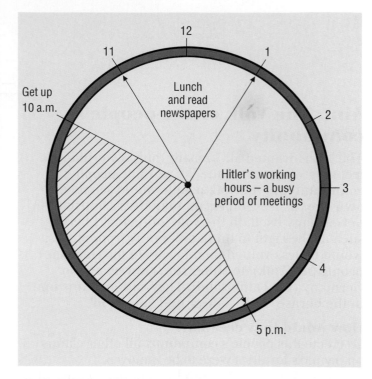

SOURCE 1 Hitler's working day

SOURCE 2 Written after the war by Fritz Wiedemann, one of Hitler's personal assistants

66 *I sometimes secured decisions from him, even ones about important matters, without his ever asking to see the relevant files. He took the view that many things sorted themselves out on their own if one did not interfere. But the question was how did they sort themselves out? The Party leaders found it easiest to get something out of him. If they belonged to the top ranks they could always come to lunch. During coffee they quickly explained their problem to him and normally got the decision they wanted.*

He let people tell him the things he wanted to hear, everything else he rejected. Hitler refused to let himself be informed … How can one tell someone the truth who immediately gets angry when the facts do not suit him? Perhaps that may have been part of his strength. 99

1. What can we learn from Source 2 about the way Germany was run?
2. What information, not in Source 2, would you need to know to judge how well Germany was run?
3. Do you think Fritz Wiedemann thought Hitler was a strong leader or not?

How did the Nazis run Germany? The reality

It might not have mattered that Hitler opted out of many decisions. It was not possible for one person to control all aspects of government. However, the problem was that below Hitler was a very chaotic power structure.

SOURCE 3 The power structure in Nazi Germany. Some of these 'power blocs' became more important during the 1930s, particularly the SS. Others like the army and big business became less powerful. The arrows show when their power increased or decreased

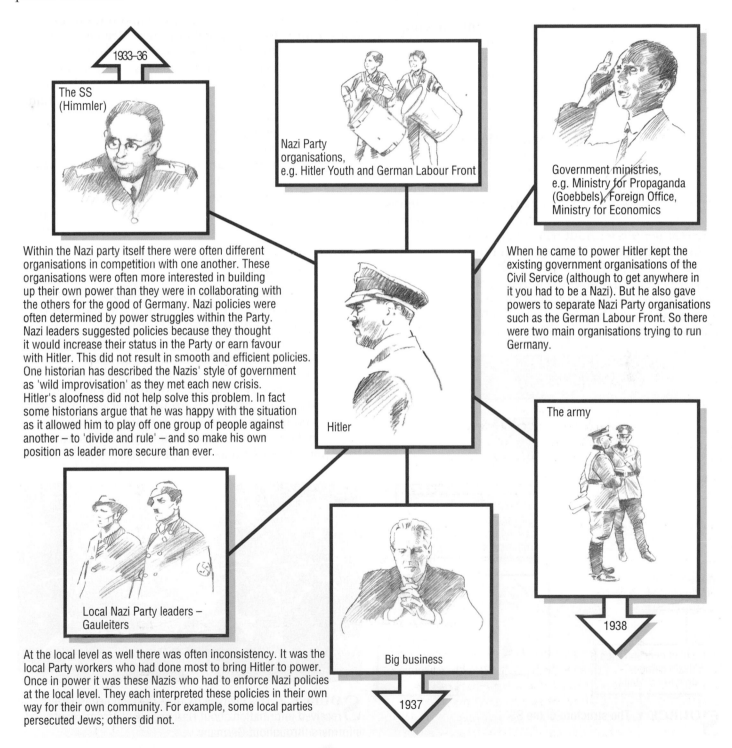

1933–36

The SS (Himmler)

Nazi Party organisations, e.g. Hitler Youth and German Labour Front

Government ministries, e.g. Ministry for Propaganda (Goebbels), Foreign Office, Ministry for Economics

Hitler

The army

Local Nazi Party leaders – Gauleiters

Big business

1938

1937

Within the Nazi party itself there were often different organisations in competition with one another. These organisations were often more interested in building up their own power than they were in collaborating with the others for the good of Germany. Nazi policies were often determined by power struggles within the Party. Nazi leaders suggested policies because they thought it would increase their status in the Party or earn favour with Hitler. This did not result in smooth and efficient policies. One historian has described the Nazis' style of government as 'wild improvisation' as they met each new crisis. Hitler's aloofness did not help solve this problem. In fact some historians argue that he was happy with the situation as it allowed him to play off one group of people against another – to 'divide and rule' – and so make his own position as leader more secure than ever.

When he came to power Hitler kept the existing government organisations of the Civil Service (although to get anywhere in it you had to be a Nazi). But he also gave powers to separate Nazi Party organisations such as the German Labour Front. So there were two main organisations trying to run Germany.

At the local level as well there was often inconsistency. It was the local Party workers who had done most to bring Hitler to power. Once in power it was these Nazis who had to enforce Nazi policies at the local level. They each interpreted these policies in their own way for their own community. For example, some local parties persecuted Jews; others did not.

Why was the SS so important?

ONE ORGANISATION did eventually emerge as the most powerful in Germany – the SS. It became the overseer of all aspects of the Nazi police state.

What was the SS?

Originally the SS had been a private bodyguard for Hitler and other Nazi leaders. SS stands for *Schutz-Staffel* or 'protection squad'. It had only 500 men. In four years Heinrich Himmler built it into an elite force of 50,000 tall, blond, blue-eyed Aryan 'supermen'. The physical standards were very strict. Until 1936 even a filling in a tooth was enough to keep a man out of the SS.

The SS were ruthless and fiercely loyal to Hitler. In 1934 they helped Hitler crush the SA in the 'Night of the Long Knives' (see page 72). He then made them into a separate organisation. They replaced their brown uniforms with black ones.

The role of the SS also changed. They became the main means of terrorising or intimidating Germans into obedience. The SS had almost unlimited power to arrest people without trial, search houses, or confiscate property. They also ran the concentration camps.

By 1936 they had many different sections (see Source 1). When the war began the SS became even more important. They had their own fighting units, the Waffen SS, which soon rivalled the power of the army.

Concentration camps

The first concentration camps were temporary prisons set up by the SA and the SS in disused factories or warehouses or in hastily erected barbed-wire enclosures in the countryside. Some were local camps taking overflow from nearby jails. Others specialised in particular kinds of prisoners such as trade unionists or young people.

Opponents of the regime were taken there for questioning, torture, hard labour and 're-education' in the early days of the Nazi regime. If someone was killed at a concentration camp family members would receive a note saying that the victim had died of pneumonia or some such disease, or that he had been shot while trying to escape.

By 1939 they had built up a massive business using their prisoners as slave labour, extracting raw materials and manufacturing weapons. Later these concentration camps became the scenes of mass GENOCIDE, but in the early days of the regime – although there was great cruelty and suffering – they were not death camps as they were in the later years.

The Gestapo

This was originally the Prussian secret police run by Goering. After June 1936 it became the state secret police under the command of Himmler.

The Gestapo tapped telephones, intercepted mail, and spied on people. They had a network of informers throughout Germany. Anyone who so much as whispered any opposition to Hitler could be reported to the Gestapo by an informer and arrested.

They could strike anywhere at any time against ordinary Germans. It was probably the Gestapo that the opponents of Nazism most feared.

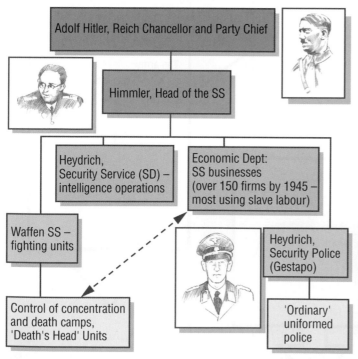

SOURCE 1 The structure of the SS

- Adolf Hitler, Reich Chancellor and Party Chief
- Himmler, Head of the SS
- Heydrich, Security Service (SD) – intelligence operations
- Economic Dept: SS businesses (over 150 firms by 1945 – most using slave labour)
- Waffen SS – fighting units
- Heydrich, Security Police (Gestapo)
- Control of concentration and death camps, 'Death's Head' Units
- 'Ordinary' uniformed police

SOURCE 2 This teletype room in Gestapo headquarters received information about Nazi opponents from agents and informers throughout Germany

SOURCE 3 Elsbeth Emmerich was eight years old in 1942. She wrote down her memories after the war

It was the Gestapo who came that morning – to arrest granddad! He had been known to them since before the war for his anti-Nazi activities and being a trade union shop-steward and a member of the Communist Party ...

The Gestapo kept arresting him but always released him after a while. He was one of the best men in his engineering works and was desperately needed there ...

They tortured my grandfather at the prison, trying to make him give them the names of those who were working against the Nazi regime. It didn't succeed. They took grandma, mum and two of her sisters to the prison and made them cry out for granddad to hear. That didn't work either.

The police, the courts and the prisons

When they came to power the Nazis did not get rid of the existing police forces and legal system. They simply took control of them. The police were under the command of the SS. The judges took an oath of loyalty to Hitler. The conventional courts could be used by the Nazis against their opponents, for example by arresting people on a 'technicality' such as currency violations.

The number of crimes punishable by death rose from 3 in 1933 to 46 in 1943. They included listening to foreign radio stations or publishing anti-government leaflets.

1. Why do you think each of the following was considered by the Nazis to deserve the death penalty:

   ■ breaking into the house of a soldier during the war
   ■ having a sexual relationship with a Jew
   ■ telling an anti-Nazi joke
   ■ stealing towels, a sheet and a pillow from an air-raid storage depot
   ■ a mugging committed by someone who had a criminal record and came from a family of criminals?

Informers

The Nazi Party had a strong local structure. Every town was divided into small units called blocks which included only a handful of homes. Their local Nazi – the Block Warden – visited them weekly, collecting donations and checking up on them.

In the police state these local leaders were also intended to act as the eyes and ears of the Party. They had to write reports on the 'political reliability' of their block residents. These reports could determine whether someone got a job. They could report on any person who was showing signs of independent thinking, for example if they were telling anti-Hitler jokes, refusing to support the Party, hosting illegal political meetings, or not flying a Nazi flag on celebration days.

Heinrich Himmler

Himmler was formerly a chicken farmer. He was interested in German folklore and the occult. He was said to be so sensitive that he felt sick when he witnessed a killing and could not bear to see an insect harmed. Yet he led the SS, who were feared for their callous brutality, and supervised the extermination of six million Jews. In 1942 he told his SS leaders: 'We need other people as slaves. Whether or not 10,000 Russian women collapse from exhaustion while digging a tank ditch interests me only in so far as the tank ditch is completed for Germany.'

■ TASK

Listed below are a number of Nazi objectives. The Nazis wanted to:
a) rebuild the army
b) rebuild the economy
c) eliminate non-Aryans from Germany
d) create the Volk
e) eliminate opposition.
From what you know about the methods of the Nazis, in which of these aims do you think they will be most successful? Put them in order from 1 to 5, with 5 as the most successful. Explain your choice.

As you study the rest of this book you will be able to decide whether you were right.

chapter

6

HOW EFFECTIVELY DID THE NAZIS CONTROL GERMANY FROM 1933 TO 1939?

AS YOU SAW from pages 78–81, the image of Nazi Germany as a well-oiled machine – smoothly run by efficient leaders and obeyed by scared and subservient people – may not be completely accurate. In Chapter 6 you are going to investigate this in more detail, in particular how successfully the Nazis dealt with particular groups in German society, from those who were their out-and-out opponents to those who simply 'got in their way'.

You will see how they used the carrot and the stick to control one town (Northeim, which you first visited on pages 55–59), destroy the socialists, suppress the churches and persecute the Jews; and how they used an overwhelming barrage of propaganda to keep ordinary Germans in favour of Nazi policies. You will consider how successful the Nazis were in each of these areas.

How effectively did the Nazis deal with their political opponents?

SOURCE 1 Hitler, in a speech to Nazi leaders in 1926

66 *A movement which wants to fight Marxism must be just as intolerant as Marxism itself. It must have no doubts that if we are victorious Marxism will be completely destroyed. We too know no tolerance. We shall not rest until the last newspaper has been destroyed, the last organisation liquidated, the last centre of education wiped out and the last Marxist converted or exterminated. There is no half-way house.* 99

As you can see from Source 1, Hitler did not wait till he came to power to start his campaign against the Marxists. You have already found out how the Nazis intimidated and terrorised opponents (see pages 50, 53, 64). They also gathered detailed information about the leading Marxists: where they lived, where they worked. By the time of the Reichstag fire (see pages 64–66) the Nazis knew exactly who the Communists were, and so were able to arrest thousands of the most active ones in a single night.

Phase 1: March–April 1933

The Reichstag fire marked the beginning of a two-month purge of the Nazis' most feared opponents. Well over 25,000 people were taken to local prisons and hastily erected concentration camps (the first was in the grounds of a disused gunpowder factory in Dachau). These were the 'official' detention centres but there were also countless other unofficial prisons. The SA set up prisons and torture chambers in homes, or in cellars or bunkers.

Supposedly, this was a purge of the Communists, but in practice the SA arrested anyone whom they wanted to get. Again this was supposed to be 'preventive detention' (imprisoning people to prevent them doing harm to the state), but in fact what the Nazis were after was for people either to convert to Nazism, or to become so terrified of the Nazis that they would never again dare do anything to oppose them.

Some prisoners were held for a few days, questioned, or tortured, or both; others spent many years in detention. Fifty-seven Communist members of the Reichstag or the local state assemblies were executed in the official camps. In the unofficial SA prisons many others were murdered or tortured.

Phase 2: May–July 1933

By Marxism the Nazis did not just mean Communism. They also accused the Social Democrats, and even the centre parties, of being Marxists. In May the Nazis began their purge of these other bodies. They arrested everyone from Social Democrats to members of the other nationalist parties. Jewish writers and lawyers, and industrialists, were included. In fact, Himmler's department sent instructions to arrest all 'those persons who have been particularly active in party politics'.

By the end of summer 1933 the Nazis had achieved many of Hitler's aims in Source 1. They had wiped out any organisations where their opponents were strong. They had closed the trade unions and confiscated their money and equipment. They had banned all other parties. It became an offence to hold a political meeting of any sort. Those they did not arrest had fled the country, or 'gone underground'.

There was little real political resistance for the next twelve years.

Case study: Hermann Schulze

The Nazis' success is best explained by looking at individuals.

Source 2 tells the story of a Northeim socialist. Similar stories could be told about individuals all over Germany. This everyday, routine brutality and intimidation was the Nazis' way of grinding down and demoralising their opponents to the point of powerlessness. In Northeim there were no more political arrests after 1935. There was no need for them. The opposition had been tamed.

SOURCE 2 The experiences of Hermann Schulze, who lived in the town of Northeim (see page 55). This story-strip is based on an interview he gave to W.S. Allen in the 1960s

(see page 55)

■ TASK

Study the story of Hermann Schulze.

1. What do you think happened to Hermann Schulze next?
2. List the different methods used to control him.
3. What Nazi measure do you think most affected him?
4. The Nazis wanted to win the hearts and minds of the German people. How successful do you think they were in Hermann Schulze's case?

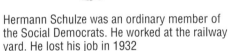

> You're fired. Only Nazis can have jobs here now.

Hermann Schulze was an ordinary member of the Social Democrats. He worked at the railway yard. He lost his job in 1932

> I can't afford to employ a socialist any longer. The Nazis won't buy from me if I do.

He worked as a farm labourer. In exchange for a meal he and his children would do a day's work, until …

> At least they didn't find my socialist banner.

Hermann's house was ransacked by the Gestapo

> We know you have a socialist banner here . . .

The Gestapo came back another twenty times to question him

> We'll give you a job at the quarry if you promise to give up politics.

> I haven't really got a choice!

In the summer of 1933 the Nazis offered Hermann a job

Almost all his old socialist friends were there. Every morning …

> The pay is less than the dole and the conditions are awful … but if I leave I get nothing.

Hermann's cousin died through exposure, working through the winter at the quarry

> I'm running away from the Gestapo. Can you tell me where I can find some loyal socialists?

> No! I'm through with it … I've had enough. All I can do is give you a bed and food. I'd do the same for any human being on a night like this.

Hermann later went to work on an Autobahn team. The Gestapo searched his house seven times. Then one day …

> He's an SS officer! I might have known.

In the morning the 'fellow socialist' got ready to leave. At the door he turned back his lapel

Case study: How did the Nazis take control in Northeim?

1... by taking over the council

ONE-THIRD OF Northeimers had voted for the Social Democrats, not for the Nazis. The elections gave the Nazis a 15:5 majority on the local council. This would have been a working majority, but they were not satisfied. Their goal was to eliminate opposition.

Before the first council meeting they arranged for one Social Democrat councillor to be arrested by the local police and put in prison 'for spreading reports of an anti-governmental nature'. As a prisoner he was barred from being a councillor so he had to resign.

They got rid of the others through sheer bullying. The Nazis moved the first council meeting from the town hall to the ballroom of the local hotel, which they decorated with swastikas and pictures of Hitler. They packed the room with SA and SS men. The Nazis sat at a long table, centre stage, the socialists at a tiny one to one side. When the socialist leader stood up to speak he was told he would not be allowed to. The socialist councillors left the room in protest. As they walked down the gangway SA men spat upon them.

On 27 June 1933 all Social Democrat councillors had to resign because their party was banned throughout Germany. For the next twelve years Northeim council was run entirely by members of the Nazi Party. Anti-Nazis were dismissed from council employment.

2... by terror

Controlling the council did not give the Nazis control of individuals. To do that the Nazis needed to convince Northeimers that the violence with which they dealt with their political opponents was also what anyone who stepped out of line could expect.

They set up a search of all houses in Northeim, supposedly looking for guns and ammunition. They ransacked homes and arrested twenty-two people. Seven were taken to the local concentration camp at Moringen. Other Northeimers were arrested for minor offences such as insulting the SA or 'spreading false rumours' about the Nazis.

For example, on 24 May, 51-year-old Johannes Grote, a socialist from Northeim, was arrested. He was held for three days at the county jail. Each day he was questioned for three or four hours, with his face pressed against the wall as he was beaten from behind. His wife was also arrested and his house ransacked. He lost his job and his ID papers. Eventually he left Northeim for another town where he might be able to make a better life.

People began to warn each other what not to do. 'Be careful what you say' was the message passed on by ordinary Northeimers. There were rumoured to be five Gestapo informers in the town.

3... by 'co-ordination'

In Northeim there were more than fifty separate clubs and organisations which the Nazis wanted to get rid of or take over. To justify this they used the argument that since there was now a Nazi majority in the Reichstag, all other organisations in Germany should have the same. They called this co-ordination or GLEICHSCHALTUNG. The aim was that whenever even a small group of people got together, it would be under the watchful gaze of a Nazi.

The sports clubs were co-ordinated. The gym club, the two football clubs, and the swimming club were merged into one Nazi-led sports club led by Hermann Denzler, head of the SA in Northeim. He immediately declared a new focus on military training. Membership of the sports club soon fell by half.

There were a number of choirs and singing groups in Northeim, including one for the working class, one for the middle class, and an upper-class one. They all had to elect a Nazi leadership but rather than do that the working-class one, run by socialists, dissolved itself. A new classless 'Mixed Choral Singing Club of 1933' was created.

The same happened to the town bands, the trade unions, the Red Cross, the Museum Society, the town library (a quarter of the books were burned because the Nazis disapproved of them) and, as you will see on pages 94, 130 and 134, the churches, the schools and the youth groups were all taken under Nazi control.

Co-ordination destroyed the social life of Northeim. By autumn 1933, there was hardly anywhere that ordinary Northeimers could go to enjoy themselves with friends which was not Nazi-run. This meant that honest discussion of the Nazi regime or planned opposition became almost impossible.

4... by persecuting Jews

Northeim had about a hundred Jews. On 1 April the Nazis announced a boycott of all Jewish businesses. SA men were posted outside the doors. The Nazis ran newspaper advertisements telling people to boycott these stores, and included a clip-out coupon listing Jewish businesses for people to carry with them at all times.

Some Northeimers, particularly socialists, went out of their way still to shop at Jewish-run businesses, but they were a minority. Most Northeimers isolated the Jews. Dr Ballin's medical practice declined quickly because of the boycott. Jews who had previously been a part of the many organisations in Northeim now quietly resigned to avoid the hatred of the Nazis, giving false reasons such as pressure of work.

5... through propaganda

Northeimers quickly learned that there was to be no let-up in the propaganda effort which had brought the Nazis to power. The intense round of meetings and marches would continue throughout the spring and summer.

They kicked off in March with a massive parade featuring the ceremonial burning of the Weimar flags and the hoisting of the Nazi banner all over Northeim including at the city hall, the fire station and the post office. A torchlight parade of 3000 Northeimers ended in a public park with a speech by Ernst Girmann – 'The individual is nothing! The Volk is everything! Once we unite internally, we shall defeat the external enemy! Then Germany really will be "on top" [*über alles*]!'

Adolf Hitler's birthday, 20 April, became a celebration day with the necessary parade, speeches and singing.

On 26 May was book-burning day. Northeimers purged their own book collections, bringing banned works such as *All Quiet on the Western Front* to be burned publicly in the market square.

In six months there were literally hundreds of events. There were theatre presentations, concerts, films, military manoeuvres by the SA. The biggest of these events attracted thousands of people in a town with a population of only 10,000. Nazi Party members were forced to attend. All Northeimers were encouraged to. The average Northeimer might have three or four such meetings in a single week.

If you missed the events, you could not avoid reading about them, for they were written up along with all the other news in the Nazi-controlled newspaper. The Nazis started their own newspaper and Nazi supporters were told to cancel their subscriptions to the other newspapers. These newspapers quickly realised that if they were not to go bankrupt they needed to print pro-Nazi news.

Local businesses helped out by selling swastikas, organising pro-Hitler speeches in the cafés and restaurants, creating patriotic window displays and giving preferential treatment to Nazis.

6... by tackling unemployment

Many Northeimers had voted for the Nazis because of the Depression. The Nazis needed to do something very quickly about unemployment which was the most obvious symbol of the Depression.

In June 1933 there were more than 500 registered unemployed. In July the Nazis used money from central government to set the unemployed to work. In July 450 people were employed by the council to repair roads, and tidy up the woods and forests around the town. The moat around the old town was drained and made into a ring of swan ponds and parks. They subsidised local builders to decorate flats. A Book of Honour was started, listing the names of businesses which had taken on an unemployed worker.

On 24 July Ernst Girmann announced at a press conference that the Nazis had eliminated unemployment in Northeim. The truth behind this claim was somewhat different.

- Most of the money to pay for the new jobs had in fact been allocated to the town by the Weimar government before the Nazis took over – but it had taken months to come through.
- Socialists or Communists who had been dismissed from their jobs could not register as unemployed so were excluded from the scheme. Their jobs were given to Nazis.
- All unemployed were forced to join the new work schemes, regardless of skills or previous occupation. If they did not join the schemes they got no unemployment benefit.

The rush to join the Party

Party membership had been rising steadily since 1930. In the early months of 1933 it rocketed. People could see that to get anywhere in Hitler's Germany they would have to join. The local party had 300 members in January. By May it had 1200. Some Northeimers were pressurised to join by their families. Others wanted to protect their jobs. Some believed passionately in Hitler and the Nazis and were thrilled by what they were doing in Northeim.

The rush to join the Party posed a problem for the Nazis. Were the new members really committed Nazis, or were they just jumping on the bandwagon? The old-timers gave the new members a name – the March casualties – and were always very suspicious of them.

■ TASK

1. Which of the Nazis' six methods do you think would be most important in Northeim in
   a) destroying opposition
   b) increasing the power of the Nazi Party?
2. Pages 84–87 are based on the research of historian W.S. Allen. He identifies two aspects of the Nazis' actions which particularly helped them take control without much opposition:

   - They made everything they did appear to be legal and authorised.
   - They achieved what they wanted step by step; no one individual action seemed too extreme in itself.

Explain how far the evidence supports each point, using examples from these four pages.

Did the Nazis win the hearts and minds of the German people?

PAGES 82–87 SHOW how thoroughly the Nazis dealt with political opposition. However, opposition can take many forms.

How could people show their opposition in Nazi Germany?

1 Attempted coup d'état

The Nazis could not be voted out. The only way to get rid of a dictator like Hitler was by a coup d'état: killing or imprisoning the leader and replacing him with an alternative leader.

2 Underground resistance and open opposition

People campaign against the government or deliberately disrupt its policies.

3 Passive resistance

People are prepared to publicly declare their opposition by not co-operating with the Nazis.

4 Private grumbling

People grumble among family, friends or colleagues at work and in private, but never in the hearing of someone who might report them to the Nazis.

■ TASK

Work in pairs. Listed on the left you can see examples of different kinds of opposition. We have graded them on a scale of 1–4.

1. Decide where on this scale you would place each of the people or examples of opposition described in Sources 1–10. In each case explain your answer.

	1	2	3	4
The Northeim societies				
Elsbeth Emmerich's mother				
Von Blomberg and von Fritsch				
Shipyard worker				
People in a Berlin café, 1934				
Workers on a train				
Anna Rauschning				
Anti-government leaflets				
Schröer, the delicatessen owner				
Pastor Grueber				

2. Explain why each one might be a danger to the Nazis.
3. Do you think the Nazis saw people who were simply apathetic as opponents?

SOURCE 1 Information about Gleichschaltung in Northeim from W.S. Allen

66 *One organisation – the Beautification Society – did not want the Nazis to get hold of their large funds, so they bought a hut in the forest before they were co-ordinated. Another organisation held a drinking party just before the hand-over to the Nazis so they could drink up all their funds.* 99

SOURCE 2 Elsbeth Emmerich was eight years old in 1942 and later remembered when her mother, a talented sports coach, had a visitor. Elsbeth's mother disliked the Nazis. Elsbeth's father had died fighting in the German army in Russia

66 *There was another knock at the door and a stranger entered. A strange man with a notebook and pencil and a Nazi pin in his lapel. He said he had heard about my mother's achievements. He had assumed that she was a member of the Party and only found out that she was not when he checked his records. No doubt that was just an oversight, he went on, and she would join? He had his pencil at the ready but my mother froze over and said firmly 'NO'. She did not want to become a member of the Party. 'You realise you cannot keep your position as coach to our young girls, unless you are a member of the Party?' My mother said surely coaching had nothing to do with politics … My mother had to give up her much-loved job.* 99

SOURCE 3
In 1937, when Hitler told the army of his plans to conquer Germany's neighbours, the leader of the army, General von Fritsch (centre), and the War Minister, Field-Marshal von Blomberg (left) argued against Hitler's plans as they feared a fatal war. Hitler decided to remove them. It was 'discovered' that von Blomberg's wife had a criminal record as a thief and a prostitute. Von Blomberg was dismissed. Then von Fritsch was falsely accused of homosexual offences. Hitler removed von Fritsch and made himself Commander-in-Chief of all the armed forces. A further sixteen generals were retired and forty-four demoted

SOURCE 5 Philip Gibbs, a journalist, was visiting Berlin in 1934

❝ I remember being in a big Berlin café when Hitler was announced to speak over the microphone. The loudspeaker was turned on. Next to me was a group of German businessmen. They went on talking in low voices. At another table was a woman writing a letter. She went on writing. The only man who stood up was a little fellow with his tie creeping over his collar at the back of his neck. No one in this crowded café listened to Adolf Hitler. ❞

SOURCE 6 Bert Engelmann recalls a conversation he heard on a train in Berlin between a working man (speaking here) and a loyal Nazi woman

❝ Listen, at the beginning of 1933 there were over six million unemployed, and now there's only two million – that much is true. But it's also true that at the beginning of '33 I was still earning good money in my own trade and was home – and now we work ourselves to the bone and the wages keep going down – it's 16 marks net per week now. The whole thing stinks, and somebody's got to say it! ❞

SOURCE 7 Anna Rauschning, the wife of a German civil servant, remembers a visit from the SA

❝ I went into the kitchen to see what was being prepared for the Eintopf, the one-dish meal demanded by Nazi law on Sundays. A young Hitler Youth in uniform was standing at the stove, lifting the lids from the pots.
'What is this?' I said, in surprise.
'It is the usual inspection,' the cook said.
I pointed to the door. 'It's not necessary to check on this house,' I said sharply. 'My husband is a servant of the State.'
The boy stood his ground but his jaw dropped open in amazement. I took him by the shoulder. 'Get out. I'll be responsible for this house. You don't need to check here.'
He left like a creature in a dream. ❞

SOURCE 4 In 1936 shipyard workers in Hamburg gave the Heil Hitler salute at the launch of a new ship – with the exception of one man who stood with his arms folded, risking immediate arrest and imprisonment. Can you find him?

SOURCE 8 Statistics on anti-government leaflets seized by the Gestapo

❝ Gestapo records show that they seized 1,643,000 anti-Nazi leaflets in 1936. ❞

SOURCE 9 Ludwig Schröer, the owner of this confectionary shop, was arrested for telling jokes about Hitler. He was sent to Buchenwald concentration camp. He later hanged himself to escape a second term there

SOURCE 10
Pastor Heinrich Grueber. In 1936 Pastor
Grueber formed a secret organisation to protect Jews. He helped many to emigrate by providing forged passports and visas. He was arrested in 1940 and sent to a concentration camp where most of his teeth were knocked out. His work was carried on by others including Pastor Zwanziger who is credited with smuggling 56 people out of Germany in February 1940 alone

So how much opposition was there?

Attempted coups d'etat: *hardly any*
Through the first ten years of Nazi rule there were no attempted coups. It was only in the last years of the war (when the regime was collapsing anyway due to the war effort) that plots against Hitler gathered any support.

Underground resistance and open opposition: *not a lot*
There was more underground resistance than most people realise. Throughout the regime working-class groups produced anti-government leaflets. People like Pastor Grueber helped Jews. There was sabotage of factories, railways and army depots. Some Germans acted as spies passing on industrial or military secrets to other countries. Within the churches there were a number of leaders who openly criticised the Nazi dictatorship. For example, they led a public outcry against the Nazi policy of EUTHANASIA, and got it stopped. However, when critics of the government could be arrested, tortured and even executed most opponents preferred to get involved in underground opposition movements rather than publicly oppose the Nazis.

Passive resistance and non-cooperation: *quite common*
Many people refused to join the Party. Some refused to give the 'Heil Hitler' salute; a few people were even executed for this. Some refused to contribute to Nazi funds. Members of banned political parties continued to meet in secret throughout the 1930s, although such meetings could result in their being imprisoned or even executed. In 1936 the Gestapo broke up a reported 1000 meetings of underground socialist groups.

Private grumbling: *very widespread*
All the evidence suggests that ordinary Germans greatly resented many aspects of the Nazi regime – the intrusion into people's private lives; the bully-boy tactics of the SA; the grating propaganda. The Block Warden was seen as a pest. When he (Block Wardens were nearly always male) came round collecting money or promoting the latest Nazi scheme people would pay up or sign up – but only for an easy life. As for the endless meetings, parades and demonstrations, even by the end of 1933 these were treated with apathy and indifference. People attended because their jobs might depend on it, but the show of support became an increasingly elaborate pretence. Grumbling was a national pastime – but it was rarely done in public. The greatest show of opposition many Germans ever managed was to pass on an anti-Nazi joke! Anything else just seemed too risky.

Why didn't private grumbling become open opposition?

Germans were afraid
The SS and the Gestapo could destroy people's lives if they did not toe the line. The Nazis wanted people's hearts and minds, but as long as people did not rock the boat, and kept their groans and grumbles to themselves, they were tolerated. However, if those grumbles became open opposition then the apparatus of the police state was there to deal with it.

The opposition was divided
Left-wing groups such as the Communists and the Social Democrats were the natural enemies of Nazism. They were both banned in 1933.

However, these groups did not trust each other and so did not co-operate to resist the Nazis. Each decided to resist in different ways. The Social Democrats did little more than meet in small groups, talk, start whispering campaigns against the Nazis. For a long time the Communists simply assumed that the Nazis would fall – as had previous governments. Later they decided on a more active campaign of spreading discontent amongst factory workers.

People did not know what was going on
Censorship and propaganda stopped people receiving reliable information. Some of the extremes of Nazi policy were kept secret. Those who did suspect had learned not to ask questions for fear of their own lives.

People were pleased with the Nazis
Many German people were genuinely pleased with what the Nazis were doing. Even if they did not agree with something the Nazis did they would tolerate it for the sake of the stability and prosperity they believed the Nazis were creating.

Quibbles were minor
Even those who were dissatisfied with the Nazis often had very minor criticisms. For example, in Northeim the decision to merge the four sports clubs into one raised much more opposition than the victimisation of the Jews.

The Nazis did drop unpopular policies
The Nazis did sometimes moderate their policies if they seemed to be alienating ordinary Germans. In 1938 the Nazi assault on the Jews – Kristallnacht (pages 107–109) – produced such widespread condemnation among ordinary Germans that from then on all measures against the Jews were kept secret. In 1940 their programme of euthanasia was halted after a popular outcry against it led by Church leaders.

'We did vote for them, after all!'
Because the Nazis had achieved electoral success, most Germans (and most people in other countries) saw the Nazis as having the legal authority to do what they wanted.

There was no organised opposition
Since the Nazis had dismantled or taken over virtually all other organisations, there were no groups which people could join to resist them. The main exceptions to this were the Christian churches, and it is no surprise therefore that they formed some of the most public opposition to the Nazis in the early years. You will look at the churches in detail on pages 94–99.

Case study 1: Why did this German doctor keep his fears to himself?

The following source explains the reaction of a German doctor to the Nazis. Use it to answer the following questions.

1. How did the doctor's attitude to his Jewish neighbours differ from that to Jews in general?
2. Does Source 11 provide evidence that doctors welcomed the Nazis?
3. Why did the doctor not oppose the Nazis?
4. Do you believe the doctor's claim that he was not a Nazi? Is there any evidence to doubt this claim?
5. What evidence is there in Source 11 of Nazi methods of rule?
6. What problems faced the young doctor in 1933–34?
7. Do you have any sympathy for him?
8. What factors make this source reliable or unreliable?

■ TASK

On pages 88–92 you have come across many examples of people grumbling about or criticising the Nazis. As you study the rest of this book build up your own record of German people showing enthusiasm for the Nazis or praising them for their achievements.

SOURCE 11 In 1981 Bert Engelmann listened to this explanation from a German doctor on how he reacted to the persecution of the Jews in the early days of Nazi rule in 1933 and 1934

❝ At the time I did wonder whether Hitler's seizure of power might not prove helpful to me. In my medical school my fellow students were often complaining that opportunities for doctors were getting worse every year, because Germany had so many doctors. But if Hitler came to power he would 'eliminate' our Jewish competition, and then we 'Aryans' could have a profitable practice …

Many viewed the mere 10,000 Jewish doctors as a serious threat to our profession. People were envious of the Jews because they attracted more patients and because so many of the most distinguished physicians were Jewish. For someone like me, a civil servant's son without independent means, the prospects for setting up in private practice were not exactly rosy … Please don't misunderstand! At home we had Jewish neighbours with whom we got along splendidly; and whenever one of us was sick my parents would call our old Jewish family doctor, Dr Marcuse. No, I wasn't prejudiced! Besides, when the Nazis promised to 'eliminate' the Jewish competition, I pictured something quite harmless, perhaps a temporary limit on the licensing of Jewish doctors or something of that nature … But perhaps I was just fooling myself, because in fact it wasn't hard to guess what the Nazis really had in mind. I was scared of the Nazis. They had such a brutal manner, a penchant for violence, and that bloodthirsty way of expressing themselves. On the evening of January the 30th when I was on duty in the emergency room I got a taste of what was in store for anyone who resisted them. I had my hands full with all the injured people who were brought in – Communists, members of the socialist organisations, several Jewish shopkeepers, the administrator of the co-operative society. They had been beaten up by the SA men, drunk with victory.

Like most people, I took the path of least resistance. I said 'Heil Hitler!', like a good boy when it seemed called for, and joined the National Socialist Physicians' Association and a few of the many other Nazi organisations besides – but only as a dues-paying member. Our head physician, who was a devoted Nazi, almost persuaded me to apply for admission to the SS as a battalion doctor. Fortunately I was a few centimetres too short for the SS and not blond enough. I acted as though I were terribly disappointed … To be honest with you, I wasn't really against the Nazis at that particular time. I often found their methods appalling – their total disregard for the law, and the brutality with which they terrorised innocent people. But I was too afraid of getting myself into political hot water. I avoided all conversations about politics and kept my mouth shut. The truth is, all that business about the 'unity of the German people' and the 'national rebirth', the sense of a new vitality and purpose in 1933 – that really impressed me. And I thought it was high time something was done about the massive unemployment. To my mind, no measure could be considered excessive when it was a question of eliminating poverty and bringing about stability. At the time I didn't realise that most of it was simply propaganda; and as for the many unpleasant side effects, I told myself they were none of my business. After all, I wasn't Jewish, nor was I a Social Democrat, nor a Communist. So I kept quiet and consoled myself with the thought that this must be a passing phase. I dare say most people felt as I did. ❞

Case study 2: Why did people tell anti-Nazi jokes?

There were many anti-Nazi jokes circulating privately among the German people in the 1930s, despite the fact that telling jokes about Nazi leaders could be severely punished. Anti-Hitler jokes were punishable by death. Sources 12–16 give some examples.

■ TASK

Which of these jokes do you think is
a) the funniest
b) the cleverest
c) the most dangerous to Hitler and other Nazi leaders
d) the most useful piece of historical evidence about attitudes to the Nazis?
Explain your choices.

SOURCE 12

66 *Dr Goebbels was drowning in a lake when a young boy saved him. Goebbels said, 'How can I repay you, my young fellow?'*

'Well, I think I would like to have a state funeral,' said the boy. Goebbels was surprised.

'At your age? Why, you're not going to die so soon.'

'Oh, no?' said the boy. 'Just wait till I get home and tell my father whom I saved from drowning!' **99**

SOURCE 13

66 *Someone opens his mouth too wide and as a result spends several weeks of 'ideological training' in a concentration camp. After his discharge he is asked by a friend what life was like there. 'Excellent!' he replies. 'At 9 a.m. we were served breakfast in our bedrooms: real coffee or cocoa, whichever we preferred. Then some light work for those who wanted to work, and some sport for those who didn't. Next we had elevenses: bouillon and open sandwiches. Lunch was plain but good: soup, meat or fish, and a sweet. After a siesta of two hours, in bed, we had coffee and cake, and afterwards again some light work. For supper we were served some open sandwiches and pudding. In the evening we had lectures or a film, or we played games.' The questioner is much impressed. 'Incredible!' he says. 'All those lies we're told about the concentration camps! The other day I met Meier who had just been released from one; he told me rather different stories about his camp!'*

'Well, yes, but then Meier is back in his camp again!' **99**

SOURCE 14

66 *It is early in 1933. One Stormtrooper whispers to another, 'Have you heard the latest? The Reichstag is aflame!' The other Stormtrooper hisses, 'Shhh! Not before tomorrow!'* **99**

SOURCE 15

66 *Since 1933 law and order in the Third Reich have been simplified:*

1 *The German people consist of the Leader and the Misled;*
2 *There are no longer any social classes;*
3 *Anyone who does or omits to do anything will be punished;*
4 *The punishment will be determined by the sound feeling of the people;*
5 *The sound feeling of the people will be determined by the Gauleiter.* **99**

SOURCE 16 A cartoon with the caption 'Germany, the tidiest country in the world'

■ TASK

'The Nazis failed in their attempt to win the hearts and minds of the German people.' Write an essay to explain whether you agree or disagree, using evidence from pages 88–93.

Why didn't the Nazis destroy the churches?

1. Sources 1 and 2 provide evidence of Hitler's view of religion. Do they contradict each other?
2. If so, how can you account for this?

Should the Nazis destroy the churches?

As you can see from Sources 1 and 2, there were conflicting views among Hitler and the Nazis on how to deal with the churches.

Destroy them!

The Nazis saw the churches as a threat. They wanted total control over German life, and the churches stood in the way of this.

- In 1933 nearly all Germans were Christians. Roughly one-third were Roman Catholic and two-thirds were Protestants. The Protestant Church had more members than any other organisation in Germany, including the Nazi Party.
- Religious beliefs were powerful ones. People who believed in God might be less likely to worship Hitler as the leader of Germany. The Church taught its people very clear rules of behaviour and attitude. What if they conflicted with what the Nazis wanted?
- Church meetings could be used for spreading anti-Nazi ideas.

These, the Nazis argued, were reasons for destroying the Church as they had destroyed all other independent organisations.

Use them!

On the other hand, the Nazis needed the churches.

- Many Church members had voted for Hitler, Protestants in particular. Protestant church pastors were among the most popular and successful Nazi election speakers.
- There was also common ground on several issues, such as the importance of family life. The Church supported the Nazi emphasis on the military; in 1936 priests accompanied the troops as they re-entered the Rhineland.
- The church was often the local power base for the Nazis. If they could build on it then they would be stronger still.

Some Nazis therefore argued that, far from destroying the Church, they should try to use it.

Agreements with the churches: 1933–35

When he came to power in 1933 Hitler chose not to provoke a conflict with the churches until he was sure he could win. In a speech to the Reichstag on 23 March 1933 Hitler said that Christianity was 'the unshakeable foundation of the moral life of our people'.

In June 1933 the Catholic Church signed a Concordat (understanding) with Hitler. Hitler promised that the Catholics could carry on their religious work, and that Catholic schools and youth groups would be left alone. The Pope promised the Vatican would stay out of politics. Catholic Bishop Bürger said: 'The aims of the Reich [Nazi] government have long been the same as those of the Catholic Church.'

Hitler united all the Protestant churches together into one Reich church under a pro-Nazi Reich Bishop, Müller (see Source 3). They became known as the German Christians. They adopted Nazi-style uniforms, salutes and marches. Their slogan was 'The swastika on our breasts and the cross in our hearts'.

SOURCE 3 Reich Bishop Ludwig Müller, leader of the German Christians, making a speech in September 1934. You can see their flag – a cross with a swastika imposed on it – at the top of the steps

The Faith Movement

The German Faith Movement was the Nazis' alternative to Christianity. It involved pagan-style worship of nature centred on the sun. The movement's flag was a golden sun on a blue background, often with a Nazi swastika attached.

SOURCE 5 A pagan-style Nazi festival, 1934

Many of the SS especially were anti-Christian. New marriage, 'baptism' and burial services were devised. Sources 6 and 7 show what these services were like.

SOURCE 7 A Nazi altar

SOURCE 4 The ending of a speech at a meeting of the Faith Movement. The Faith Movement saw the Catholic and Protestant churches as the enemy

❝ *Our faith is in blood and earth, we want to be pure heathen, not contaminated with Christianity. We don't talk about Christians or heathens, but only about Germans. Adolf Hitler! [This was followed by cries of 'To the gallows with the Bishop', 'Shoot him', 'Throw them out of the churches', 'Away with the monasteries', 'Shoot the priests', 'String up the nuns', 'We don't need Christianity', 'Away with Christ'.]* ❞

SOURCE 6 A newspaper account of a Nazi marriage ceremony

❝ *The central point was the wedding table which was decorated with two figures. On the table lay a yellow sun disc made of flowers on a blue background; to the left and right stood torch-bearers and behind the table a bowl, containing fire, and the pulpit. German songs and music were played. Then the bridal pair were offered bread (representing the germinating force of earth) and salt (the symbol of purity) on silver vessels.* ❞

3. Do Sources 4, 5 and 6 support Source 1 or Source 2?
4. Study Source 7. How does this altar differ from a Christian altar?
5. In not more than 50 words explain how the Faith Movement would help the Nazis control the churches.

Did the churches oppose the Nazis?

Many Christians sided with the Nazis. A small minority did not, as you can see from the sources below.

■ ACTIVITY

1. Complete this table to show what aspects of the Nazis' policies each person opposed:

	Catholic/ Protestant/ Other	What did they oppose?	How dealt with?
Martin Niemöller			
Paul Schneider			
Cardinal Galen			
Josef Fath			
The Jehovah's Witnesses			

2. Choose one individual or group who you think posed a particular danger to the Nazis and write a paragraph to explain your choice.

Martin Niemöller

Martin Niemöller was a First World War hero – as a U-boat commander he had won Germany's highest decoration for bravery. During the 1930s he became the Nazis' most prominent critic among Church leaders. He disliked the 'German Christians' and the Nazis. With other Protestant ministers (including Dietrich Bonhoeffer – see page 152) he formed an alternative 'Confessional Church'. Niemöller and hundreds of other ministers were put in concentration camps.

> **SOURCE 8** Sermon preached by Niemöller to his congregation, Sunday 24 March 1934. There were members of the secret police in the congregation
>
> 66 *We see more and more clearly how there is a spread of new heathenism which wishes to have nothing to do with the Saviour who was crucified for us, while the Church which acknowledges the Saviour as its only Lord is attacked as an enemy of the state ... we must obey God rather than men.* 99

Paul Schneider

Schneider was a pastor in a small town. He criticised the Nazis, especially Josef Goebbels. In 1934 he was arrested and warned not to make speeches hostile to the Nazis. He ignored this warning.

Finally in 1937 he was sent to Buchenwald concentration camp. He smuggled out letters warning that the Church must not compromise with the Nazis. He refused to take off his cap when the Nazi swastika flag was hoisted so he was stretched on a rack and whipped. He was tortured and strung up by the arms for hours at a time. Soon he was little more than a bruised skeleton, dressed in rags and crawling with lice. Still he refused to sign a promise not to preach. Then he was put in a cell which looked out, at ground-level, on the camp parade ground. He prayed aloud for the other prisoners, and when he saw SS guards shoot prisoners he would cry out, 'I have seen this! And I will accuse you of murder before God's judgement-seat!' He was kept in the camp for two years.

This photograph shows Pastor Niemöller with an American GI immediately after his release from Dachau in 1945

While awaiting trial in a Nazi prison he was visited by the prison chaplain who asked him, 'But brother! Why are *you* in prison?' Niemöller replied, 'And, brother, why are you *not* in prison?'

In 1938 he was sent to a concentration camp and although Hitler ordered his death shortly before the end of the war, he survived.

Cardinal Galen

Catholic Cardinal Galen publicly attacked the Nazi policies as early as 1934.

In 1941 he revealed that the Nazis were secretly killing mentally and physically handicapped people. Galen led a campaign which made Hitler call a halt to this euthanasia programme.

The Nazi Party did not want to make Galen into a martyr so they took no action against him, but three Catholic priests were executed for distributing copies of Galen's sermons to soldiers. Some Nazis urged Goebbels to hang Galen, but Goebbels pointed out: 'If anything were done against the bishop, the population of Münster could be regarded as lost to the war effort, and the same could be said of the whole of Westphalia.'

Cardinal Galen

Josef Fath

In many rural areas the local priests clashed with Nazi schoolteachers and leaders of the Hitler Youth movements who were trying to lure young people away from Catholic beliefs. The village of Leidersbach was looked after by the young Catholic priest Josef Fath.

SOURCE 9 An account given by the local Nazi schoolteacher when, in 1937, fifty parents demanded she be sacked

66 *Positive work on behalf of the National Socialist State and Party has recently become completely impossible. This is attributed to hostile local cleric Chaplain Fath ... A few facts serve to show this ... on Church feast days despite express ban, some seventy yellow and white church flags were hung out ... on the appointment of a Hitler Youth leader stones were thrown at their headquarters and the leaders were loudly and violently abused ... Chaplain Fath agitated in the Catholic Mothers' Association against the teacher, saying the teacher hung a picture of Hitler at the front of her classroom and the crucifix at the side. He agitates, in secret, against the youth organisations. This is proved by the fact that despite the greatest recruitment drive, the number of girls in the Hitler Youth is seventeen while 'his' fledglings in the Congregation of Mary number almost two hundred ... This time my own person is the target and the brains behind the demonstration is again Chaplain Fath, who up to now has succeeded in getting rid of everything in his path.* 99

The Jehovah's Witnesses

Germany's 30,000 Jehovah's Witnesses believed they should live according to their religious beliefs and not by what the government said they should do. Most Jehovah's Witnesses ended up in concentration camps and one-third of them died.

Did the Nazis succeed in controlling the churches?

After 1935, once they felt more secure in their overall control of Germany, the Nazis became bolder in their attempts to control the churches.

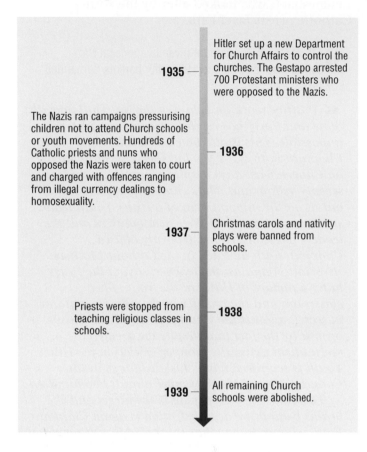

1935 — Hitler set up a new Department for Church Affairs to control the churches. The Gestapo arrested 700 Protestant ministers who were opposed to the Nazis.

The Nazis ran campaigns pressurising children not to attend Church schools or youth movements. Hundreds of Catholic priests and nuns who opposed the Nazis were taken to court and charged with offences ranging from illegal currency dealings to homosexuality.

1936

1937 — Christmas carols and nativity plays were banned from schools.

Priests were stopped from teaching religious classes in schools.

1938

1939 — All remaining Church schools were abolished.

However, even in this period policy was chaotic. The Nazis improvised, changed their minds, and bowed to public pressure. At the local level it was local leaders who set policy. Some local Nazi leaders sent their SA men to beat up and murder priests; others went to church every Sunday and sang in the choir. It is no surprise therefore that the Nazis' success varied very much from place to place.

In the 1939 census of the Greater German Reich, when people had to state their religious faith, the results were:

Roman Catholic	1,944,000
Protestant	42,636,000
Jewish	308,000
Without belief	1,208,000
Neo-pagan	2,746,000

Even the majority of the three million Nazi Party members still paid Church taxes and registered as Christians.

■ TASK

Case study: Bavaria

Sources 10–15 are evidence about Bavaria. Bavaria had been the birthplace of the Nazi Party, but in the elections of 1933 the Nazis had not done well there. It was a mainly Catholic area.

Work in pairs. One of you is going to argue that the Nazis succeeded in controlling the Church in Bavaria, the other is to argue that they did not. Do this by first selecting what you think are the four best sources or points to support your argument.

You have one minute each to present your argument. Then you have a further two minutes in which you should argue with each other. At the end you should decide on who put forward the better argument.

SOURCE 10 In 1934, when the Nazis tried to control the Protestant churches in Bavaria, they met with strong opposition from the bishops and the people. A church newsletter reported:

66 *We witnessed a miracle here in Nuremberg. There was enormous commotion going on in the town. We only gave out hand notices at twelve o'clock and in the evening sixteen churches were full to bursting. Everywhere, often at the most inconvenient times, churches were full.* 99

SOURCE 11 By 1937 the Protestant Church in Bavaria noted:

66 *The danger which threatens our parishes is of being ground down, of becoming dispirited. The vast majority of our parishes believe that 'one cannot do anything' against the new forces and give up ... Above all, youth is losing the habit of going to church regularly.* 99

SOURCE 12 Comments from police reports in Bavaria in 1937 and 1938

66 *a) ... the influence of the Church on the population is so strong that the National Socialist spirit cannot penetrate.*
b) ... the local population is as ever under the strong influence of the clergy and behaves indifferently towards the National Socialist government and its measures.
c) These people much prefer to believe what the priest says from the pulpit than the words of the best speakers. 99

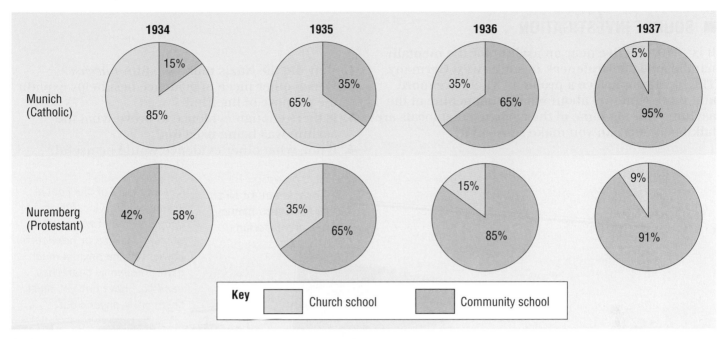

S OURCE 13 In two cities in Bavaria the Nazis held an annual vote of parents to decide if they wanted a church school or a non-church 'community school'. These were the results

S OURCE 14 When in 1941 the Nazis tried to remove crucifixes from Catholic schools in Bavaria they met with fierce opposition. This was often led by women who organised school strikes and got soldiers on leave to forcibly return the crosses to schools. The government compiled this table

	Crosses removed	Crosses returned
Mühldorf district	all from 43 schools	all except one
Ebersberg district	none	–
Upper Bavaria as a whole	389 from 977 schools	282

S OURCE 15 The role of the clergy in Catholic Bavaria is explained by Ian Kershaw in his book *Popular Opinion and Public Dissent in the Third Reich – Bavaria* (1983)

❝ *In the Catholic clergy, Goebbels met his propaganda match. Clergy took the lead in many outward signs of opposition – use of the 'Grüß Gott' greeting and avoidance of 'Heil Hitler', omitting to put out the swastika flag on official celebrations or continuing to show the banned Church flags ... The reports of the Nazi authorities are littered with cases of priests being arrested and punished in one form or another for such behaviour.* ❞

1. Many of the soldiers referred to in Source 14 had shown little or no interest in the Church before the war. Why do you think they helped return the crosses to schools?

■ **TASK**

Using all you have found out about the Nazi policy towards the churches write an essay with the title 'Did the Nazis succeed in controlling the churches?' You should cover:

■ why Nazis were divided on this issue
■ the different measures they used to control the churches
■ whether in your opinion the Nazis were successful.

What is happening at Grafeneck Asylum?

■ SOURCE INVESTIGATION

It is 1940. You live near an asylum for the mentally handicapped at Grafeneck in south-west Germany. The local people face a problem. There are more and more rumours about what is happening at the asylum. Here is some of the evidence that locals are talking about. Can you make sense of it?

1. Why did the Nazis make the film *I accuse?*
2. Which other piece of evidence best helps explain the purpose of the film?
3. Is there enough evidence to prove what the asylum was being used for?
4. If not, what other evidence would be useful?

A The asylum at Grafeneck

B There is smoke all the time from the chimney of the crematorium.

C Grey vans of the Postal Transport Service, full of people, some of whom are in straightjackets or handcuffs, now enter the asylum much more frequently than they used to. I have not yet seen them bring anyone out.

E Many families with relatives in the asylum are receiving letters of condolences such as this one:

D Families with relatives in the asylum have been informed of their deaths, but odd things have happened such as:

■ One family received two urns of ashes for one dead relative
■ Hairpins have turned up in the ashes of males
■ People who had their appendix removed years before have been declared dead due to appendicitis
■ Parents who have removed their children from the asylum have received a letter notifying them of their death
■ Families have put death notices in newspapers such as:

Today the asylum accounting office received your credit transfer of twenty Reichmarks intended for flowers for the grave of your little daughter Irmgard. We can report that Irmgard was still overjoyed with the little coat, and above all with the lovely dolly, which she had in her arms to the very end.

> ...his sudden death will always remain a mystery to us.

F Some staff at the asylum drink in the local inn and when drunk have suggested their work is most unusual and make sick jokes about the quality of local fertilisers.

G You remember this cartoon which appeared in 1938 claiming the fertility rates of the criminal and educationally backward were higher than the 'ideal German family'.

■ ACTIVITY

Work in groups of four. Either role-play or write a short conversation that might take place in the home of a family living in Grafeneck. One member of the family should be pro-Nazi; another anti-Nazi; the other two should be undecided about the Nazis.

In your conversation use the evidence on this page and your wider knowledge of Nazi policies.

The Menace of the Subhumans

Male criminals: 4.9 children

A marriage between criminals: 4.4 children

Parents of Special School children: 3.5 children

The German family: 2.2 children

A marriage between academics: 1.9 children

H A new film called *I accuse* has been released. The hero is a medical professor whose young wife Hanna suffers from multiple sclerosis. When he fails to find a cure, he decides to kill her with an overdose to end her suffering. He is accused of murder, there is a big court case and he is found innocent.

A scene from *I accuse*. Professor Heyt comforts his wife Hanna whom he is about to kill.

I The Nazis are encouraging everyone to see the film. The local Catholic priest is against your seeing it. Other films you have seen tell about the cost of keeping people in asylums.

J Someone told you about a speech Hitler made in 1929 in which he said:

If Germany was to remove 700,000–800,000 of the weakest people then the final result might be an increase in strength.

K In 1940 Heinrich Himmler, head of the SS, wrote to an official concerning the asylum at Grafeneck:

The population recognises the grey vans of the SS and believes it knows what is going on in the perpetually smoking crematorium. What is happening there is supposed to be secret, but it is not any more. Because of this, the mood there is very ugly. In my opinion, the only alternative is to cease employing the asylum in this way, and, if need be, to enlighten people there intelligently and rationally, by allowing films to be shown about the hereditarily and mentally ill.

Why did the Nazis persecute many groups in Germany?

THE STORY OF Grafeneck Asylum reveals one of the most disturbing aspects of Nazi policy in Germany. On pages 82–87 you have already studied how the Nazis dealt with their potential opponents, but alongside this, gradually and systematically, the Nazis began to get rid of some of the weakest and most vulnerable members of German society. What were the Nazis worried about?

Why did the 'master race' fear 'inferiors'?

Like many people in the early years of the twentieth century Hitler believed in a form of Social Darwinism. Charles Darwin was a nineteenth-century scientist who argued that all living creatures had changed over time. The way they changed was that only the fittest and strongest survived. The weak or vulnerable species died out because they could not compete with the strong.

Some people who applied Darwin's ideas to human society believed that war between individual races was a natural part of history. The strongest and most ruthless would win this struggle. Hitler believed the Germanic people (what the Nazis called the Aryans) were the strongest. According to Hitler, Aryans were superior not just because of their intelligence but because of their capacity to work hard and sacrifice themselves for their country.

However, if the Aryans were the master race Hitler believed them to be, then why did they lose the First World War? Part of the reason, according to Hitler, was that the German nation had been divided and weakened. If the Nazis did not take action to prevent this weakening of the German race then Germany could not become strong again.

The problem was intensified because more than a million of Germany's healthiest young men had been killed in the First World War. Throughout the 1920s there was a shortage of Aryan men to father children. This further helped to explain the weakness of Germany. If the Nazis were to rebuild Germany they would need to encourage all available Aryan men to have lots of healthy children, but equally to make sure that those who did not fit the Nazis' ideal did not.

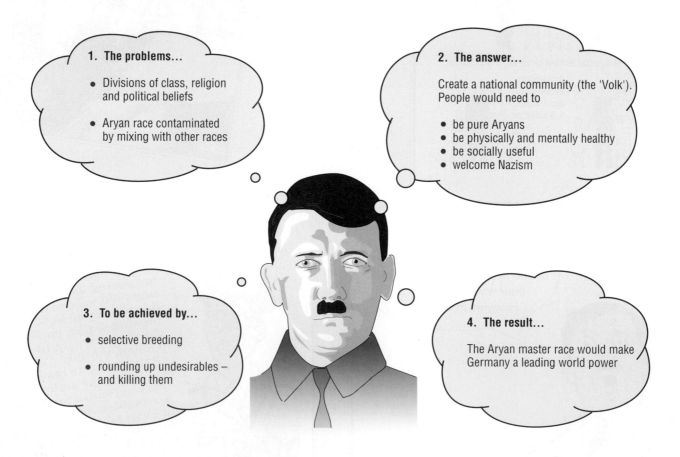

1. The problems...

- Divisions of class, religion and political beliefs

- Aryan race contaminated by mixing with other races

2. The answer...

Create a national community (the 'Volk'). People would need to

- be pure Aryans
- be physically and mentally healthy
- be socially useful
- welcome Nazism

3. To be achieved by...

- selective breeding

- rounding up undesirables – and killing them

4. The result...

The Aryan master race would make Germany a leading world power

SOURCE 1 Hitler's beliefs about how Germany was weakened, and what needed to be done about it

The ideal German – physical features!

Tests were developed to decide who were ideal Aryans. They included matching hair colours and measuring the dimensions of the face.

■ TASK

Use Sources 2 and 3 to decide which of the people in Source 4 the Nazis would have described as pure Aryan and which they would have rejected as being from an inferior race.

S**OURCE 2** The Nazi weekly *Racial Research* explained

  66 We demand of a member of this noble race that he marry only a blue-eyed, oval-faced, red-cheeked and thin-nosed blonde woman. We demand that he take a wife, a virgin only … We demand that the blue-eyed Aryan hero marry an Aryan girl who like himself is of pure and unblemished past. 99

S**OURCE 3** *The Nazi Race*, 1929, provided more detail

  66 The Nordic (Aryan) race is tall, long-legged, slim … male height of above 1.74m. The race is narrow-faced, with a narrow forehead, a narrow high-built nose and a lower jaw and prominent chin, the skin is rosy bright and the blood shines through … the hair is smooth, straight or wavy – possibly curly in childhood. The colour is blonde. 99

S**OURCE 4**

The ideal German – social features

Ideal Germans were 'socially useful' in that they had a job and they contributed to the Volk or national community. Anyone else was seen as a 'burden on the community'. Those who could not or would not work (the 'work-shy'), the unhealthy, the severely disabled and mentally handicapped, tramps and beggars should not be tolerated in the Third Reich.

These people were seen not only as worthless, but as expensive. With the advances of modern medicine many more 'unproductive' people with serious illnesses or hereditary defects were being kept alive. The cost of caring for them was increasing as their numbers grew.

Other groups, such as alcoholics, prostitutes, homosexuals and juvenile delinquents, were seen by the Nazis as asocial and undesirable. They were therefore dangerous; if the Nazis wanted everyone in Germany to fit their ideal, the presence on the streets of Germany of those who did not would undermine and threaten the Nazi programme.

The Gypsies

The Nazis had a particular fear of the Gypsies, who failed both their tests. They were non-Aryan but also seen as homeless and work-shy. There were only about 30,000 Gypsies in Germany but the Nazis were determined to prevent them mixing with Aryan Germans. Nazi racial experts particularly feared what they classed as half-Gypsies, and in 1935 banned marriage between Gypsies and Germans. In 1938 a Decree for the 'Struggle against the Gypsy Plague' was issued. The aim was to register all Gypsies and so be able to ensure the racial separation of Gypsies from Aryans.

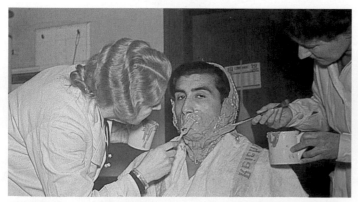

SOURCE 5 The Nazis sent teams of specialists to establish the racial characteristics of Gypsies. This included blood testing, checking eye colour against charts and taking wax masks of faces

How did the Nazis deal with 'burdens on the community'?

The Nazi campaign against those they considered to be burdens on the community built up step by step.

Step 1: Propaganda

A propaganda campaign was started which tried to stir up resentment against people who were burdens on the community.

Step 2: The Sterilisation Law

In many countries in the 1920s and 1930s the idea of preventing 'undesirables' from having children had become popular. In the USA a few persistent criminals were compulsorily sterilised so they could not have children.

In July 1933, only months after coming to power, the Nazis passed a Sterilisation Law. It allowed the Nazis to sterilise people with certain illnesses such as 'simple-mindedness' and 'chronic alcoholism'. These terms were interpreted very freely. In September 1933 a massive round-up of 'tramps and beggars' began. Many were sterilised. Between 1934 and 1945 between 320,000 and 350,000 men and women were compulsorily sterilised.

Step 3: The concentration camps

By 1936 the 'work-shy', tramps and beggars, alcoholics, prostitutes, homosexuals and juvenile delinquents were being sent to concentration camps. A special youth concentration camp was set up in 1937. In 1938 another round-up netted about 11,000 beggars, tramps and Gypsies, most of whom were sent to Buchenwald concentration camp. Many Germans welcomed this removal of what were seen as 'awkward customers'.

Step 4: The euthanasia campaign

In 1939 the Nazis secretly began to exterminate the mentally ill in a euthanasia programme. Six thousand handicapped babies, children and teenagers were murdered by starvation or lethal injections. The Nazis also devised a new method of killing, using carbon monoxide gas. Gas chambers were built in six mental asylums; one was at Grafeneck. German officials busied themselves calculating how much money and food had been saved by these killings and how to make 'better' use of the hospital beds and buildings which had been freed up. Some 72,000 people had been murdered before public protests made Hitler stop the programme in 1941, although some Germans must have approved. Ordinary Germans sent Hitler letters asking for 'mercy killings'. These included a woman dying of cancer, a man blinded and maimed after falling into a cement mixer, and pleas from parents with handicapped children.

Hashude

The idea

The city of Bremen in northern Germany carried out an experiment to try to make difficult families become useful members of society rather than burdens. Some of the city's worst families were placed in a camp of modern terraced houses. Here they could be controlled and 'educated'.

The camp

There were 84 family houses, a bathing area and a children's home. There was also an administration building with an observation cabin which controlled the large iron gate – the only entrance and exit to the estate.

What was life like?

The men were made to work.

The women were taught how to look after their children and had to keep a clean and orderly household.

The houses were inspected daily.

The children attended school.

The houses had no back doors.

Alcohol was prohibited.

The 'welfare workers' (guards) could enter houses at any time.

Punishments included extra drill and being locked up in a dark cell for up to three days with little or no food.

A family usually stayed for a year. For the first six months no contact with other families was allowed.

The families were under constant surveillance.

Who was sent to Hashude?

People could be sent to Hashude for being unwilling to work, alcoholics, begging, disturbing community life, neglecting their children or getting into debt. One such family was that of Heinrich H. who was 'a former Communist, had rarely worked, an alcoholic, a rabble rouser and a danger to the community'.

How did a family leave?

If the family could show improvement they were released into normal society, but if not they might be sent to a concentration camp. It was a last chance for 'asocial' families.

Did Hashude succeed?

The war led to a shortage of houses, so Hashude was closed in July 1940 and became a normal housing estate. Of the 84 families there when it closed, only 18 were recorded as making no improvement. But Hashude was branded a failure. It was very costly and opponents argued that families could not be educated to behave correctly as such bad characteristics were hereditary. The SS were already sending such people to concentration camps.

SOURCE 6 The nursery at Hashude

1. Where would the project at Hashude fit into the Nazis' step-by-step campaign to deal with 'burdens on the community'?
2. What kind of improvements do you think a family would need to make to be released?

■ TASK

Produce a report for the Nazi leadership on 'undesirable' groups in Germany
a) explaining why each group poses a danger to the Nazis
b) suggesting how they should be dealt with.

How did Nazi persecution of the Jews lead to Kristallnacht?

THE NAZIS' RACIAL policy was applied most extremely and most horrifically to the Jews.

Background

Anti-semitism (hatred of the Jews) had been common in Europe for many centuries. In the early twentieth century it was particularly harsh in Russia and many Russian Jews moved to Germany and other European countries where the attitude to Jews was more tolerant.

Many German Jews were poor but some had done well. In 1933 although Jews made up less than 1 per cent of the German population they were prominent in some professions – for example 16 per cent of lawyers and 17 per cent of bankers were Jews. There were 10,000 Jewish doctors.

How did the Nazis treat the Jews from 1933 to 1939?

From its birth the Nazi Party had campaigned against the Jews (see page 33). However, many people who voted for them did not really think that the Nazis would act on their anti-Jewish ideas. Even many Jews did not and some Jews actually supported the Party themselves.

However, within days of taking power the Nazis made their intentions obvious by calling for a boycott of all Jewish businesses (see page 85). The Nazi press, particularly the newspaper *Der Stürmer* run by the Nazi Julius Streicher, continued to pour out a stream of anti-Jewish propaganda as it had done for the previous ten years.

For the first two years of Nazi rule, however, there was little organised persecution of the Jews.

SOURCE 1 A Nazi children's book illustration encouraging children to read *Der Stürmer*

In 1935, Hitler had achieved many of his initial aims. He felt he was in a stronger position to advance some of the Nazis' more extreme measures and took the first steps towards using the law to keep Aryans and Jews separate.

On the timeline below you can see the measures taken by the Nazis from 1933 to 1939.

1933
April Official one-day boycott of Jewish shops, lawyers and doctors all over Germany.

1934 Anti-Jewish propaganda increased.

1935
May Jews forbidden to join the army.

September *The Nuremberg Laws*
Law for the Protection of German Blood and Honour – banned marriages between Jews and Aryans, and forbade them to have sexual relations outside marriage.
Reich Citizenship Law – made Jews 'subjects' rather than citizens, i.e. they lost certain rights.

1936 There was a lull in the anti-Jewish campaign as the Olympic Games were taking place in Berlin. Anti-Jewish signs were taken down.

1937
September For the first time in two years Hitler made an outspoken attack on the Jews. The Aryanisation of business was stepped up – more Jewish businesses were confiscated.

1938
April Jews had to register their property, making it easier to confiscate.

June–July Jewish doctors, dentists and lawyers were forbidden to treat Aryans.

October Jews had to have a red letter 'J' stamped on their passports.

9–10 November Kristallnacht – Nazis destroyed synagogues, Jewish homes and shops.

■ SOURCE INVESTIGATION

What happened on Kristallnacht?

Would you make a good investigative journalist? Here is your chance to find out.

Sources 2 and 3 tell us about Kristallnacht ('Crystal Night'), also known as the 'Night of Broken Glass', which took place on 9–10 November 1938. Many Jews were attacked and much of their property destroyed. It marked an increase in Nazi persecution of the Jews.

SOURCE 2 Jewish shops with shattered windows. Some historians have calculated that up to 400 synagogues and 7500 shops were destroyed, 91 Jews killed and 30,000 sent to concentration camps. Compare their estimates with Heydrich's statistics in Source 7.

SOURCE 3 Report in the London *Times*, November 1938

" The murder in Paris of Herr von Rath led in Germany today to scenes of systematic plunder and destruction which have seldom had their equal in a civilised country since the Middle Ages. In every part of the Reich, synagogues were set on fire or dynamited, Jewish shops smashed and ransacked, and individual Jews arrested or hounded by bands of young Nazis through the street ... other gangs of young men, all in plain clothes but evidently acting according to a systematic plan, toured the streets of Berlin, smashing the windows of every Jewish shop which they encountered ...

But destruction and looting did not begin in earnest until this afternoon. A large café in the Kurfürstendamm had been plundered of its bottles of wines and spirits and these were being gleefully thrown at what remained of the windows, or at anything breakable in the establishment. The active participants in this display were youths and little boys of the Hitler Youth – the only uniformed body which I actually saw taking part in this destruction ...

During the entire day hardly a policeman was to be seen in the streets where the 'purge' was in progress, save those few who were directing traffic. In no case, so far as can be learned, did the police dare to interfere with the demonstrators. In the Kurfürstendamm, army officers in uniform did try to bring the fanatics to reason, but were forced to leave because of threats ...

It is impossible to say how many synagogues may have been burned in Germany during the past 24 hours. "

Source 3 was written by the correspondent of *The Times* in Berlin. It describes the destruction of Kristallnacht but it leaves many questions unanswered. For example:

1. Who was Ernst von Rath (whose killing supposedly sparked off Kristallnacht)?
2. Why was von Rath killed?
3. Were Jews killed on Kristallnacht?
4. Was Kristallnacht planned?
5. Which unidentified groups were involved?
6. What did the fire brigade do?
7. What did ordinary Germans think?

Sources 4–7 give more information about the events of 9–10 November. They were not available to the writer of Source 3 but they do help answer questions 1–7. Your task is to use them to answer the questions.

Then you should rewrite Source 3 to include the answers to questions 1–7. Your revised report should tell what really happened on Kristallnacht.

SOURCE 4   Karl Hartland, the son of a wealthy Jewish banker in Essen, remembered the events of 9–10 November in his autobiography. He was aged twelve at the time

66 *On the wireless it said that a Jewish lad had shot and seriously wounded a German Embassy official in Paris, Ernst von Rath. 'If he dies there will be serious trouble,' said my Father ... Very early in the morning there was a telephone call. 'They have set fire to the synagogue and they are arresting everybody. We must get out of the house,' my father said ... As we came near the synagogue ... there were clusters of people just standing about and watching. Smoke was coming out of the roof ... There was no sign of the fire brigade.*

'I think I will have to disappear for the night,' said Father. 'I'll sleep in the secret place in the loft. If anyone asks, say I have gone away on a trip.' Later on Father went into hiding. The doorbell rang. Two policemen in civilian clothes had come to collect any arms there might be in the house. I said, 'There is only my air gun and the toy guns.' 'We will take those,' they said ...

I was asleep when the doorbell rang again. Not the usual ring but long, long rings that just went on. I rushed downstairs. There was also a crashing sound from the back door. A group of Stormtroopers pushed their way in. 'Any weapons in the house?' they asked. The men were in brown uniforms and carried pistols and daggers ... The men charged up the stairs. There were crashes and bangs all over the place. One of the men went up to a chest of drawers and pulled it open ... 'Look at what these Jews have got,' the Stormtrooper said. 'They wallow in everything and we have got nothing.' They rushed from room to room. I saw one trooper with my camera. 'That's my camera,' I shouted. 'You are stealing my camera.' The trooper turned on me and took my shirt and twisted it round and round so that it was tight round my throat. 'Listen, Jew boy, the Stormtroopers don't steal' ... Later I saw my camera; it had been stepped on and the lens pushed right in ... 'Please sir,' I begged, 'please don't burn this house.' 'We'll let you off this time,' said the officer. 'Come on everybody, we have got lots of work to do.' And they all went out. Grandfather rang the police. The police said there was nothing they could do, but they might send someone later. In the meantime the bell rang again and this time a group of SS men came in.

'So they have been here before us,' one of them said. 'We are supposed to protect this house. We want to be able to use these good houses. Got anything to drink?'

The doorbell rang and a policeman appeared. The SS man said, 'Will you guard this place?' The SS men left carrying Father's brandy bottle. I went round the house. Every room had been turned inside out ... paintings had been slashed and a lot of crockery had been broken. 99

SOURCE 5   The American Consul in Leipzig, David Buffum, wrote a report (dated 21 November 1938) on the events of Kristallnacht in Leipzig

66 *At 3 a.m. on 10 November was unleashed a barrage of Nazi ferocity. Jewish buildings were smashed into and contents demolished or looted. An 18-year-old Jewish boy was hurled from a third-storey window to land with both legs broken on a street littered with burning beds and other household furniture ...*

A small dog was thrown four flights on to the street with a broken spine ... looting of cash, silver, jewellery and other easily sold items is apparent. The main streets of the city were a litter of shattered plate glass. According to reliable testimony, the débâcle was executed by SS men and Stormtroopers not in uniform, each group having been provided with hammers, axes, crowbars and incendiary bombs. Three synagogues were fired, no attempts whatsoever were made to quench the fires, the fire brigade only played water on adjoining buildings ... At the Jewish cemetery the temple was fired, tombstones uprooted and graves violated ... Jewish males aged between 16 and 60 were arrested and transported to concentration camps ... All of the local crowds observing were obviously benumbed and aghast over the unprecedented fury of Nazi acts. 99

SOURCE 6 Heydrich sent the following instructions

" Secret
Copy of Most Urgent telegram from Munich,
of 10 November 1938, 1.20 a.m.
To:
All Headquarters and Stations of the State Police
All Districts and Sub-districts of the SD
(Security Police)
Urgent! For immediate attention of Chief or his
deputy!

Re: Measures against Jews tonight
Following the attempt on the life of Secretary of the
Legation von Rath in Paris, demonstrations against
the Jews are to be expected in all parts of the Reich in
the course of the coming night, November 9/10 1938.
The instructions below are to be applied in dealing
with these events:

The German Police has received instructions detailed
below.
a)   Only such measures are to be taken as do not
*   endanger German lives or property*
*   (i.e. synagogues are to be burned down only*
*   where there is no danger of fire in neighbouring*
*   buildings).*
b)   Places of business and apartments belonging to
*   Jews may be destroyed but not looted. The police*
*   are instructed to supervise the observance of this*
*   order and to arrest looters.*
c)   In commercial streets particular care is to be
*   taken that non-Jewish businesses are completely*
*   protected against damage.*
d)   Foreign citizens – even if they are Jews – are not
*   to be molested.*
The demonstrations are not to be prevented by the
Police, who are only to supervise the observance of
guidelines. "

SOURCE 7 Report of Reinhardt Heydrich, Chief of Security Police, on the damage, dated 11 November

" Shops – 815 destroyed
Synagogues – 276 destroyed
Jews – 20,000 arrested
Foreigners – 3 arrested
Looting – 174 looters arrested. "

Heydrich noted: 'The true figures must be several times greater than those reported.'

Why did Kristallnacht happen?

One reason for Kristallnacht was the power struggle between leading Nazis. Goebbels was out of favour with Hitler because of Goebbels' affair with a Czech actress and he decided to win his way back into Hitler's favour. He suggested to Hitler that Kristallnacht should take place to satisfy the hatred many Nazi hardliners had for the Jews. Hitler agreed and decided to use it to speed up the removal of Jews from German economic life. Other Nazi leaders, especially Goering and Himmler, disapproved and were irritated by the events of Kristallnacht. This is an example of the chaotic way in which the Nazis made up policy.

1. Did Kristallnacht happen as the Nazis intended? Consider which parts of Heydrich's orders were followed and which were not.
2. What does this tell us about Nazi control?
3. There are some points on which the sources seem to contradict each other. Can you find any and suggest why they might do so?

From persecution to genocide

After Kristallnacht the position of German Jews got rapidly worse, as is shown in the timeline below.

1938

12 November	Much of the property damaged on Kristallnacht was only rented by Jews from German owners. The Nazis 'fined' the Jews one billion Reichmarks for the damage.
15 November	Jewish pupils only allowed to attend Jewish schools.
December	Remaining Jewish businesses confiscated.

1939

January	All Jews had to add new first names – Sarah for women, Israel for men. Reich office for Jewish Emigration was established to promote emigration 'by every possible means'.
September	The Second World War began.

On 12 March 1939 the first mass arrests of Jews took place and nearly 30,000 Jewish men and boys were sent to concentration camps. With the onset of war the mistreatment of the Jews quickly escalated. You will study the next phase of this awful story in Chapter 8, pages 156–59.

Why was propaganda so important to the Nazis?

YOU HAVE NOW looked at different areas of Nazi policy – their treatment of political opponents, of the churches, and their persecution of minorities. Behind all these was a massive propaganda campaign which aimed to convince the German people that all the Nazis did was right and good.

Not everyone was like the woman in Source 1, as you will already have realised. However, for those who were, much of the blame can be attached to the Nazi propaganda effort and to its overseer Josef Goebbels. In the next few pages you are first going to look in overview at the propaganda for which he was responsible. You will then look at two case studies on aspects of the Nazis' propaganda programme – art and architecture, and the Berlin Olympics.

■ TASK

The diagram on the opposite page summarises the problems facing Goebbels when the Nazis came to power in 1933. How might he deal with each of these problems?

Write out your own ideas, then compare them with what Goebbels actually did – which you can find out about on page 112.

SOURCE 2 Josef Goebbels, appointed as Nazi Minister of Propaganda and National Enlightenment on Hitler's rise to power. He was vain and ambitious, a womaniser and a bitter anti-semite. This photograph was taken in 1931. It shows him leaving a polling station after voting in a general election. The photograph was banned after 1933 because it showed Goebbels' club foot

What were the problems facing Goebbels in 1933?

Newspapers

Germany had no real national newspapers in 1933 but had 4700 local newspapers. Some were owned by big Jewish publishing firms. All the political parties had newspapers. The circulation of Nazi newspapers was small.

Radio

Hitler and Goebbels believed the spoken word was more effective than the written word, so radio was very important. The problem was that much radio was local. States like Prussia and Bavaria had their own radio. Hermann Goering, who was Minister for Prussia, was determined he should control radio in Prussia. Goebbels wanted control of all radio in a Reich Radio Company.

The other problem was to make sure people listened to the radio. Few people owned radios as they were expensive.

Films

These were seen as another very important means of propaganda. The problem was that Germans were used to films which were made to a high standard and were very entertaining. The 1920s had been a golden age in German film-making, with Germany producing some of the most celebrated directors and stars. Would people watch political films if they were used to such good films?

Festivals and celebrations

Goebbels had successfully used marches, rallies and festivals to attract people in the battle to win power. Now they had to be used to keep people loyal, to make people feel important and part of the new Germany. They needed to be impressive. But what should the rallies and parades be like? What events from the history of the Nazi Party could be celebrated each year?

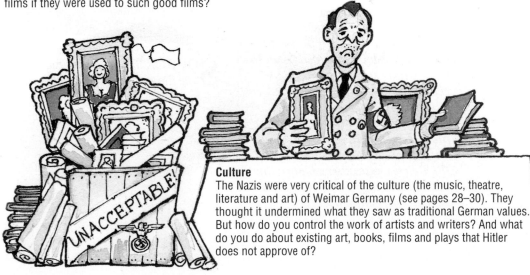

Culture

The Nazis were very critical of the culture (the music, theatre, literature and art) of Weimar Germany (see pages 28–30). They thought it undermined what they saw as traditional German values. But how do you control the work of artists and writers? And what do you do about existing art, books, films and plays that Hitler does not approve of?

Goebbels' solutions

Compare your own answers to the task on pages 110–111 to the solutions which Goebbels came up with.

Newspapers

Goebbels took over most of the publishers, put controls on what journalists could write and set up a press agency to tell newspapers what the news should be.

The Propaganda Ministry issued daily orders to newspapers, such as that in Source 3.

> **SOURCE 3** Orders from the Propaganda Ministry, 6 April 1935
>
> *66 Photos showing members of the Reich government at dining tables in front of rows of bottles must not be published in future. Recently, because of a great number of photos, the utterly absurd impression has been created among the public that members of the government are living it up. 99*

Anti-Nazi newspapers were closed. By 1944 there were only 1000 daily newspapers and most of these were controlled by the Nazi Party. Newspapers were put up in public display boxes. Some Nazi newspapers threatened people who cancelled their subscriptions. Even newspaper sellers at train stations were checked on to see if they were following Nazi instructions.

Films

The cinema was popular so Goebbels encouraged new films. Well over a thousand films were made during the Third Reich. Most of these were love stories, comedies or adventure films; the rest were political films. Two examples of propaganda films are *Jud Süss*, which told the story of an 'evil' Jew, and *Ohm Kruger*, an anti-British film about the Boer War. Admission to cinemas was only allowed at the beginning of the entire programme, so you also had to watch newsreels and short documentary films which carried the Nazi message.

> **SOURCE 4** An official account of the filming of the celebrations for Hitler's 50th birthday for a newsreel in 1939
>
> *66 The spirit of the hour must be captured also, the whole atmosphere of discipline and of concentrated power. The programme begins. The Führer driven between lines of troops to the parade ground. Immediately on his arrival the march past begins … cheerful marching tunes resound, the camera lingers lovingly on the Goebbels children all clothed in white, who stand, curious but well behaved, next to Hitler, thus strengthening his reputation as a true lover of children – a special shot for women in the audience. Now the picture turns to the crowd. Now Hitler appears on the balcony of the Reich Chancellery before the crowd, which breaks out into a repeated ovation. 99*

Goebbels believed that propaganda succeeded best if people were entertained, so he wanted films to be well made. Two Nazi propaganda films are now regarded as great masterpieces of cinema – *The Triumph of the Will*, about the 1934 Nuremberg Rally, and *Olympiade*, about the 1936 Olympic Games. They were directed by a woman, Leni Riefenstahl.

SOURCE 5 A poster for the film *The Eternal Jew*

Radio

Goebbels won the power struggle for the control of radio and formed the Reich Radio Company which controlled all local radio stations. Millions of very cheap radios called 'The People's Receiver' were made. These could not pick up foreign broadcasts. By 1939 70 per cent of German households had a radio. For those who did not, 6000 loudspeaker pillars were erected in public squares all over Germany where Nazi propaganda programmes could be heard.

Local radio wardens encouraged the spread of radio and made sure orders such as the newspaper announcement in Source 6 were obeyed.

SOURCE 6 Newspaper advertisement, 16 March 1934

66 *Attention! The Führer is speaking on the radio. On Wednesday 21 March, the Führer is speaking on all German stations from 11 a.m. to 11.50 a.m. The district Party headquarters have ordered that all factory owners, department stores, offices, shops, pubs and blocks of flats put up loudspeakers an hour before the broadcast of the Führer's speech so that the whole workforce and all national comrades can participate fully in the broadcast.* 99

1. Why would the Nazis make radios which could not pick up foreign broadcasts?

SOURCE 7 A poster with the caption 'All Germany hears the Führer with the people's receiver'

Typical broadcasts were Hitler's speeches, German music and programmes about German history. The Nazis also invented the idea of frequent news flashes and community programmes. They had children's programmes which taught children about how to serve their country.

Festivals and celebrations

People were encouraged to celebrate a new list of important days. On such days people were expected to attend parades and speeches and hang out flags.

January	'Day of Seizing of Power' – mass torchlight processions
February	Founding of the Nazi Party Day
March	War Heroes' Day
April	Hitler's birthday – army parades, flowers for Hitler's portrait in schools
July	German Culture Day
September	Reich Party Day – a week's rally at Nuremberg
November	Anniversary of the Munich Putsch – silent march through Munich

The Nuremberg rallies

The week-long rally at Nuremberg was the highlight of the year, with thousands of people watching parades and displays and listening to speeches.

■ ACTIVITY

Design a Nazi propaganda poster for one of the festivals or celebration days.

SOURCE 9 German Culture Day in Munich, 1938

SOURCE 8 Hitler speaking at the 1938 Nuremberg Rally

Culture

Goebbels set up the Reich Chamber of Culture. Musicians, writers and actors had to be members of the Chamber. Goebbels could stop any musician, actor, writer or artist from working by ending his or her membership of the Chamber of Culture – many who were thought to be unsuitable were banned. Some left Germany in protest, some buckled under and started to produce work which was acceptable to the Nazis. You can see what he wanted from music, theatre and literature below. There is a special case study of art and architecture on pages 116–17.

Music

Goebbels drew up guidelines for what was acceptable. Music should be German: folk songs, marching music and classical music by Bach, Beethoven and Mozart were to be preferred. Some popular music was permitted, but never jazz which was 'black' music and therefore racially inferior.

Theatre

Theatre should concentrate on German history and political drama. Cheap theatre tickets were available. If you joined the Nazi 'Cultural Association' you could see ten plays at half price, but you could not choose which plays or when, because Goebbels controlled that too.

Literature

Goebbels drew up a list of banned books which were removed by the Gestapo from bookshops and libraries. In May 1933 the Nazis encouraged students to burn the books they believed were un-German and Jewish. Goebbels wanted books about race, war and the Nazi movement. One popular topic was the heroic actions of German soldiers in the First World War. Such books described the thrill of combat and how Germans should be prepared to die for the Fatherland.

A model Nazi book was written by Goebbels in 1929. A novel with the title *Michael*, it contained the following Nazi themes:

- The comradeship of the battlefield
- The superiority of Nordic blood
- The evil influence of Communists and Jews
- The ideal of motherhood and the home
- The inspired leadership of Hitler
- The heroic way of life under the Nazis.

TASK

Study Sources 3–11.
1. Which are examples of Nazi propaganda?
2. Why would Hitler have approved of each one?
3. For each example of Nazi propaganda explain

   ■ who it was aimed at
   ■ what message it contained.

4. Explain which you think was the most effective means of propaganda.

Museums

SOURCE 10 1935 book cover showing how the Nazis had turned an anti-war museum into a war museum

SOURCE 11 'The Eternal Jew', an anti-semitic propaganda exhibition

Propaganda case study 1: Art and architecture

HITLER TOOK A particular interest in two aspects of culture – art and architecture.

Architecture

Hitler believed architecture was the finest of the arts and that it could influence people's lives. In his later years as leader he became more involved in his pet architectural projects. He favoured two styles:

- The 'monumental style' for public buildings. This meant they were to be large and built of stone. Often they were copies of the buildings of ancient Greece and Rome with plenty of columns and steps.
- The 'country style' for family homes and youth hostels. These were traditional folk-style buildings using wood and stone, and with shutters and pitched roofs.

1. Which of the styles would support each of these Nazi aims:

   - To show Nazi power
   - To encourage the role of the woman as mother and home-maker and the man as the provider
   - To show that the state was more important than the individual?

Art

Hitler had tried to earn a living as an artist and had very definite ideas on art. He disliked modern art and sculpture and preferred art which showed heroic German figures, the power of the 'master race' or rural family scenes. He despised the art of Weimar Germany, which he attacked as degenerate (perverted), unpatriotic and Jewish. He wanted art to reject the weak and ugly and glorify healthy and strong heroes.

In 1937 the Nazis opened the House of German Art to show officially approved art. At the same time they also put on an exhibition of unacceptable 'Degenerate Art' which had been banned by the Reich Chamber of Culture. The pictures were often hung without frames and labelled with rude explanations or filthy jokes. This exhibition was very popular and attracted five times as many visitors as the approved German Art exhibition.

2. Why do you think the 'Degenerate Art' exhibition was so much more popular than the German Art exhibition?

SOURCE 1 A poster advertising the 'Degenerate Art' exhibition. The caption reads 'What we see in this interesting exhibition was once taken seriously'

ACTIVITY

Work with a partner to decide which of Sources 2–7 Hitler and Goebbels would include in their 'Degenerate Art' exhibition and which in their German Art exhibition. Explain your choice.

SOURCE 2 *Kahlenberg farmer and his family*, a painting from 1939

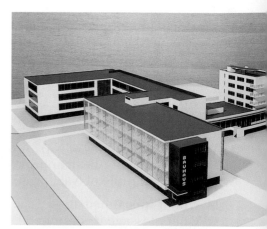

SOURCE 3 Architect's model for a building built in Dessau, Germany

116

SOURCE 6 *Carnival* by Max Beckmann

SOURCE 4 Two sculptures entitled *Girl with blue hair* and *Bather*

SOURCE 7 Architect's model of the Königsplatz in Munich

SOURCE 5 *The Guardian* by Arno Breker

Propaganda case study 2: The Berlin Olympics

THE OLYMPICS WERE due to come to Berlin in 1936. They had been planned years earlier, before the Nazis came to power. Some Nazis wanted to cancel them, but Goebbels argued that this was a great opportunity. With the media of 49 countries there in strength the Olympics could be a showcase for Nazi ideas: they could show the world that Germany was a modern, well organised and civilised society and that Aryans were racially superior.

While other countries sent amateurs who had to take time off work and lose pay to attend, the Germans were full-time athletes who had been carefully trained for the Games, much as athletes are today.

Hitler's persecution of the Jews was well known by this time. There were attempts to boycott the games. In answer to foreign criticism the German team contained one token Jewish athlete.

■ SOURCE INVESTIGATION

1. List all the different kinds of propaganda which Goebbels used at the Olympic Games.
2. How far do Sources 2–4 agree about reactions to the opening and closing ceremonies?
3. Which reactions would have
a) pleased
b) displeased
the Nazis most?
4. Why did the performance of Jesse Owens matter to Hitler?
5. Do you think Hitler successfully showed:
a) that Germany was a modern country
b) that Germany was well organised
c) that Germany was a civilised society
d) that Aryans were superior?
You may want to draw a chart to help you decide:

Source	Modern	Organised	Civilised	Aryans superior

The stadium

SOURCE 1 The Olympic stadium in Berlin, 1936, which held 100,000 people. The Nazis built 150 other new buildings

The ceremonies

SOURCE 2 R. Hart-Davis, *Hitler's Games*, 1986

66 Everyone who saw the opening ceremony agreed that it had been magnificently planned and executed. Foreign visitors were astonished and not a little unnerved by the colossal scale of the stadium and all the arrangements – by the huge number of soldiers lining the route to the stadium, by the continuous saluting, by the overt military nature of the regime. Another feature which shook strangers was the hysterical adulation accorded to the Führer wherever he went: men who saw him yelled themselves hoarse, women gave piercing screams, wept with excitement, fainted. 99

SOURCE 3 William E. Dodd, U.S. Ambassador to Germany, described the closing ceremony, 6 August 1936. Dodd was opposed to Nazism

66 I have never seen such an elaborate show … How much the Olympics cost one can hardly imagine, though I would guess 75 million marks. The propaganda of it may have pleased the Germans. It had a bad influence on foreigners, as reported to me, in spite of the fine entertainment of all concerned. 99

SOURCE 4 Godfrey Brown, a 400-metre runner in the British team

66 The fact is that some of us went to Berlin with a mistaken idea – that we were going to take part in a sports meeting. Instead, we were treated to a piece of political propaganda … On the last day we were inflicted with the sight of thousands of gross, flabby Germans, so-called Hitler Youth, clad in nothing but shorts and performing ridiculous evolutions on the grass. We cried, 'Sweep on, you fat and greasy citizens' and made a dash for the first train home. 99

Jesse Owens

SOURCE 5 Jesse Owens wins the 100 metres, second is Metcalfe (USA), third is Osendarp (Holland). Owens was the greatest athlete of the Games. He won four gold medals – in the 100 metres, 200 metres, long jump and 4 x 100 metres relay. He broke Olympic records eleven times. Jesse Owens was very popular with the German crowd. In all, the ten black members of the U.S. track and field team won between them seven gold, three silver and three bronze medals. This was more than any national team won for track and field

SOURCE 6 The Reich Youth leader, Baldur von Schirach, later claimed that after Owens' victory Hitler said

66 The Americans should be ashamed of themselves, letting Negroes win their medals for them. I shall not shake hands with this Negro … Do you really think that I will allow myself to be photographed shaking hands with a Negro? 99

The technical facilities

SOURCE 7 R. Hart-Davis, *Hitler's Games*, 1986

66 The one disappointment of the day was the performance of the television cameras, which had been set up with a great deal of publicity. Television was in its infancy, and this was the first occasion on which it was used to cover a sporting function. The pictures were scarcely recognisable; they resembled very faint, over-exposed film and were so hard to follow that many people turned away in disappointment.

Television apart, the technical facilities devised for the Games seemed faultless. The photo-electric timing mechanism worked perfectly and a constant source of fascination for the crowd was the immense stopwatch mounted on the Marathon Gate, the largest stopwatch ever built. 99

SOURCE 8 The historian Z. Zeman describes the achievement of German radio at the Olympics in his book *Nazi Propaganda, 1964*

66 In 1936 the Germans took great pains to make available as many radio facilities as possible. Four hundred and fifty additional wireless workers were ordered to Berlin. Three hundred microphones, 220 amplifiers, 20 transmitting vans were put at the disposal of foreign broadcasters. These facilities were used by 32 foreign countries. Ninety-two foreign reporters described races. During the 16 days of the Olympic Games 2500 reports were broadcast in 28 languages. The effort and the accomplishment was indeed impressive. The majority of the foreign radio representatives sent telegrams to Goebbels, full of admiration for the achievements of the German broadcasters. A director of the American NBC said 'the work done by German radio remains without precedent in the history of broadcasting'. 99

The results

SOURCE 9 The medal table for the 1936 Olympics

Nation	Gold	Silver	Bronze
1. Germany	33	26	30
2. United States	24	20	12
10. Great Britain	4	7	3

The convert

SOURCE 10 R. Hart-Davis, *Hitler's Games*, 1986

66 One member of the South African team, boxer Robie Leibbrandt, was won over by the Nazis. He was an eccentric character who slept on bare boards and every two weeks fasted for 24 hours, during which he ate nothing but sand and charcoal. After the Games he was given a scholarship in Germany and he stayed there. During the Second World War, after being trained in sabotage and espionage techniques, he was landed by U-boat on the coast of South-West Africa and blew up bridges and railway lines until he was captured. At his trial he shouted 'Heil Hitler!' 99

Images of Hitler

ON PAGES 52–53 you examined the ways in which the Nazis built up Hitler in the 1920s and early 1930s. One of the Nazis' greatest successes during their years in power was the way they managed to maintain Hitler's popularity.

Hitler was presented as a man …

- who worked tirelessly for Germany.

  He was actually a rather unreliable worker.

- who abstained from pleasures that many 'ordinary' Germans enjoyed.

  He was a vegetarian, very concerned about his health, and was not very interested in sex.

- who was generous and refused his official salary.

  He could afford to do this because of his massive royalties from Mein Kampf and because he charged for the use of his portrait on postage stamps!

- who was fond of children.

  This was true.

- who had been a brave soldier in the First World War.

  He was indeed brave – he could undergo painful dental treatment without anaesthetics.

SOURCE 1 'Loyalty, Honour and Order'. A 1934 Nazi poster

Above all he was presented as a gifted man with the skills needed to lead Germany.

Many women were attracted to Hitler. He received adoring letters from them. Many people felt they could identify with him – soldiers, farmers, craftsmen and workers could all find something in Hitler's past or in his promises which made them believe in him as a leader. Many people worshipped him; they believed he could do no wrong and refused to blame him for any mistakes made by the Nazis. Even people who disliked Nazi policies still had a personal respect for the Führer.

■ TASK

1. For each of Sources 1–5 explain what impression it gives you of Hitler.
2. Why do you think Source 3 was censored?
3. Why was Hitler's image so important to the Nazi propaganda effort? Refer to Sources 1–5 in your answer.

SOURCE 2 A 1930s poster entitled 'Long Live Germany'

SOURCE 3 Hitler at work. Hitler wore glasses in private but never in public. This picture was in fact censored – as shown by the cross

SOURCE 4 Hitler photographed with two children

■ TASK

For this task you will need to look back over all your work from chapters 5 and 6.

Do you think that Nazi Germany was:

a) a true TOTALITARIAN state with total control

b) on the way to becoming a totalitarian state, as it was successful in most areas

c) trying but failing to be a totalitarian state, as its control in many areas was incomplete?

To help you decide, fill out a chart like this:

Nazi aim	Totally successful	Partly successful	No success
To eliminate opposition			
To win the hearts and minds of ordinary people			
To get people to worship the leader as a hero			
To control the media – radio, newspapers, films, etc.			
To eliminate freedom of speech			
To control people's leisure time			
To eliminate non-Aryans from Germany			

SOURCE 5 A portrait of Hitler painted towards the end of the war in 1944

Was everyone better off under the Nazis?

THERE WAS LITTLE effective opposition to the Nazis. Most historians explain this by claiming that the Nazis brought prosperity and political stability. Is this really the case?

1. Small businesses

The Nazis had found many supporters among small businessmen such as shopkeepers and self-employed craftsmen, and had promised them much.

Many small shops were finding it very difficult to survive because of competition from large department stores. The Nazis passed laws to ban new department stores, stop existing ones growing and enable craftsmen to control their trade. Competing Jewish businesses were closed down.

Between 1936 and 1939 the number of self-employed skilled craftsmen fell from 1,650,000 to 1,500,000, but the value of their trade nearly doubled between 1933 and 1937.

2. Farmers

The Nazis told farmers they were one of the most important groups in Germany. Some farm debts were written off and all farmers benefited from an increase in food prices. But farmers resented the government's meddling – it was ordered, for example, that each hen had to lay 65 eggs per year. Farmers also suffered from a shortage of labour as workers left to go to better-paid jobs in the towns.

3. Big business

Large firms benefited from the massive rearmaments programme and the destruction of the trade unions. The value of German industry rose and big profits were made. The average salary of managers rose by nearly 70 per cent between 1934 and 1938. But industrialists had to pay for these benefits; the government took control of prices, wages, profits and imports, and decided who should receive scarce raw materials. They also made industry produce what they wanted.

4. Unskilled workers

This group had been the hardest hit by the Depression. They formed the bulk of the six million unemployed. They were immediately put to work on government programmes. They had no option. If they did not accept the work they would receive no unemployment benefit. However, wages on the government's work schemes were sometimes lower than the rate of unemployment benefit. For others the government's scheme was a lifeline. It allowed them to feed and clothe their families adequately once more. As the local councils took action to provide more cheap flats (there had been a severe shortage of affordable housing during the Depression), another of their problems was solved.

■ TASK

Which of these four groups were better off under the Nazis? Put the groups in order of how much they benefited from the Nazis' rise to power.

Case study: Were the working classes better off under the Nazis?

Most working-class people had not supported the Nazis before 1933. They had voted for the socialists. Now the Nazis were in power they needed to control the workers.

Workers had to join the DAF (Deutsche Arbeitsfront) headed by Dr Robert Ley. It put them to work building new autobahns (motorways), hospitals, schools and other public buildings. Both employers and employees belonged to the DAF, which settled any disputes between them. The DAF became a massive organisation to control the workers.

To help win over the workers Dr Ley set up two organisations within the DAF:

- 'Beauty of Labour' to persuade employers to improve working conditions in factories. It organised campaigns such as 'Good ventilation in the workplace' and 'Hot meals in the factory'.
- 'Strength through Joy' (Kraft durch Freude') to organise the leisure time of workers. Source 1 shows the activities arranged. It proved popular with workers.

In another organisation, the Reich Labour Service (RAD), all 18–25 year old men had to do six months' work service. It was unpopular because it was hard, manual labour and poorly paid. The Nazis tried to use the RAD to indoctrinate young adults.

Overall the attitude of workers to the Nazis varied. Some were thankful for a job and remembered there had been six million unemployed, but the attitudes in Source 9 were common. Sources 1–10 will help you decide if industrial workers were better off.

SOURCE 1 The number of participants in various activities organised by 'Strength through Joy' in 1938

Concerts 2,515,598

Popular entertainments 13,660,015

Operas 6,639,067

Theatre 7,478,633

Films 857,402

Variety shows 7,980,973

Exhibitions 1,595,516

Cruises 131,623

Hikes 1,937,850

Various sports (total) 22,379,631

Other activities 13,776,791

Other holidays 8,259,238

SOURCE 2 Hitler speaking about the new 'People's Car' – the Volkswagen. 'Strength through Joy' offered workers the chance to start paying towards one. Many started paying but no cars were delivered

SOURCE 3 A 'Strength through Joy' instructor organises physical exercise for swimmers

SOURCE 4 The average working week for industrial workers, excluding overtime

1933 43 hours

1939 47 hours

SOURCE 5 Unemployment in Germany. However, refer back to page 87 to see this in context

1932 5,603,000

1935 2,151,000

1939 119,000

SOURCE 6 Workers assemble to begin work on the first autobahn, September 1933

SOURCE 7 A 'Strength through Joy' ('Kraft durch Freude') poster encouraging Germans to save up for travel. It reads 'Now you too can travel!'

SOURCE 8 The daily programme at an RAD camp in Saxony, May 1938, from a Social Democratic Party report. The report commented 'The young people are deadened by physical exertion. The daily wage is not enough to buy a beer'

4.45 Get up

4.50 Gymnastics

5.15 Wash, make beds

5.30 Coffee break

5.50 Parade

6.00 March to building site. Work until 14.30 (30 minutes break for breakfast).

15.00 Lunch

15.30–18.00 Drill

18.10–18.45 Instruction

18.45–19.15 Cleaning and mending

19.15 Parade

19.30 Announcements

19.45 Supper

20.00–21.30 Sing-song or leisure activity

22.00 Lights out

1. The Nazis also used the RAD to prepare young men for something else. Can you work out what from the routine in Source 8?

SOURCE 9 Bert Engelmann recalled a conversation he heard on a train in 1936

66 *Two autobahn workers were grumbling about the back-breaking work, poor housing and bad food they had to put up with. Then a woman aged about thirty and wearing a Nazi Women's League badge entered the train compartment. The two men continued their conversation. After just a few minutes she gazed sternly at the two workers, and remarked, 'Is this whining really necessary? You should be grateful that you have work and thank the Führer for getting rid of unemployment!'*

The older of the two said quietly, 'Listen here, young woman: we work outdoors in all kinds of weather, shovelling dirt for 51 pfennigs an hour. Then there are the deductions and the "voluntary" contributions they take out automatically, and 15 pfennigs a day for a straw mattress in a draughty wooden barracks, and 35 pfennigs for what they ladle out of a cauldron and call dinner – slop you wouldn't touch, I guarantee it! Six months ago we were still getting 66 pfennigs an hour, and now they're pushing us harder and harder.'

'Let it go, Karl,' the younger one said, but his friend forged ahead. 'I'm trained as a printer. In the summer of '33 I lost my job. I collected unemployment until the spring of '34 – and that was a lot better than what I'm doing now. At least I was home, with my family, and now and then I could pick up some odd jobs, or I could work in the garden. Now I'm in compulsory service, with ten days' holiday a year! That's enough to do a man in, I'm telling you!'

'Forget it, Karl,' the younger one intervened again, 'The lady isn't interested.'

'But she should be,' the older one continued, undeterred. 'Listen, at the beginning of '33 there were over six million unemployed, and now there's only two million – that much is true. But it's also true that at the beginning of '33 I was still earning good money in my own trade and was home – and now we work ourselves to the bone and the wages keep going down – it's sixteen marks net per week now. The whole thing stinks, and somebody's got to say it!'

The woman remained silent for a while. What he said had clearly affected her. But she soon felt compelled to reply, chiefly for the benefit of the 'young foreigner' in the compartment. 'You can't expect that the misery brought about by fourteen years of mismanagement will be cured in the twinkling of an eye! But now people have hope. They're off the streets, and Germany is strong and powerful again. We've regained our honour – that's the main thing! In three years Adolf Hitler has accomplished miracles, and from year to year things are getting better. Maybe next year you can take a holiday with your family in Madeira with "Strength through Joy" ... You must have faith in the Führer!' 99

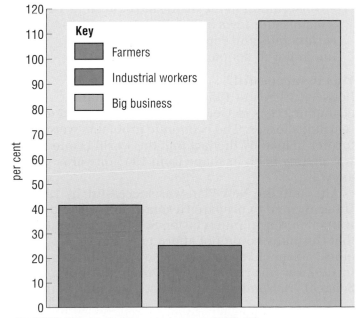

SOURCE 10 Increase in income 1933–38

■ ACTIVITY

Prepare for a debate. First divide Sources 1–10 into two groups – those which support the argument that industrial workers were better off, and those which do not.

Then look again at your lists. Most of these sources can be used to support either argument. Can you work out how?

Finally, prepare for a class debate by writing two speeches using the sources, one arguing industrial workers were better off, the other arguing they were not.

HITLER WANTED GERMANY to regain the land lost in 1919 and to dominate Europe. To do this he knew that Germany had to recover its economic strength.

Aims

1. To reduce unemployment. In 1933 it was six million.
2. To build up the German armaments industry and to rearm and enlarge the German army, navy and airforce.
3. To make Germany economically self-sufficient so it could not be blockaded in times of war.

Problems

In 1933 Germany faced major economic difficulties:

1. It was difficult to export goods as world trade had collapsed in the Great Depression.
2. Germany was short of certain essential raw materials.
3. Germany could not afford to pay for many imports.

Dr Hjalmar Schacht – the New Plan

When the Nazis took power Hitler entrusted Germany's economy to Dr Hjalmar Schacht. He was made President of the Reichsbank in March 1933 and in 1934 he was made Minister of the Economy. He had been a loyal supporter of Hitler before the Nazis came to power. He was also a brilliant financial expert and was trusted by business people in Germany and by foreign leaders and bankers. He devised what he called the 'New Plan'.

How the New Plan worked

- **Imports were limited:** How much and what materials could be imported were carefully controlled.
- **Trade agreements** were made with individual countries (for example, Hungary exchanged butter, vegetable oil, fodder and raw materials for industrial products in 1934) to supply the raw materials Germany wanted in return for German goods.
- **Government spending** was channelled into a wide range of industries, but the government did not try to control those industries.
- **Unemployment was reduced by:**
  – work creation projects such as rebuilding German cities and building the new autobahns
  – the compulsory Labour Service
  – conscription to the army, introduced in 1935
  – dismissing Jews and political opponents from certain jobs and replacing them with unemployed people.

Was it successful?

Between 1934 and 1936 this plan solved the economic crisis in Germany and enabled Hitler to rearm his forces. The economic problems were further helped by the fact that the world economy was getting back in shape from 1933 onwards anyway.

Although the New Plan was successful, by 1935 Hitler wanted to prepare Germany for war and wanted to rearm much faster. Schacht told Hitler that Germany could not afford to rearm so quickly. Schacht soon lost his power and resigned in 1937. He was replaced by Hermann Goering. Schacht later ended up in a concentration camp.

Hermann Goering – the Four-Year Plan

Goering was probably the second most important person in the Nazi Party after Hitler. He was also head of the German airforce, the Luftwaffe, and President of the Reichstag. He had been a First World War fighter pilot and was a loyal supporter of Hitler. However, he was not an expert in economics or business.

The aim of the Four-Year Plan was to prepare for war within four years. Hitler was well aware that in the First World War the British naval blockade had starved Germany of the food and materials it needed. The Four-Year Plan aimed to make Germany self-sufficient in materials essential for war such as oil, rubber and steel, and set targets for the production of these materials. This policy was known as 'Autarky'.

How the Four-Year Plan worked

- Increase production of the raw materials needed for rearmament: coal, iron ore, oil, metal and explosives.
- Persuade big business to produce key synthetic raw materials such as rubber, fuel and textiles.
- Reduce imports even further.
- Tighten controls on prices and wages.
- Used forced labour if needed.
- Build new industrial plants such as the Hermann Goering Works – a huge mining- and metal-works.

Was it successful?

The government poured billions of Reichmarks into the Four-Year Plan. But by 1939 Germany still depended on foreign imports for one-third of its raw materials.

Arms had taken precedence over developing agriculture. 'Arms not butter' was Goering's slogan. But in 1939 butter was still rationed in Germany.

The only way for Germany to become fully self-sufficient was to conquer countries which could provide the raw materials and food it needed.

Did the Nazis achieve an economic miracle?

■ SOURCE INVESTIGATION

This is an unusual source investigation. It is entirely based on statistics. The charts and graphs in Sources 1–8 record the economic performance of Germany between 1933 and 1939.

Stage 1
To help you decide if Germany achieved an economic miracle answer the questions below. For each question you will first need to identify which source will help you. Some sources will help you answer more than one question. For some questions you will need to refer back to the information on pages 122–27.

Imports/exports
For a strong economy you need to export more than you import.

1. What happened to Germany's balance of trade?

Unemployment
For a strong economy you need to reduce unemployment.

2. What happened to unemployment under the Nazis?
3. How do the figures for industrial production help explain the trend in unemployment?

Government spending
For a strong economy the government needs to spend its money wisely.

4. Why did the government debt rise?
5. What was the government spending its money on?

Investment
For a strong economy you need to invest money in industry.

6. When did investment return to the level it was at before the Depression (in 1928)?

Production
A strong economy needs a wide range of industries and should not be too dependent on one sector.

7. When had most industries overtaken 1928 production levels?
8. Which industry recovered the most slowly?

Workers
For a strong economy you need to pay good wages to your workers, so that they in turn can become consumers.

9. Did people's earnings increase or decrease between 1933 and 1938?
10. When were earnings at their highest between 1928 and 1938?
11. Were people better off under the Nazis than before?
12. Did the diet of working-class families improve or get worse between 1927 and 1937?
13. Why do you think this was so?

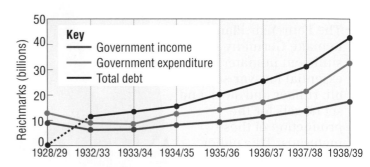

SOURCE 1 Government income, expenditure and total debt 1928–38

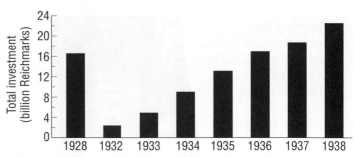

SOURCE 2 Investment by government and private institutions 1928–38

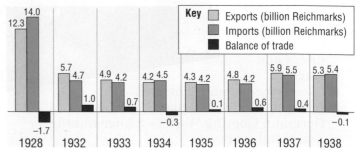

SOURCE 3 German trade 1928–38

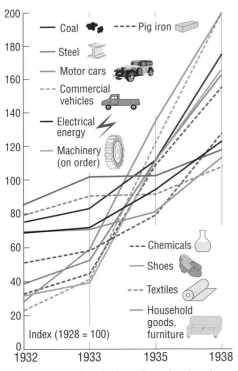

SOURCE 4 Index of production for selected German industries 1932–38

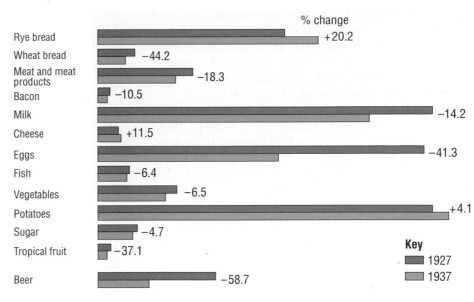

SOURCE 5 Annual food consumption in working-class families, 1927 and 1937

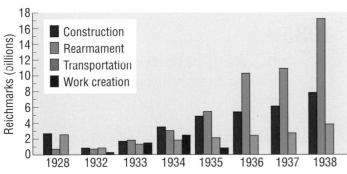

SOURCE 6 How the government spent its money 1928–38

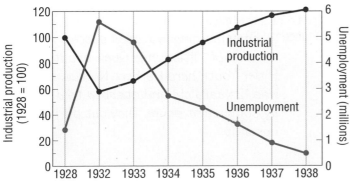

SOURCE 7 Industrial production and unemployment 1928–38

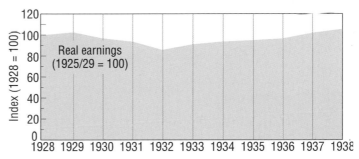

SOURCE 8 Real wages in Germany 1928–38 (that is, wages adjusted to allow for inflation)

Stage 2

When you have completed the questions write your own account by describing:

a) how the economy improved between 1933 and 1939

b) how the economic situation compared with that of 1928.

Reach your own conclusion as to

c) whether the Nazis had achieved their own objectives

d) whether they had created a strong economy.

e) Finally, explain

■ the strengths
■ the weaknesses

of statistical information such as Sources 1–8 in answering these questions.

What was life like in the Hitler Youth?

HITLER WANTED TO turn the young into loyal Nazis. The three greatest influences on young Germans were their families, their schools and youth movements. The Nazis tried to control all three.

Youth movements had been popular in Germany for a long time. They usually involved hiking, singing folk-songs, camping and sport. There were many groups to choose from – most were political or religious groups. The Nazis had formed their own Hitler Youth in the 1920s.

After 1933 young people were encouraged to join the Hitler Youth and most other political youth organisations were closed down. By 1936 it was almost impossible not to join the Hitler Youth.

There were separate organisations within the Hitler Youth for boys and girls, all under the command of Reich Youth Leader, Baldur von Schirach. Girls were encouraged to join the League of German Maidens. The Nazis believed the girls' youth organisations were less important than those of the boys because girls were not prepared for military service. Nevertheless, girls had to do similar activities and tests to the boys.

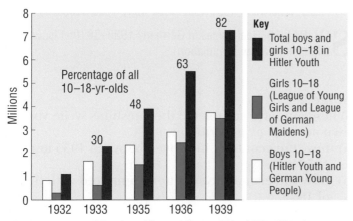

SOURCE 1 Membership numbers of the Hitler Youth organisations 1932–39

Many former members of the Hitler Youth have written about their experiences. The following is a fictitious diary of a young boy in the Hitler Youth which pulls together details from many different accounts. All the entries record events and activities which actually happened. The boy's attitudes to these events are those Hitler would have wished of a boy in the Hitler Youth.

1934

JAN Joined the German Young People. I am on probation for four months.

FEB My first cross-country march. It was hard work.

APRIL My probation period is up. I had to pass a special test – I had to run 60 metres in 12 seconds, jump 2.75 metres, throw a ball 25 metres and complete a cross-country march of one and a half days. That was easy! But the test also included close combat, questions on the history of the Party and finally a courage test – we had to jump in full battle-dress from a window of a first-floor block of flats. I passed, those who did not are weaklings. I can now wear the knife, shoulder strap and insignias.

1935

This year is dedicated to physical training. I reached medal standard in athletics.

APRIL I swore the oath of loyalty as we do every year: 'I promise in love and faithfulness in the Hitler Youth to help the Führer, to do my duty, so help me God, at all times'.

Sunday morning: watched special showing of 'Hitlerjunge Quex' about the Hitler Youth hero Herbert Norkus. He was 12 years old and stabbed to death by Communist scum. They cut off his upper lip.

1936

This year is 'The Year of German Young People'. We should get our friends to join up as a present for the Führer's 47th birthday.

Good news! Saturday school lessons were cancelled so we can do physical training and military games all day.

MAY Great day, I am 14 and moved up to the Hitler Youth.

AUG Went to the Olympic Games where we showed our superiority – Germans won both the men's and women's javelin.

NOV Received our fortnightly folder; this one told us about the injustice of the Treaty of Versailles. The last one explained how the Jews are trying to take over the world.

1937

JULY Today was the first day of camp. Today's password is 'Adolf Hitler', and the motto is 'Germany must live even if we die'. The camp leader explained that we all have to become fighters for Germany. We sang 'Behind the flag we march …'. During the community hour we read about the brave German fighter pilots in the First World War. We also learnt how to throw hand grenades, read semaphore, lay telephone wires and shoot a pistol. We were allowed to write home, but we had to hand our letters in to the officers' tent without sealing the envelope.

SEPT I told our leader about my grandfather who refuses to greet people with 'Heil Hitler' and raise his right arm. I wonder what will happen to him.

1938

NOV There was a big parade to remember the heroes who died in the Munich Putsch. There were thousands of flags, we marched and sang. It was exciting, I am so proud to be German.

DEC We were taken to the film 'The Eternal Jew'. Jews are vermin! At today's meeting we had to discuss 'Mein Kampf'; we have a test on it tomorrow. It is Wednesday and I listened to the Hitler Youth educational hour on the radio. I learnt about the great German air ace in the First World War, Baron Manfred von Richthofen.

1939

FEB I had a great week in a Hitler Youth hostel in Austria. We were learning how to be soldiers. I enjoyed the river crossing best – we had to build a raft. I have joined the Hitler Youth Rifle School. I now know how to look after a rifle.

MARCH I had to explain to my younger sister that the fairy story 'Cinderella' is really about a racially pure prince who rescues a pure princess from her alien unpure stepsisters. I will join the SA or army when I am eighteen.

OCT I'm enjoying the war and am doing my bit for Germany. Yesterday we delivered the monthly ration cards. Today we painted the kerbs at each street corner white to help people cross the street during a black-out. We were told we will soon be going from house to house to collect scrap metal, bottles and paper.

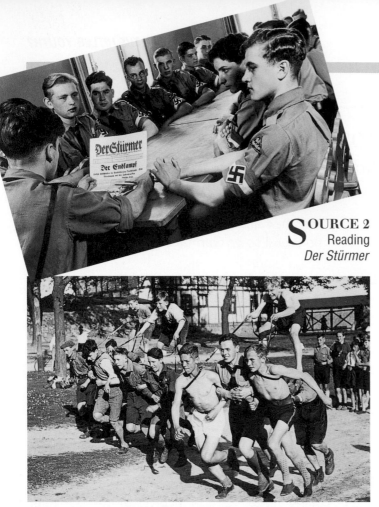

S**OURCE 2**
Reading
Der Stürmer

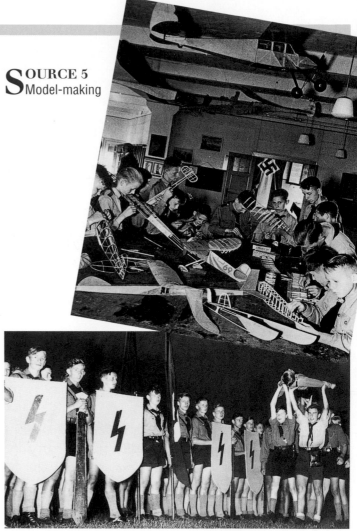

S**OURCE 5**
Model-making

S**OURCE 3** Chariot races

S**OURCE 6** Practising carrying 'dead' comrades to the
funeral pyre as part of a midsummer festival

S**OURCE 4** Hitler Youth leaping through fire at a festival to
mark the summer solstice

S**OURCE 7** Forming a swastika

■ ACTIVITY

Sources 2–7 show other activities of the Hitler Youth.
Either:
a) Use them to write four more entries for the diary;
or
b) Use Sources 8–10 on page 133 to write similar
entries for the diary of a girl in the League of
German Maidens.

SOURCE 8 A recruiting poster for the League of German Maidens declares 'Every ten-year-old to us'. The girls too had to attend camps, learn about the Nazi leaders, and memorise details of the Treaty of Versailles, German customs and stories

SOURCE 9 Javelin throwers in the League of German Maidens. Girls also had to run 60 metres in 14 seconds, throw a ball 12 metres, complete somersaults, a tightrope walk and a two-hour march or swim 100 metres; and know how to make a bed

SOURCE 10 A poster for the collection for youth hostels and homes. In fact the money went into buying armaments

■ TASK

Look back at the diary on pages 130–31. In pairs discuss these questions:

1. Which activities mentioned in the diary were intended to prepare the boys to be soldiers?
2. Select three examples of activities which were intended to indoctrinate the boys.
3. In the entry for July 1937 letters had to be handed in unsealed. Why do you think this was?
4. Why might the boy have informed on his grandfather (Sept 1937)?
5. Which activities might the boys not have been keen on?
6. Do you think that most teenagers in Germany would feel as enthusiastic about the Hitler Youth and League of German Maidens as this one?
7. What do you think most attracted young people to the Nazi youth organisations?

Were children indoctrinated at school?

THE SECOND AREA of influence over young people was their school. The Nazis used their control over teachers to influence what children learned at school. Many teachers were already very nationalistic and accepted that they should teach Nazi ideas. Those who were not were usually sacked. Many teachers attended teachers' camps which concentrated on indoctrination and physical training. Ninety-seven per cent of teachers joined the Nazi Teachers' Association.

The Nazi curriculum

The minds and bodies of young people were to be shaped to the Nazi cause. Certain subjects became more important than others:

- Physical education was given 15 per cent of school time, and some sports such as boxing became compulsory for boys. Pupils had to pass an examination, and unsatisfactory performance could lead to being expelled.
- History. This concentrated on the rise of the Nazi Party, the injustices of the Treaty of Versailles and the evils of Communism and the Jews.
- Biology explained Nazi ideas on race and population control. Pupils were taught how to measure their skulls and to classify racial types; also that Aryans were superior and should not marry inferior races.
- German. This taught pupils to be conscious of their national identity by reading about German heroes of the Hitler Youth and First World War.
- Geography taught about the lands which were once part of Germany and the need for more living space (Lebensraum) for Germans.
- Religious Studies became less important and by 1937 pupils could drop the subject.

Girls usually had a different curriculum from boys. They also studied domestic science and eugenics (how to produce perfect offspring by selecting ideal qualities in the parents).

1. Explain how each of Sources 1–4 was meant to influence young people.
2. Which of the following values and qualities do you think the Nazis wanted to develop in young people: duty, honour, physical courage, endurance, gentleness, intellect, obedience, strength, love of peace, humanity?

SOURCE 1 From a book for fourteen-year-olds, *The Battle of Tannenberg*. This excerpt describes a German soldier in the First World War

" A Russian soldier tried to stop Otto, but Otto's bayonet slid gratingly between the Russian's ribs, so that he collapsed groaning. There it lay before him, simple and distinguished, his dream's desire, the Iron Cross. "

SOURCE 2 Some questions from a Mathematics textbook

" 1. To keep a mentally ill person costs approximately 4 RM per day, and there are 300,000 mentally ill in care.
a) How much do these people cost to keep in total?
b) How many marriage loans at 1000 RM each could be granted from this money?
2. A modern night bomber can carry 1800 incendiaries.
a) How long (in kilometres) is the path along which it can distribute these bombs if it drops a bomb every second at a speed of 25 km per hour?
b) How far apart are the craters from one another?
c) How many fires are caused if one-third of the bombs hit their targets and of these one-third ignite? "

SOURCE 3 Essay title

" Analyse the structure and plan of Adolf Hitler's speech of 17 May 1933 "

SOURCE 4 Girls salute the flag at a Nazi leadership school in 1935

Leadership schools

New types of schools were also created to prepare the best of Germany's boys and girls for leadership. 'Napolas' (National Political Institutes of Education) controlled by the SS educated future chiefs for the government and the army. Future political leaders were prepared in 'Adolf Hitler Schools'. These schools provided a military-style education, pupils belonging not to classes or tutor groups but to a platoon or squad. Not surprisingly, there were many complaints about falling academic standards.

Education for the Jews

For those who were not Aryan, particularly Jews, life in school became very difficult. Source 5 shows how Karl Hartland, who was the son of a Jewish banker, later remembered his time at school in Nazi Germany.

3. Read Source 5. Explain why the Geography teacher was embarrassed.
4. Why was Karl deeply envious of Brett?
5. Why do you think the History textbooks had been withdrawn?
6. Why was a Jewish boy not allowed to visit the army barracks?
7. How far does Source 5 suggest that the boys in this school accepted Nazi ideas?
8. Look back over all the sources on pages 130–135. Which do you think is the most useful source to the historian studying Nazi Germany?

SOURCE 5 Extracts from *A Boy in Your Situation*, 1988

❝ **A**   The new school was not a happy place. Karl's new teacher introduced himself. He wore a button with a swastika on it in his lapel buttonhole.

'I must now make up the register. Hartland, the banker? Are you Jewish?'

'Yes.'

'What a pity. I had hoped for a completely Aryan class.'

B   Later there were to be more 'free' periods because lessons were included to increase the boys' Germanic self-awareness and it was not thought right that Jews should attend these. There had been an embarrassing incident in the Geography class when the teacher had picked out Karl to demonstrate the Aryan type.

'You see,' he said, 'here we have the blond hair and blue eyes – and notice the head shape. Not round like negroes but high at the back denoting intelligence.' The class listened in appalled silence. No one liked the Geography teacher so they said nothing.

'Sit down, boy. What is your name?'

'Hartland.'

'The banker Hartland?'

'Yes.'

'Oh my God, sit down.'

C   Karl had a new problem at school – the German teacher, Mr Bartholomeus. He had a little swastika badge in his lapel that Karl came to dread. Teachers who wore that badge always seemed to go out of their way to say something unpleasant to Karl, in front of the whole class.

D   Brett, the brightest boy in the class, had taken to wearing his Hitler Youth movement uniform in class. Karl was deeply envious. There was not only the brown shirt, the black trousers, black neckerchief and armband with the lightning rune on it, but a dagger. A dagger, a real dagger which he pulled out in front of a group of admirers. The dagger was short, set in a black hilt and had 'Blood and Honour' engraved on the blade. Brett saw Karl and waved the knife at him. 'This is not for dirty Jews,' he said. 'This is for real enemies.'

E   In the History classes the French were the hereditary enemy and all the lessons were about the wars against the enemies of Germany. There were no History textbooks. They had all been withdrawn and until new National Socialist versions came out there was nothing but the teacher, who dictated notes and gave inspiring addresses. He was a reserve officer in the army. He told boys all about it. 'We have got marvellous tanks now, fantastic; and good guns to use against French tanks.'

The boys were all enthralled when he drew battle plans on the blackboard. 'Tell you what,' he said, 'I'll take you all to my barracks.' Soon after that he said it was all fixed up and would they all bring one mark for expenses. They filed past his desk and put their money into a box. He looked up. 'You, Hartland, you are a Jew. Jews can't come into army barracks.' Brett grinned at him and hissed, 'You would sell our secrets to the enemy.'

F   Then one day the newspaper said: 'No Aryan German child will in future risk being contaminated by having to sit next to a Jew in school.' That was it. Karl felt an enormous sense of relief. He would not have to go back to school. ❞

What did the Nazis want from German women?

GERTRUDE SCHOLTZ-KLINK was the Nazi Party's ideal German woman. She had classic Aryan looks: blonde hair and blue eyes; she had four children, was devoted to her family and accepted without question the leadership of the Party. In 1934 she was made Head of the Women's Bureau but she never had any real political power. The Nazi Party was run by men who believed politics was not part of a woman's world. One of their first edicts was to ban women from positions of leadership in the Party. Gertrude did as she was told!

In Weimar Germany women had been freed from many of the restrictions of the pre-war years. By 1933 there were 100,000 women teachers, 13,000 women musicians, and 3000 women doctors. One-tenth of Reichstag members were women. For the Nazis this was yet another sign of how degenerate and corrupt Weimar Germany was. What the Nazis wanted from women was something much more traditional. In 1933 they wanted mothers.

1933: The Nazis need mothers ...

The Nazis believed women and men had different roles in life. A man's role was that of worker or soldier – provider and defender. A woman's place was in the home, having children and caring for her family. When a deputation of women came to Hitler to discuss women's rights, Hitler's reply was to promise them that in the Third Reich every woman would have a husband!

The Nazis were very worried by the decline in the birth rate. In 1900 there had been over two million live births per year but this had dropped to under one million in 1933. Families were getting smaller because of contraception and because women wanted paid work. If Germany was to become a great power once again, its population needed to increase.

Nazi attitudes to women may seem strange today but they were not so unusual in the 1930s. Many countries in Europe were acting to reverse falling birth rates. France began rewarding mothers who had several children long before Germany did, and also made contraception and abortion illegal.

A massive propaganda campaign was launched to promote motherhood and large families. The government offered special loans to new brides who agreed not to take a job. Eight hundred thousand took these up. To improve women's fertility they were encouraged to stop smoking, stop slimming and to do sport. Young women, especially newly married, could attend mothercraft and homecraft classes. As a result of all these measures, in 1936 there were over 30 per cent more births than there had been in 1933 (see Source 10 on page 138).

■ TASK

1. Sources 2–5 and 8 and the information above show various measures taken to encourage women to have children. List these measures.
2. Were Sources 2 and 8 aimed at women or men?
3. Which of these measures do you think would have had the most influence on women?

SOURCE 1 Gertrude Scholtz-Klink, Head of the Nazi Women's Bureau

SOURCE 2 'The Honour Cross of the German Mother'. This was awarded to women as follows:

■ *Gold for eight children*
■ *Silver for six children*
■ *Bronze for four children*

Holders of the award were given an honoured place at Nazi meetings

SOURCE 3 Official guidelines for the employment of women civil servants and teachers, 5 October 1933

❝ I consider it fundamentally right that, in the event of males and females being equally qualified for employment in public service, the male applicant should be given preference. ❞

SOURCE 4 The Nazi Rudolf Hess speaking in May 1936

SOURCE 4 The Nazi Rudolf Hess speaking in May 1936

❝ We are opposed to women going into the professions which make them 'mannified'.

What National Socialists want are women who are genuine comrades and mothers. The ideal woman is one who, above all, is capable of being a mother. ❞

SOURCE 5 Hitler, speaking in 1934 at the Reich Party Conference

❝ Woman has her battlefield too; with each child that she brings into the world for the nation she is fighting her fight on behalf of the nation. ❞

SOURCE 6 A German rhyme addressed to women

❝ Take hold of kettle, broom and pan,
Then you'll surely get a man!
Shop and office leave alone,
Your true life work lies at home. ❞

SOURCE 7 An advertisement in a German newspaper, 1935

❝ 52-year-old pure Aryan doctor, fought in First World War, wishes to settle down. Wants male children through marriage with young, healthy virgin of pure Aryan stock, undemanding, suited to heavy work and thrifty, with flat heels, without earrings, if possible without money. ❞

1. Do you think the Nazis would approve or disapprove of Source 7? Give reasons for your answer.

. . . but not just any kind of mothers

These campaigns were particularly aimed at Aryan women. They were the ones whom the Nazis really wanted to have large families. They wanted to mould Aryan women into their ideal mothers who:

■ **did not go to work.** In all the jobs they directly controlled they began to get rid of women: 15 per cent of teachers, all women doctors and civil servants were sacked
■ **looked like this:** blonde, heavy-hipped, and athletic, in a full skirt, wearing flat heels and no make-up
■ **cooked like this:** always using up left-overs; once a month on a Sunday they had to prepare a one-dish meal, a sort of stew made of cheap meat and left-overs that everyone was meant to eat. The SA could come round and check on whether this was being observed
■ **dressed like this:** always using home-produced substitutes for imported wool, cotton and silk
■ **behaved like this:** there was public pressure to stop women smoking. In many cities police chiefs put up posters in restaurants forbidding women to smoke. One police chief told people to stop women who were smoking and remind them of their duty as German women and mothers
■ **brought their children up like this:** as loyal Nazis, encouraging them to worship the Führer and join the Hitler Youth.

SOURCE 8 An advertisement for the German pharmaceutical industry, exhorting girls to 'look after their health and beauty, as future bearers of the nation's children'

■ ACTIVITY

In groups design and produce a Nazi wall display or booklet promoting:
a) the ideal German woman
b) large families.
Include your own posters, advice and a message from Hitler.

1937: ... but we also need women workers!

Historians argue that Nazi Germany was full of contradiction and chaos. Policies were wildly improvised for each new crisis the government faced. For example, after years of trying to get women out of work they suddenly discovered they needed them back!

Germany was rearming. Men were joining the army. Now the Nazis needed **more** women to work. They abolished the marriage loans and introduced a compulsory 'duty year' for all women entering the labour market.

This usually meant helping on a farm or in a family home in return for bed and board but no pay. More women did get jobs but not nearly as many as the Nazis hoped. In 1939 there were fewer women working than there had been in Weimar Germany before the Great Depression. Many women did not like the thought of working in the factories where the wages were low and the working conditions poor. Employers often preferred foreign labour and protested that they had no suitable lavatories, washing facilities or even soap for women. Hitler worried about women working; he continued to believe that a woman's place was in the home and that work would harm the chances of giving birth.

... but don't stop having children

Even with their need for workers the Nazis could not give up on their other aim: for women to produce more children.

In 1938 they changed the divorce law – a divorce was possible if a husband or wife could not have children. Even when the husband had made the wife infertile by infecting her with venereal disease he was allowed to divorce her. The Nazis also set up the *Lebensborn* programme whereby specially chosen unmarried women could 'donate a baby to the Führer' by becoming pregnant by 'racially pure' SS men.

■ TASK

Study Source 10.

1. Was the number of marriages increasing under Nazi rule?
2. Was the population rising?
3. Why might there have been more marriages in 1939?
4. Throughout the 1930s the Nazis both increased the birth rate and got more women working. Does this suggest that their plans were a success? Explain your answer.

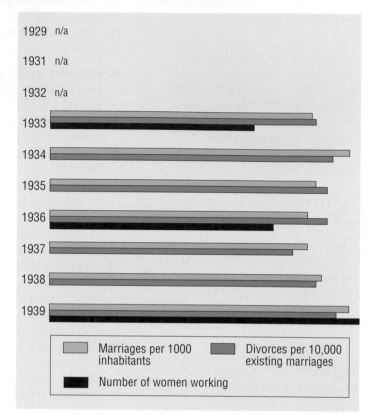

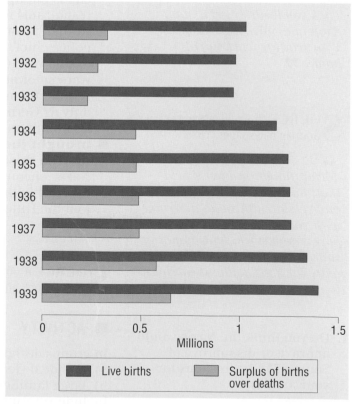

SOURCE 10 Employment, marriages, and births 1929–39

So what was life like for women in Nazi Germany?

With the conflicting pressures of home and work you might expect that the 1930s were a stressful time for women; for some they were. The pressure to bear children was so great that one woman, who could not have a child, kidnapped a baby so she could be seen to be providing a child for Germany.

However, for many women these were good times. Those who had been hardest hit by the Depression were much better off by 1935. Despite Nazi propaganda women's employment actually increased. Employers preferred women workers because they were cheaper. Those who had a job found their wages rising faster than prices, although women's wages were only two-thirds of a man's.

Many women were keen supporters of the Nazis. One former teacher who supported the Nazis recalled: 'Everyone was honest. At night we could leave all doors unlocked. No one would come inside. One could let the washing hang on the line. One could leave a car on the street with the key inside.'

Hitler received many letters from women. Some asked him to father their children. Some even cried out his name when giving birth. Observers at Nazi rallies in the 1930s described scenes where screaming women wanted to touch Hitler.

Sources 11 and 12 give different women's viewpoints on this period.

SOURCE 13 A mother and her child in the 1930s

3. How typical do you think Source 13 is? Explain your answer.

SOURCE 11 A description by an Australian visitor to Germany of a camp where young women were doing their 'duty year'. They got free bed and lodging but no pay

66 *The girls live in houses, not barracks, and spend most of the day working for farmers' wives, learning to milk cows and make cheese and the like.*

Their routine is a rigorous one. Rising at five-thirty, they have exercises and singing until seven o'clock. After breakfast they have to work from half-past seven until three o'clock, either in the settlement or on a neighbouring farm with half an hour for lunch. They have an hour's compulsory rest and classes until half-past six. The evening is always devoted to singing or lectures, and they have to go to bed at half-past nine. 99

1. Compare this routine with the routine of the young men in the RAD camp (Source 8 on page 124). Who had the harder time?

SOURCE 12 Wilhelmine Haferkamp was 22 in 1933. She lived in the industrial city of Oberhausen. Her husband worked in a quarry

66 *When one had ten children, well not ten, but a pile of them, one had to join the Nazi Party; 1933 it was and I already had three children and the fourth on the way. When 'child-rich' people were in the Party the children had a great chance to advance. I got thirty marks per child from the Hitler government and twenty marks per child from the city. That was a lot of money. I sometimes got more 'child money' than my husband earned.* 99

2. Which of the following factors would most affect what life was like for a woman in Nazi Germany: what race she belonged to, how old she was, whether she had a job, whether she lived in a town or in the country?

■ ACTIVITY

In groups (four or five per group would be ideal) write or devise a play set in 1938. The main characters should be members of a single family, although you can add other characters if you wish.

Mother (mid-30s – working in a factory)
Father (mid-30s – also working in a factory)
Daughter 1 (aged 18 and serving her 'duty year' – working on a farm)
Daughter 2 (aged 9)

Try to include details from the sources in your play. It should attempt to show what life was like for women in Germany in 1938.

You will need to write down your play, as you will later be writing a second scene set in wartime Germany.

WHAT WAS THE IMPACT OF THE SECOND WORLD WAR ON NAZI GERMANY?

SINCE 1935 THE Nazis had been preparing Germany for war. However, for all the Nazi emphasis on the glories of war, the war when it came was not greeted with enthusiasm. Even many supporters of Hitler and the Nazis still had vivid memories of the First World War. There were no cheering crowds when the garrison marched out of a small town like Northeim. Many feared the worst.

However, the first year of the war went unbelievably well for Hitler. In twelve months the German army swept through eastern and western Europe, meeting very little resistance. The first conquests quickly brought extra food and riches back to Germany.

But from 1942 onwards the war began to go very badly for Germany. In this chapter, you will investigate how, piece by piece, the Nazi state began to collapse. The war disrupted Nazi policies on women and on the economy. It sharpened opposition. It intensified the Jewish 'problem' because it brought millions more Jews under the control of the Third Reich. It led directly to the Holocaust. The persecution of the Jews itself also sharpened opposition to the Nazis from the churches. Even army leaders plotted to assassinate Hitler.

And behind all this, all over Germany the war was slowly draining German resources, leading to shortages, illness and civilian deaths on a scale never known in any war before it. You are going to begin with that story of ordinary Germans on the home front.

What was life like on the home front?

1939–41	*1941–43*	*1943–44*	*1944–45*

1939–41: The war goes well for Germany

In September 1939 the Germans prepared for their first winter of the war. Rationing was introduced for most foodstuffs and for other items. Many more items were rationed than in wartime Britain. Germans received seven food ration cards, colour-coded for different foods.

SOURCE 1 The normal food ration for one week in 1939

> *Meat   453g*
> *Bread   2.2kg*
> *Fats   340g*
> *Sugar   340g*
> *Ersatz coffee (made*
> *from barley seeds*
> *and acorns)   453g*

1. Extra rations were given to workers in heavy industries such as mining; to expectant or nursing mothers; sick people; vegetarians and donors of blood or breast-milk.
   For each group explain why they might be given extra rations.

As a result of rationing, two out of five Germans ate better than before the war! However, the diet became increasingly monotonous – vegetables and black rye bread, with small amounts of meat, butter and a single egg each week. Bread was usually sold when it was one day old because that way it took more chewing and people ate less. Adults received no milk ration although children received a generous one.

Clothes rationing was introduced in November 1939. There was a complicated points system. Some items such as new shoes and winter coats were almost impossible to buy.

Hot water was permitted on only two days per week. Soap was also rationed.

SOURCE 2 The observations of an American radio reporter, Howard K. Smith, in 1941

66 In the subway [underground railway] you smell the people. There is not enough time nor enough coaches for coaches to be properly cleaned and ventilated every day, so the odour of stale sweat from bodies that work hard, and have only a cube of soap as big as a penny box of matches to wash with for a month, lingers in their interiors. In summer, it is asphyxiating ... dozens of people, whose stomachs and bodies are not strong anyhow, faint in them every day. Sometimes you just have to get out at some station halfway to your destination to take a breath of fresh air between trains. 99

One newspaper advised that soap was not necessary for a bath and suggested that the liquid from stewed pine needles could be used instead. Stewed and strained ivy leaves were recommended for washing clothes. Toilet paper was not available.

SOURCE 3 A humorous rhyme of the time

66 No butter with our eats.

Our pants have no seats.

Not even paper in the loo

Yet, Führer – we follow you. 99

Tobacco was difficult to find. Many people were so desperate for it that tobacco became a kind of substitute for money. People could buy other things in exchange for tobacco. Farmers would trade one egg for a cigarette.

Shop windows displayed goods which were labelled 'Nur Attrapen' – for decoration only. Dairies displayed rows of milk bottles full of white salt to look like milk.

The first year of war went well for Germany. As Germany conquered other countries, food as well as huge stocks of luxury goods such as dresses, stockings, furs and perfumes were imported from those countries. People could buy these on the black market if they had money, but most of the goods went to loyal or high-ranking Nazis.

2. Germans were told to save all their rubbish and separate it into paper, rags, bottles, old metal, and other items. Why do you think they were told to do this?
3. Which aspect of life on the home front in these early years do you think people found hardest to bear?

| *1939–41* | *1941–43* | *1943–44* | *1944–45* |

1941–43: The tide turns against Germany

In June 1941 Hitler ordered the invasion of the USSR. This was a massive gamble. He was hoping for the kind of lightning victory he had achieved in western Europe. He got the opposite. His army became bogged down in a four-year battle for survival that tore the heart out of the army. By the end of 1942 Germany's war was going badly. New hospital trains brought thousands of wounded Germans home from the war in the Soviet Union. People got more used to seeing wounded soldiers and women in mourning.

Propaganda
Various propaganda campaigns were launched to keep up morale and to encourage people to support the war effort (see pages 146–47). Goebbels claimed that between December 1941 and January 1942 Germans gave 1.5 million furs and 67 million woollen garments to help clothe the German army in Russia. Other campaigns urged people to save fuel, work harder and even to try to avoid tooth decay. Extra food rations were given out at Christmas 1942 to help keep up morale.

SOURCE 4 Goering, speaking in 1942

66 The worst is over, things will improve for we possess the territories with the most fertile soil. We shall send our best agriculturists to follow the fighting troops, and they will provide our troops and the homeland with the produce of the land ... If there is any hunger, it will not be in Germany. 99

| *1939–41* | *1941–43* | *1943–44* | *1944–45* |

1943–44: Total war

By 1943 it was clear that the war was not going Germany's way any longer. The government began preparations for 'total war' with every part of German society geared to the war effort, producing arms, growing food, caring for the sick or fighting.

SOURCE 5 In September 1943 Goebbels wrote in his diary:

66 *We are now carrying out my idea of 'total war'. We are stopping the production of anything that does not help us in the war. This means that another eight million workers can go into making things for the war, and 300,000 other workers will now be able to join the army. All factories will soon be making war materials.* 99

Anything that did not contribute to the war effort was eliminated. In March 1943 professional sport was ended. Magazines not important to the war were closed. Non-essential businesses were closed, though the result of this was not always what the government intended. For example, sweet shops had to close (see Source 6), even though many of them also sold food.

SOURCE 6 A confectioner from Hanover told an official in the German Foreign Office:

66 *The majority of sweet shops in Hanover are kept by little old ladies, who run tiny businesses in their own homes with a minute turnover. They are far too old and fragile to undertake any other sort of work; but their shops have been closed and the only one to suffer is the state, which has to assume responsibility for the board and lodging of these old ladies.* 99

Hair-dyeing and perming were banned in some parts of Germany. Some women who could afford it travelled a great distance just to go to the hairdresser's. In August 1943 clothes rationing was suspended and the manufacture of civilian clothing was ended. Exchange centres were opened where people could swap furniture and clothes.

SOURCE 7 Children try on shoes at an exchange centre

The cutbacks did not, of course, extend to propaganda. In June 1943 Goebbels commissioned the film *Kolberg*, which told of heroic German resistance to Napoleon in 1807. It was first shown in January 1945. It cost 8.5 million marks, 187,000 soldiers were employed as extras, 6000 horses were used, and 10,000 uniforms were made for it. The chief of the German navy was overruled when he refused to provide 4000 sailors. Railway trucks were in short supply but one hundred trucks of salt were sent to the set to provide 'snow' for one scene.

Labour shortages

With most German men in the armed forces there was a severe shortage of workers. More women were drafted into the labour force (see page 144).

In the concentration camps Jews and political prisoners were worked to their deaths to supply the demands of the German war effort. Millions of captured foreign workers and prisoners of war were also forced to work in factories and on farms. By May 1944 there were over seven million such people. Those from France, Belgium and Holland were given a certain amount of freedom, but workers from Russia and Poland were treated as slaves.

Germans had to be careful how they treated them, as acts of kindness were punished. A landowner who attended the funeral of a 'slave' worker who died on his own farm was imprisoned for six months.

4. Why were prisoners from different countries treated so differently?

Air raids

The first air raid on Berlin had been in August 1940. By 1942 the raids were more frequent and more intense. At the same time the number of doctors available to treat victims was going down. In Berlin, the number of doctors available to the civilian population fell from fifteen doctors per 10,000 people in the 1930s to one doctor per 10,000 in 1941. Most of the doctors had gone to help the army. Others had been lost because of the ban on Jews and on women doctors.

As air raids worsened many Germans left the cities and were evacuated to villages or rural towns such as Northeim (see page 55). The population of Northeim nearly doubled.

In the cities the air raids became increasingly ferocious. Sources 8 and 9 describe the reaction of Berliners to the air raids of 1943.

SOURCE 8 Ruth Andreas-Friedrich, an anti-Nazi, describes the destruction

66 *The English have made a shattering raid on Berlin, the like of which has never been seen. A hundred and sixty thousand are said to have been made homeless. The city and all the western and southern suburbs are on fire. The air is smoky, sulphur-yellow. Terrified people are stumbling through the streets with bundles, bags, household goods, tripping over fragments and ruins. They can't grasp it that they – they, in particular – should have been the ones to suffer so.* 99

SOURCE 9 Ursula von Kardorff, a journalist, recorded in her diary:

66 *November 1943: Everything goes on as usual at the office. Berlin is so large that some of my colleagues never even noticed the raid.*

February 1944: I feel a growing sense of wild vitality within myself, and of sorrow too. Is that what the British are trying to achieve by attacking civilians? At any rate they are not softening us up … The disaster which hits the Nazis and anti-Nazis alike is welding the people together. After every raid special rations are issued – cigarettes, coffee, meat. If the British think that they are going to undermine our morale they are barking up the wrong tree. 99

5. How do Sources 8 and 9 differ in their reaction to the bombing?
6. Why do you think they differ?

SOURCE 10 Victims of a Berlin air raid are laid out for identification in a warehouse

SOURCE 11 Aerial view of Cologne after the 'Thousand-Bomber Raid' on 30 May 1942

One attack on Hamburg in 1943 led to a fire storm which wiped out large areas of the city. Thirty thousand people died. The emergency services tried to supply food and shelter but after three days the services collapsed under the pressure. The government had to step in and build emergency accommodation for air-raid victims.

SOURCE 12 Emergency two-roomed houses built for air-raid victims. They were small but comfortable

SOURCE 13 A Danish reporter, P.E. von Stemann, recalls the spring of 1944

66 [It was a time of] dullness, anticipation, fear and continuous bombing. It was a soulless existence. The war seemed perpetual. The sameness of each successive day was blunting but the obliteration of beauty was even more so ... The flowers had gone, the books had been burnt, the pictures had been removed, the trees had been broken, there were no birds singing, no dogs barking, no children shrieking ... there were no small surprises, no fun, no merriment ... there was no laughter and no giggling. No face ever lit up in a warming smile, no friendly kiss or hug. 99

| 1939–41 | 1941–43 | 1943–44 | 1944–45 |

1944–45: Failure and defeat

By July 1944 Allied armies were pushing the Germans back in the west and in the east. Refugees were pouring into Germany from the areas being reconquered by the enemy. Goebbels was appointed Reich Trustee for Total War and he prepared to mobilise Germany for one final effort to win the war. He ordered the following:

- All non-German servants and all workers to go into armaments factories.
- To save fuel, railway and postal services were reduced, and all letter boxes were closed.
- All theatres, opera houses, music halls and places of entertainment (except cinemas) were closed.
- The age limit for compulsory labour for women was raised to fifty.
- The Volkssturm (Home Guard) was formed. Someone called it 'the last round-up of the old and the lame, the children and the idiots'. They marched through Berlin with borrowed weapons.

7. Why do you think cinemas were not closed?
8. How do you think these measures affected morale?

In early 1945 some of the most extreme air raids began. In two nights of bombing up to 150,000 people were killed in Dresden as Allied bombers destroyed 70 per cent of the properties in the city. Many of them were refugees from the east, newly arrived in the city. Even tiny Northeim was bombed. A raid on the railway yard killed more than thirty, mostly women and children. By the end of the war almost as many German civilians had been killed by bombing as German soldiers had died in combat.

SOURCE 14 Statistics on bombing and casualties on the German home front

- *800,000 (estimated) civilians killed by bombing*
- *2,697,473 tons of bombs dropped by the RAF and USAAF*
- *Approximately 50 per cent of bombs fell on residential areas and 12 per cent on factories and war industries*
- *3,600,000 homes destroyed*
- *7,500,000 people made homeless*
- *2,500,000 children evacuated*
- *3,640,000 German civilians died as a result of the war.*

The Nazi administration could not cope with destruction on this scale. By early 1945 government plans were in chaos. Ration cards were no longer honoured. Instead people relied on the black market or on scavenging for food. Almost anything could be bought on the black market – for example, a complete set of identity papers for 80,000 marks. Later, as the defeat of Germany loomed, you could even buy hammer and sickle badges and six-pointed stars of David as worn by the Jews.

9. Why might Germans want to buy identity papers, hammer and sickle badges or stars of David?

SOURCE 15 A report by the Nazi Security Service, early 1945

66 *In the early stages of the war the black marketeering was rejected as a form of sabotage, but since then there has grown up a practice of evading trading regulations without any consciousness of wrong-doing. People who do not join in these practices are considered stupid. Farmers profiteer, shopkeepers barter (butchers and drapers interchange meat and cloth), craftsmen carry out repairs where they are offered scarce goods, and officials dealing with the public receive gift parcels. There is a feeling that the powers that be turn a blind eye to them.* 99

Northeim: April 1945

As Allied and Russian troops advanced into Germany, in town after town they met little resistance from the local people, who were drained by the war.

As the tanks approached Northeim, Mayor Girmann ordered his SA militia to defend the town to the death but drove himself away into the hills to get drunk. The SA ignored his instructions and handed over the town without a fight.

Carl Querfurt, former leader of the socialists, was brought in to head a new emergency council for the town. Nazi flags were burned. Eight hundred and fifty-three Nazi books were removed from the library and pulped. Northeim breathed a sigh of relief and its population busily turned to the major preoccupation of most Germans who had survived the Nazi experiment: trying to prove they had opposed it all along.

Berlin: May 1945

Amid the ruins of their capital city Hitler, Goebbels and other Nazi leaders committed suicide. The war and the Nazi regime were over – but at an appalling cost in human lives and after years of unimaginable suffering for millions of people.

SOURCE 16 Two men scavenge meat from the carcass of a dead horse, 1945

Propaganda on the home front

■ SOURCE INVESTIGATION

All countries fighting the war used propaganda. Sources 17–24 are examples of German propaganda. What can we learn from them about life on the home front? Discuss each poster with a partner and then answer the following questions.

1. a) Which posters use fear to get their message across?
b) Which use patriotism?
c) Which use both fear and patriotism?
2. a) Which posters show optimism?
b) Compare the emotions shown in Sources 17 and 23.
3. a) Explain the alternatives shown in Source 22. b) How does this poster link the Jews with Bolshevism (Communism)?
4. Two of the posters were made towards the end of the war. Which do you think they are and why?
5. Why was it necessary to produce Source 20?
6. a) Which poster do you think delivers its message most effectively?
b) Which is least effective?
Explain your choices.
7. a) What image of Hitler do the posters present?
b) Are they similar to or different from the posters on pages 120–21?

SOURCE 19 An appeal to civilians to use less coal, so it can be used by German industry

SOURCE 17 A postcard publicising charitable collections for the 'Winter War Aid' campaign

SOURCE 18 A poster warning about the consequences of failing to carry out the black-out

SOURCE 20 'Traitor' is how this poster describes anyone listening to foreign radio broadcasts

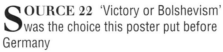

SOURCE 21 An appeal for co-operation between those working in the armaments factories and those fighting at the front

SOURCE 22 'Victory or Bolshevism' was the choice this poster put before Germany

SOURCE 23 The Volkssturm was a last-ditch defence force

SOURCE 24 *Hitler at the front*, a painting made in 1942/43

■ ACTIVITY

Some historians argue that the way the Nazis ran Germany was chaotic. Was this true of the home front in Germany? Search pages 140–147 to find examples of good organisation. Remember that every government makes mistakes, especially with the difficulties of war. Ask how well the Nazis tackled problems such as:

■ food shortages
■ the black market
■ bombing
■ evacuation
■ morale.

How did the war affect women?

ON PAGES 136–39 you investigated what life was like for women in Nazi Germany. The war further complicated Nazi policies on women. As the war intensified there was even more demand for women workers, but as the casualties mounted there was even greater pressure to increase the birth rate. There had always been a contradiction in Nazi policy on women and now it was more extreme than ever.

On the one hand women were expected to work for the war effort. Some served refreshments at railway stations to servicemen and evacuees. Others did Red Cross work or helped collect and sift scrap metal. On the other hand they were expected to have more children and to conform to the Nazi ideal in appearance: there was even a campaign against women wearing trousers!

Rationing, bombing and absent husbands made life very difficult for mothers. Under the pressure smoking and nervous fatigue increased. Many women did not want to have a child in war time when there were so many other pressures on their lives and when the risks to the child were so great. Nevertheless, the Nazis still urged women to have children whether they were married or not.

SOURCE 1 Rudolf Hess, deputy leader of the Nazi Party, writing in the newspaper *Berliner Morgenpost*, December 1939

❝ As all National Socialists know, the highest law in war, as in peace, is the preservation of the Race. An unmarried mother may have a hard path. But she knows that when we are at war, it is better to have a child under the most difficult conditions than not to have one at all ... The family is the basis of the country. During a war the highest service a woman may perform for the continuation of the nation is to bear racially healthy children.

Be happy, good women, that you have been permitted to perform this highest duty for Germany. ❞

SOURCE 2 An advertisement in a German newspaper, 1939. Brünnhilde and Siegfried were figures from Germanic legend, here representing health and strength

❝ Two vital, lusty, race-conscious Brünnhildes, with family trees certified back to 1700, desire to serve their Fatherland in the form most ennobling to women, and would like to meet two similarly inclined Siegfrieds. Marriage not of essential importance. Soldiers on leave also 'acceptable'. ❞

SOURCE 3 A new marriage law planned in 1943, but which never came into effect

❝ All single and married women up to the age of 35 who do not already have four children should be obliged to produce four children by racially pure German men. Whether these men are married is of no significance. Every family that already has four children must set the husband free for this action. ❞

1. The law in Source 3 did not actually come into effect. Does this mean the source is of no use to historians?

When the war began to go badly in 1943 the Nazis tried to mobilise all women except those with young children. Three million women aged 17 to 45 were called to work, yet only about one million took up jobs. Many tried to evade this call up – some pretended to be ill, others deliberately got pregnant. One magazine talked about 'fear of the factory' as a new disease.

The high male casualties in the war led the Nazi leaders to come up with ideas to compensate for such losses. They assumed that after the war three out of four women would be unable to marry. Hitler calculated the loss in future soldiers and began to consider the idea that after the war healthy men could have two wives.

SOURCE 4 Night after night might be spent in an air-raid shelter like this one

SOURCE 5 One young girl, Elsbeth, later wrote of her experiences in the war

66 *Now we spent a great deal of time in air-raid shelters. We went to one of the bigger shelters. This was the town prison, which was at one corner of the square where my school was. It was a very dark building which had cellars with arched ceilings and a floor of earth. There were wide backless benches for two rows of people and nothing else. It was bleak and frightening, but my mum said the arched ceilings would stand up to bombing much better than flat ceilings.*

We spent days and nights in the cellars of the prison. We were usually on the last bench in the third room. We got to know the people who went to the same place each time. We learnt to pass the time talking, reading, solving puzzles, making small things out of paper. Most women used to knit, including my mother, who became quite skilled at this new form of entertainment.

When the all-clear went, we would go home and cook a quick meal. Often my mum would leave some potato or vegetable soup on the small stove, so that when we came out, there was something warm to eat.

Because air-raid alarms were frequent, the baker had to produce his bread whenever he could, and we got used to dashing round to his bakery for hot bread. As we ran home, carrying the bread in our aprons to save us from getting burnt, it was lovely picking at the hot crusty loaves. 99

SOURCE 7 Melita Maschmann was a loyal Nazi involved in running the League of German Maidens. Here she is writing about the war years

66 *Hitler is right, I thought, we must not spare our strength for a single minute. In their enthusiasm for the Führer most Germans are still ready to make every sacrifice that he demands of them. It is only at this historic hour that Greater Germany can be built. This conviction lay behind all that I did and drove me along from minute to minute. I believe it was the political genius of the Führer which achieved all the successes of the Third Reich: the elimination of misery after the First World War; the ending of the dictated peace of Versailles and the removal of the dishonour inflicted upon us; the return of the lost territories. And finally, had he not given meaning to my own life by calling upon me to serve my nation?* 99

SOURCE 6 Members of the League of German Maidens make Christmas decorations to raise money for Winter War Aid

■ ACTIVITY

On page 139 you wrote a scene set in 1938 in a German family.

Your task is now to write a second scene set in 1942. The main characters are the same, but their circumstances have changed.

1942
Mother
Father (home on leave from the army for a weekend)
Daughter 1 (now aged 22, married with two children but her husband is away at the war)
Daughter 2 (aged 13)

You may add other characters to your scene if you wish. In your play try to use something from each of the sources on pages 148–49 and also use the descriptions of life on the home front (pages 140–47) to get you started.

Your aim is to perform the play and show the rest of your class what life was like for women in Germany and how life had changed due to the war.

Did the war increase opposition to the Nazis?

ON PAGES 82–93 you considered how the Nazis dealt with political opponents, and also investigated how much opposition there was among ordinary people to the Nazi regime. You have already seen what resources were poured into propaganda to convince Germans that they were right to support Hitler during the war. But Hitler was clearly worried about the demoralising effect the war might have (see Source 1).

> **S**OURCE 1 Hitler speaking at a dinner party with other Nazi leaders on 7 April 1942
>
> 66 *If the slightest attempt at a riot were to break out at this moment anywhere in the whole Reich, I'd take immediate measures against it. Here's what I would do:*
>
> *a) On the same day all the leaders of the opposition, including the leaders of the Catholic Party, would be arrested and executed.*
> *b) All the occupants of the concentration camps would be shot within three days.*
> *c) All the criminals on our lists – and it would make little difference if they were in prison or at liberty – would be shot within the same period.* 99

The reality was that the invasion of the USSR had failed. The war was going badly, and opposition in Germany was increasing. You are going to investigate this through two case studies.

Case study 1: Young people

The soldiers

Nazi Youth policy throughout the 1930s was directed at preparing young Germans for war. When war came the Nazis had a strong army, but the rest of their youth policy was badly harmed. The best leaders of the Hitler Youth went away into the army, leaving the organisation in the hands of teenagers. The Hitler Youth concentrated exclusively on military affairs. Members got fed up with being policed and told what to do by people hardly older than themselves.

In several ways the Hitler Youth became less and less attractive and many young people turned away from it. These young people often formed gangs or groups. There were two main 'alternative' or opposition groups – the 'Edelweiss Pirates' and the 'Swing Youth'.

SOURCE 2 The sixth-form class at a grammar school pose for the camera, 23 September 1939. Half of them would be killed in action in the Second World War. Their teacher was captured by the Russians at the end of the war and never returned

'Swing Youth'

These were middle-class youths who wanted to dance and listen to swing music which was a blend of black jazz and white dance-band music. During the war 'swing clubs' sprang up in most big cities where members met in cafés and night-clubs. They wore English-style clothes, particularly sports jackets, girls wore make-up and Jews were accepted into their groups. A common greeting was 'Heil Benny' after the band leader Benny Goodman. The Nazis were outraged and tried to stamp out such behaviour. Some of these young people were harshly punished – such as Hasso Schutzendorff, who in October 1942 was put in a concentration camp, had his hair cut off, was thrashed with an iron bar and forced to push trolleys full of earth uphill for a fortnight.

SOURCE 3 A Hitler Youth report on a swing festival in 1940

66 *The dance music was all English and American. Only swing dancing and jitterbugging took place. The dancers made an appalling sight … long hair flopping into the face, they dragged themselves round practically on their knees.* 99

SOURCE 4 One of the 'Swing Youths' summed up their aim in a letter to a friend

66 *Make sure you're really casual, swinging or whistling English hits all the time, absolutely smashed and always surrounded by really amazing women.* 99

1. Identify six things about the 'Swing Youth' that the Nazis would dislike.
2. Which of these do you think most annoyed the Nazis?

'Edelweiss Pirates'

The edelweiss flower was a symbol of opposition adopted by many groups of working-class youths. Groups such as the 'Roving Dudes' and the 'Navajos' all regarded themselves as 'Edelweiss Pirates'. They included girls and boys. At weekends they would go on hikes, meet other groups, camp, sing, talk and hope to beat up Hitler Youth patrols.

SOURCE 5 A report by a mining instructor, 1941

66 *Every child knows who the Pirates are. They are everywhere. And they all know each other, they beat up the Hitler Youth patrols. They don't agree with anything. They don't go to work either.* 99

Some of the 'Edelweiss Pirates' also got involved in direct opposition to the Nazis. In Cologne the 'Navajos' sheltered army deserters and concentration camp escapees, and attacked military targets and Nazi officials. A group of them killed the head of the Cologne Gestapo but were caught soon afterwards and executed in November 1944.

SOURCE 6 The public hanging of twelve 'Edelweiss Pirates' in Cologne, 1944

The 'White Rose' Group

This group was led by Munich students. During the war they distributed leaflets attacking the Nazis' slaughter of the Jews and Poles, and urged Germans not to help the war effort. In 1943 most of the leaders were captured and executed.

SOURCE 7 'White Rose' group members Hans and Sophie Scholl and Christoph Probst

SOURCE 8 A leaflet by the 'White Rose' group warned:

66 *Hitler cannot win the war. He can only prolong it. The German people see nothing and hear nothing … The German name will remain for ever dishonoured unless German youth rises at last to crush its torturers.* 99

3. Which of these groups do you think the Nazis feared most?
4. How is this shown in the way each group was treated?

Case study 2: Dietrich Bonhoeffer

Source 9 puts together some of the words of Dietrich Bonhoeffer. What sort of a person do you think he was?

SOURCE 9

❝ *I pray for a defeat of my Fatherland. Only through a defeat can we atone for the terrible crimes which we have committed against Europe and the world.*

The question is really: Christianity or Germanism? and the sooner the conflict is revealed in the clear light of day, the better.

Hitler is the Anti-Christ. We must therefore continue with our work and root him out. ❞

At a time when many Church leaders in Germany actively supported or at best failed to oppose the Nazis, Bonhoeffer's Christian faith led him to act against the Nazis, resulting in his death in a concentration camp a few days before the defeat of Germany.

Bonhoeffer believed that Christianity could not accept Nazi racist views; that churchmen had to be free to preach against the Nazis; and that Christians had a duty to resist Hitler and help victims of Nazi persecution.

Early opposition
From the early 1930s Bonhoeffer consistently preached and published his views against the Nazis. In 1935 he campaigned against the Nuremberg Laws. However, he failed to get even the Confessional Church (which was supposed to be anti-Nazi) to oppose them. In 1937 the Gestapo closed his training college and banned him from preaching.

He joins the Abwehr
Bonhoeffer joined the underground resistance with his brother Klaus and his brother-in-law Hans von Dohnanyi. They secretly gathered evidence of Nazi crimes.

In 1939 Bonhoeffer became involved in the Abwehr, the German army counter-intelligence service within which a secret group was working to overthrow Hitler. He helped devise the plan code-named 'Operation 7', the aim of which was to help a small number of Jews to escape from Germany. The excuse was that the Jews were needed for propaganda work in Switzerland, to show the world that there was no foundation to the allegations of cruelty to the German Jews. The plan eventually succeeded. Gradually Bonhoeffer became more involved in the plot to assassinate Hitler.

Bonhoeffer made contact with the British government to ask if they would negotiate a peace with the conspirators if they could overthrow Hitler. The British wanted unconditional surrender and were not convinced the group could succeed and so refused to make an agreement with them.

He is arrested
Nevertheless Bonhoeffer continued his resistance, but in October 1942 a stroke of bad luck led to his arrest. The Gestapo arrested a member of the Abwehr, for currency smuggling. When interrogated the man revealed the names of others in the Abwehr who were plotting against Hitler. Bonhoeffer's brother-in-law was one of them. Eventually von Dohnanyi, Bonhoeffer and his brother Klaus were arrested.

Bonhoeffer was placed in solitary confinement, given stinking blankets and denied soap and water or clean clothes. The guards were forbidden to talk to him and he was fed on dry bread thrown onto the cell floor through a slit in the door.

Concentration camp
Hitler was becoming increasingly alarmed by plots to kill him and in 1944 Bonhoeffer was transferred to a concentration camp. He continued to write letters, poems and essays. Fellow prisoners wrote remarkable descriptions of how, even in the camp, Bonhoeffer preached the word of God and resistance to the Nazis.

On 8 April 1945 Bonhoeffer was put on trial in Flossenburg concentration camp. The trial lasted half an hour. The sentence was death by hanging. It was carried out at dawn the next day. The SS doctor who witnessed the execution later wrote: 'in nearly fifty years as a doctor I never saw another man go to his death so possessed of the spirit of God'.

■ TASK

'As the war progressed, opponents of the Nazis became increasingly desperate and the Nazis increasingly cruel in their methods of dealing with them.' Explain whether you agree or disagree with this statement, referring back to pages 88–93 as well as to the sources and information on the last three pages.

The July Bomb Plot, 1944

IN 1943 AND 1944 there were several different groups plotting to kill Hitler. This is the story of the attempt in July 1944 – the closest any plotters came to succeeding.

1. Why might anyone want to plot against Hitler? List as many reasons as you can.
2. What kind of problems would such plotters face?

Why did army leaders try to kill Hitler in 1944?

You might expect that Jews and members of other groups persecuted by the Nazis would be the first to plot against Hitler. However, the most serious attempt on his life came from within the ranks of the army. Hitler had always had his critics in the army, but while the war seemed to be going his way – and in fact Germany had enjoyed enormous success – they kept quiet. There was an undercover group which worked with Dietrich Bonhoeffer (see opposite) to topple Hitler. However, by 1943 the war was going disastrously wrong for Germany and for the first time opposition to Hitler within the army became significant.

In 1944 opposition centred on a group led by General Ludwig Beck and a civilian conservative politician, Dr Carl Goerdeler. They backed plans by Count von Stauffenberg to assassinate Hitler.

SOURCE 1 Colonel Klaus Philip Schenk, Count von Stauffenberg

Why did von Stauffenberg want to kill Hitler?

In the 1930s von Stauffenberg had been a Nazi supporter. He had welcomed the Nazis as the only group who could eliminate the Communists.

During the war Colonel von Stauffenberg fought in France, Russia and north Africa. In 1942 he was seriously wounded and lost his left eye, his right arm and two fingers of his left hand.

The suffering of the German army in Russia and the brutality of the SS finally pushed him to plot to kill Hitler.

> **SOURCE 2** A description of von Stauffenberg from T. Prittie, *Germans against Hitler*, 1964
>
> 66 *All those who knew von Stauffenberg praised him as a man of compelling charm. He was a devout Roman Catholic … and was disgusted by the Nazis' anti-semitic campaign. In May 1943 he told his wife, 'You know, I feel I must do something now, to save Germany. We General Staff officers must all accept our share of responsibility.' From this decision he never turned back.* 99

3. Do your answers to question 1 correspond with von Stauffenberg's reasons for plotting against Hitler?

Operation Valkyrie

Von Stauffenberg prepared 'Operation Valkyrie'. The plan was to use two bombs in a briefcase to kill Hitler and then seize control of Berlin using the army. The problem was how to get close to Hitler.

On 26 December 1943 von Stauffenberg was summoned to the daily conference at Hitler's headquarters at Rastenburg, hidden deep in a forest in eastern Germany. Von Stauffenberg placed a time bomb in his briefcase but at the last moment Hitler decided to spend the Christmas holiday elsewhere.

In June 1944 von Stauffenberg was appointed Chief of Staff to General Fromm, the Commander-in-Chief of the Home Army. This meant von Stauffenberg would have regular access to Hitler. The plotting continued throughout July 1944, but without success:

11 July 1944: Von Stauffenberg took a bomb with him to a military conference in Bavaria but his fellow plotters told him not to go ahead with the assassination attempt as they also wanted to kill Himmler who was not there.

15 July: Von Stauffenberg attended another conference at Rastenburg but Hitler left early, before the bomb could be primed.

17 July: Hitler called for the arrest of Carl Goerdeler, a key figure in the plot. He managed to avoid capture, but time was running out for the plotters.

20 July: Von Stauffenberg was to attend another military conference at Rastenburg. This is how events developed.

6 a.m.
Von Stauffenberg drives to Rangsdorf air field.

7 a.m.
His plane takes off. In his briefcase is a bomb wrapped in a shirt. His adjutant, Lieutenant von Haeften, carries a reserve bomb. Both bombs were made in England and have a silent fuse, which is set off by breaking a glass capsule of acid. It would take the acid about ten minutes to dissolve a wire which releases the firing pin. To break the glass capsule Stauffenberg has a specially modified pair of pliers which he can hold in his three remaining fingers.

10.15 a.m.
Von Stauffenberg's plane arrives. The pilot is ordered to be ready to take them back to Berlin at any moment. They drive the nine miles to Hitler's headquarters and pass through three SS security checkpoints. Once inside they eat breakfast and then meet General Fellgiebel. He is another vital member of the plot as he is Chief of Signals at Rastenburg and is to inform the other plotters in Berlin of the result of the attempt on Hitler's life, and then cut off all communications with the outside world for as long as possible. This will allow von Stauffenberg to escape and the conspirators in Berlin to round up the SS before they know what is happening.

12.30 p.m.
The conference is brought forward half an hour to 12.30 p.m. Mussolini, the Italian leader, is to visit Hitler the same afternoon. Usually the meeting takes place in an underground room. Today is very hot and instead a one-storey building

made of wood and concrete will be used. The room is ten metres long and five metres across, and has ten windows, all of which are open. The power of the explosion will be more dispersed in such a room. The bomb will need to be close to Hitler. Von Stauffenberg and General Keitel begin the three-minute walk to the conference room. Von Stauffenberg deliberately leaves behind his cap and belt and has to hurry back alone to collect them. He breaks the bomb's acid capsule; the time detonator is running. Von

Stauffenberg rejoins Keitel who suspects nothing. They enter the conference building.

12.36 p.m.
Von Stauffenberg stops to tell the soldier operating the telephone switchboard he is expecting an urgent call from Berlin with information for his report to Hitler. This will give him an excuse to leave the conference room after planting the bomb. He and Keitel are late and the meeting has begun. Four minutes of the bomb fuse have been eaten away.

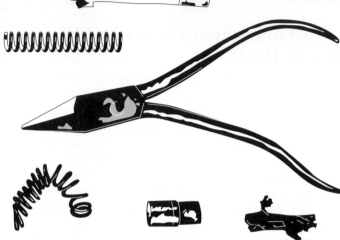

SOURCE 4
Plan of Hitler's headquarters at Rastenburg

Air-raid shelter

Mesh wire enclosures

Sentry

Hitler's bunker

Car park

Railway station

Conference room

Cinema

Sentry

Kitchen

Checkpoint II

Cement store

Checkpoint III

Officers' post

Barbed wire and trench

Minefield

Stauffenberg's escape route
→ on foot
▪▪▶ by car

SOURCE 5
Plan of the conference room at Rastenburg

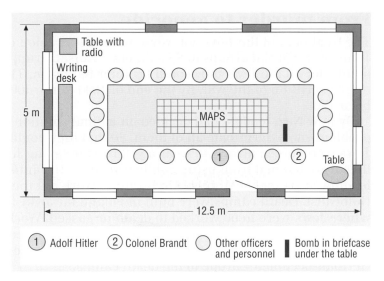

1 Adolf Hitler   2 Colonel Brandt   ◯ Other officers and personnel   ▮ Bomb in briefcase under the table

12.37 p.m.
Von Stauffenberg enters the room. Maps and diagrams are spread on the table which stands on two huge oak supports. There are 34 people already in the room. General Heusinger is in the middle of a gloomy report on the war in Russia. Keitel announces von Stauffenberg's arrival, and Hitler glances at the man with one arm and a patch over one eye. Heusinger continues.

12.38 p.m.
Von Stauffenberg puts the briefcase under the table close to where Colonel Brandt is sitting (see Source 5). Hitler is three places to the left, about four metres away.

12.40 p.m.
Von Stauffenberg makes his excuse – he needs to make an urgent phone call. Nobody suspects anything. Von Stauffenberg walks away from the building, lights a cigarette and waits. Back at the meeting Colonel Brandt leans forward to study the map, and he catches von Stauffenberg's briefcase with his foot. He picks it up and places it the other side of the heavy oak table support from Hitler. Keitel leaves the room to find von Stauffenberg.

SOURCE 6 The conference room after the explosion

12.42 p.m.
Heusinger is finishing his report: 'If our army group around Lake Pepius is not immediately withdrawn, a catastrophe ...' The bomb explodes. Bodies fly out of the windows. The roof falls in. People scream. Von Stauffenberg leaps into his car and bluffs his way past the guard posts. Hitler staggers out of the building. He is injured but still alive. His hair is singed, his right leg badly burned and his right arm is temporarily paralysed. His eardrums are damaged and his clothes are in tatters. By moving the briefcase Colonel Brandt has almost certainly saved Hitler's life. Four of those present were killed.

1.10 p.m.
Von Stauffenberg's plane is airborne and he is on his way back to Berlin for the next phase of the revolt. He believes Hitler is dead.

The aftermath
Historians are not sure what happened next. Von Stauffenberg's fellow plotters in Berlin failed to act quickly and seize Berlin. Whether they were informed that Hitler was dead or still alive is not known for certain. When von Stauffenberg arrived in Berlin very little had been done to put Operation Valkyrie into effect; troops had not been mobilised, and radio, telephone and telegraph networks had not been seized. Von Stauffenberg and Beck tried to seize control of the city. They sent troops to seize key sites and arrested army leaders who would not co-operate, but by 9 p.m. the plot had failed.

Back at Rastenburg Hitler warned:

SOURCE 7

❝ I will crush and destroy the criminals who have dared to oppose me. I'll put their wives and children into concentration camps and show them no mercy. ... These traitors deserve death and this is what they shall have. They will be exterminated once and for all. ❞

Von Stauffenberg, Beck and some of the other leading plotters were quickly executed. Hitler had his revenge – nearly 5000 of his opponents were killed by shooting, hanging, garrotting or torture.

■ ACTIVITY

It is 20 July 1944. Write a radio speech to be broadcast at 4.30 p.m. by either:
a) Stauffenberg when his plane arrives in Berlin
or
b) Hitler.

SHORTLY BEFORE THE war, persecution of the Jews had increased (see page 109). The war turned persecution into mass murder and genocide. Six million Jews and many other people who the Nazis wanted to get rid of were murdered. These events are usually known as the Holocaust, although the Jews themselves use the word Shoah.

When Germany invaded Poland in 1939 another three million Jews came under Nazi control. The war made it impossible to remove the Jews by emigration, so a huge Jewish reservation was planned in Poland. This idea was soon dropped and instead Jews were herded into ghettos in towns in eastern Poland. They were transported there from Germany. Walls were built to keep them in. The Germans allowed them only starvation rations and thousands died from hunger, the intense cold or the disease typhus. The largest ghetto was in Warsaw where 500,000 Jews died.

From murder to genocide

The treatment of the Jews got worse with the invasion of Russia in June 1941. Special groups of SS soldiers – Einsatzgruppen – were sent to murder all the Jews they could lay their hands on. This was the first mass execution of the war. By the end of 1941 some 500,000 Jews had been shot.

By now Nazi leaders had decided on a 'final solution' to their Jewish problem – to exterminate all of them. So that they could not escape, Jews were forced always to wear a yellow star saying Jew on it, and they were banned from using public transport. In January 1942 leading Nazis met at Wannsee in Berlin to work out the details of the Holocaust. Death camps were built in Poland far away from Germany where Jews were to be worked to death or gassed. Work on building gas chambers and crematoria at camps was accelerated.

A massive operation got under way to move Jews from all over German-occupied Europe to the death camps.

1. Why were the camps built far away from Germany?

SOURCE 1 Hungry children in the Warsaw ghetto

SOURCE 2 Map showing concentration and death camps and major 'euthanasia' centres

SOURCE 3 Kurt Gerstein was a young SS officer who opposed the Nazi regime and secretly tried to pass on information, and sabotage the extermination programme. He witnessed the gassing at Belzec death camp in August 1942 and wrote this account in May 1945, shortly before committing suicide. He describes an early gassing using diesel gases which were later replaced by 'Zyklon B' (hydrogen cyanide)

The train arrives: 200 Ukrainians fling open the doors and chase people out of the wagons with their leather whips. Instructions come from a large loudspeaker: 'Undress completely, including artificial limbs, spectacles etc. Give your valuables up at the counter. Tie your shoes together carefully.' Then the women and girls have to go to the hairdressers who, with two or three snips of the scissors, cut off all their hair and put it in potato sacks.

Then the procession starts to move – all naked, men, women and children, cripples. Mothers with their babies at their breast, come up, hesitate, enter the death chambers. A tough SS man tells the poor people: 'Nothing is going to happen to you. Just breathe in deeply in the chambers. It will strengthen your lungs. This is necessary because of all the sickness ... ' But the majority understand what is happening, the smell reveals their fate to them ... They climb the staircase, hesitate, but they enter the death chambers, driven on by the others behind them or by the leather whips of the SS ... People are treading on each other's toes. Seven to eight hundred in an area of twenty-five square metres. The SS push them in as far as possible. The doors shut, the others are waiting outside in the open, naked ... The people are going to be killed by diesel exhaust gases. But the diesel engine won't start! . . .The people wait in their gas chambers. One can hear them crying, sobbing ... After two hours forty-nine minutes the engine starts ... one can see through the little peepholes. After thirty-two minutes they are all dead.

The dead stand like basalt [rock] pillars pressed together in the chambers. There is no room to fall or even to lean over. Even in death one can tell which are the families. They are holding hands in death and it is difficult to tear them apart in order to empty the chambers for the next batch. The corpses are thrown out wet with sweat and urine, smeared with excrement. The corpses of children fly through the air ... dentists tear out the gold teeth and crowns with pincers and hammers ... Some of the workers check the genitals and anus for gold, diamonds and valuables.

The naked corpses are carried on wooden stretchers only a few metres to the ditches which are 100 × 20 × 12 metres in size. After a few days, the corpses swell up and then collapse so that one can throw another layer on top of this one. Then ten centimetres of sand are strewn on the top so that only the occasional heads or arms stick out.

SOURCE 4 Captain Robert Daniel, a tank commander, discovered Belsen concentration camp in April 1945. On smashing through the gates in his tank he found the following horrors – which he recalled in 1995

A trench 150 yards long, and filled with naked bodies. Parts of the corpses kept moving. You would see an arm rise, then a leg, sometimes whole bodies would come to the surface. This was the natural gases and acids from the bodies at work ...

The camp hospital, a hangar full of bunk beds eight tiers high. Every bed was occupied, but 90 per cent of the patients were dead, many of them drowned in excreta from the beds above. All had been too weak to move. The sight and the smell were completely appalling, they were all completely naked ...

In the third hangar ... the swollen, naked body of a woman, five or six days dead, and sitting on it, playing at drawing lots with straw, were a group of young children ... At the perimeter fence ... a group of prisoners who had attempted to escape were caught on the wire. Six Hitler Youths were amusing themselves by shooting them, not to kill but to cause most pain. They were shooting the men in the balls and the women in the crotch. It was an unspeakable sight. I shot four of the Hitler Youth and the other two ran away ... There were worn paths to each of the gas chambers and on the side, a pile of spectacles at least six feet high ... There were at least 3000 inmates still just alive. They were all starving, and skeletons to look at. The irony of the whole thing was that outside the wire lay the most fertile part of the German Rhineland, with fields of potatoes and green vegetables of every kind.

Some children and adults were used for hideous medical experiments. For example, in 1945 a doctor called Heissmeyer injected virulent tuberculosis organisms into twenty French and Russian Jewish children aged between five and twelve years; they became seriously ill, were injected with morphia and then, in the words of an assistant, they were 'hung like pictures around the walls until they died'.

Nearly six million Jews were killed. There were also countless other victims: political opponents of the Nazis, homosexuals, Jehovah's Witnesses, 'anti-social elements', Russian prisoners of war and Gypsies. Of the 30,000 Gypsies in Germany only 5000 survived the war. In all about 500,000 European Gypsies were murdered by the Nazis.

■ TASK

Britain's wartime Prime Minister Winston Churchill called the Holocaust 'the most horrible crime ever committed in the whole history of the world'. How did it happen? What led to it? How did the Nazis move from persecution to mass murder?

Sources 5–11 show some of the steps in the Nazi persecution of the Jews which led to the 'Final Solution'.

1. Divide them into two groups: sources from before the war and sources from during the war.
2. Explain the context for each source and what led to the event shown or described.
3. Then use the sources to write your own account of how and why the Nazi persecution of the Jews began and how it escalated to its terrifying conclusion.

SOURCE 5 1930. 'Jews are not wanted here': a banner in the village of Rosenheim, Bavaria

SOURCE 6 1940. A poem by Eva Pickova, a twelve-year-old living in the Warsaw ghetto

66 *FEAR*
Today the ghetto knows a different fear,
Close in its grip, Death wields an icy scythe.
An evil sickness spreads a terror in its wake.
The victims of its shadow weep and writhe.

Today a father's heartbeat tells his fright
And mothers bend their heads into their hand.
Now children choke and die with typhus here,
A bitter tax is taken from their bands. 99

SOURCE 7 April 1933. SA Stormtroopers plaster the window of a Jewish-owned shop with posters to persuade people not to buy from it

SOURCE 8 April 1945. Buchenwald concentration camp is liberated. There was no active extermination policy here, but some 63,500 inmates died

SOURCE 9 1924. In *Mein Kampf* Hitler wrote:

66 *The existence of our own nation is a thousand times more important to us than an alien race … Had we put under poison gas, before the [First World] War or during its course, 12,000 or 15,000 or more of those Hebrew [Jewish] corrupters, we would have saved a million German lives so dear for the future.* 99

How did the Jews resist?

SOURCE 12 Jews in Hungary are taken away for transportation

SOURCE 10 1942. A gas chamber in Auschwitz death camp

Photos such as Source 12 give the impression that Jews did not resist death at the hands of the Nazis. Indeed many did not; families wanted to stay together as long as possible and die in dignity. Others, however, did resist even though it was futile against such overwhelming odds. Some Jews who escaped the Nazi round-ups fought in resistance (partisan) groups and attacked German soldiers.

In Poland there were at least 28 groups of Jewish fighters. Armed resistance developed in nearly all the large ghettos – the longest struggle was in Warsaw where some 15,000 Jews armed with makeshift weapons held out for four weeks against a Nazi force twice their size and vastly better armed. When their resistance ended some fighters took their own lives, while others escaped through the sewers. There were also armed uprisings in five concentration camps. In Auschwitz, Greek Jews blew up one of the gas ovens.

Resistance did not only mean fighting the Nazis. In the ghettos and camps Jews could resist in many ways, as is shown by Sources 13 and 14, which were written by children.

SOURCE 11 1942. Jews in Poland are rounded up and murdered by SS Einsatzgruppe soldiers

SOURCE 13 A young resistance fighter, Chaim Lazar, wrote:

66 *Struggling to stay alive another day was a form of resistance. Escaping from the ghetto or hiding in a bunker was resistance. Resistance was giving birth to a child in the ghetto, sharing food with others, praying in a congregation, singing in a chorus, studying the Bible, planting flowers in the ghetto, keeping a diary under the shadow of death.* 99

SOURCE 14 Another young resistance fighter remembered:

66 *When we attacked we would move like lightning, and I used to shoot Germans on the left and on the right. Sometimes I threw grenades at them. The best thing was the dynamite, though with dynamite we always worked at night. We used to creep on all fours to the railway tracks, attach the wires and hide them. Then we hid in the bushes and behind the trees and waited for the train whistle. Sometimes they let me light the fuse. You had to time it just right, so that the whole train would go boom!* 99

1. Why do you think the Jews resisted when the odds against them were so overwhelming?

CONCLUSION

'Alone in a silent ghost town': the experiences of Christabel Bielenberg

■ SOURCE INVESTIGATION

Christabel Bielenberg was English but married a young German lawyer, Peter Bielenberg, in 1934. They lived in Germany until 1945. They were opposed to the Nazis and Peter was arrested after the July Bomb Plot in 1944, but he was released shortly before the end of the war. During the war Christabel and her children were evacuated to different parts of Germany. These are extracts from her book *The Past is Myself* (1968).

You are going to use them as a way of revising the material you have studied.

1. Can you name two of the political parties with fighting units that Christabel refers to in Source 1?
2. Who were the Stormtroopers referred to in Source 2?
3. Who do you think were being chased by the Stormtroopers in Source 3?
4. How do Sources 4 and 5 help us understand why people voted for Hitler?
5. What does Christabel mean when she refers to a 'phoney religion' in Source 5?
6. Can you date the events described in Source 6 by what happened to Professor Bauer?
7. What event is Source 7 describing?
8. Do you think as a Block Warden Herr Neisse (Source 8) was of any importance in the Nazi control of the people?
9. Who suffered most and who suffered least due to rationing (Source 9)?
10. Explain why the German and British reports in Source 10 differed so much.
11. What are the brown uniforms referred to in Source 12 and why were they being given to the Winter Help charity when clothes were rationed?
12. Do you think the bombing as remembered in Source 11 was the worst experience of the war for most Germans?

SOURCE 1

❝ In 1932 I thought I understood just about all I would ever understand about politics in Germany. I could recite the names of half a dozen of the innumerable political parties, and recognise the various uniforms of the Kampfverbande, which were the fighting units attached to these parties.

I had also learned, by 1932, that no government in Germany remained in power longer than a few months, because no single party or coalition of parties could ever muster enough votes to enable them to govern. ❞

SOURCE 2

❝ Autumn 1932. Hitler himself was to speak to an open-air rally. A huge area had been cordoned off, and rows of burly Stormtroopers wedged the milling crowds into orderly rectangles ... community singing, the rolling of drums, the National and Party anthems ... Peter said, 'You may think that Germans are political idiots, Chris, and you may be right, but of one thing I can assure you, they won't be so stupid as to fall for that clown.' ❞

SOURCE 3

❝ It was an incident in May 1933 which made Peter apprehensive about the future. He was strolling across the Lombardsbrücke ... when there was a sudden commotion and two small figures came running towards him. They were clutching briefcases, sweating and obviously terrified, darting and dodging like hares in and out through the passing traffic. Several hefty Stormtroopers followed panting on their heels. ❞

SOURCE 4

66 The change of scene when I returned in 1935 [after a year in England] came not only from the fact that the cheerful hikers were now dressed in uniform of a particularly nasty colour, that the boys' hair was clipped much shorter and the girls had grown rather massive plaits, nor from the small moustaches 'au Führer' on the upper lips of so many, nor the ... hideous Nazi flag which fluttered and flapped from every public building. It seemed to me that the change lay deeper. Street fighting, unemployment, fear of civil war, fear of another inflation had been burning problems when I left; when I returned they no longer seemed to exist. Instead a certain air of modest prosperity pervaded the streets. Manners in public (never a very strong point in Germany) had improved beyond recognition. I did not find that everyone I met was enthusiastic about every aspect of the regime, they were not; but most were ready to admit that there was quite a lot to be said for the New Order, and deemed it an improvement on what had gone before. 99

SOURCE 5

66 Hitler understood his Germans well. There was a titbit for all in his political stew pot. Work for the unemployed, an army for the generals, a phoney religion for the gullible, a loud, insistent and not unheeded voice in international affairs for those who still smarted under the indignity of a lost war: there were also detention camps and carefully broadcast hints of what might be in store for anyone who had temerity enough to enquire into his methods too closely, let alone openly disapprove of them. 99

SOURCE 7

66 It was rumoured that many arrests were made in the night and that there were many dead, and whoever was in town early that morning brought back the news that gangs of young ruffians, obviously working to orders, had systematically moved from shop to shop, smashing windows and hurling the wares into the streets. No passer-by had thought of trying their hand at looting; the glass, the toys, the coats, the shoes and the handbags lay strewn about the pavements until the shopkeepers came out to sweep them aside in the morning.

I was often in town during the following week, in the shops and in the trams; all eyes and ears as befits an incurable busybody. No one to whom I spoke rejoiced in the shambles; on the contrary, those who were supposed to have been spontaneous about it stood around the newspaper kiosks registering puzzlement, perturbation, even disgust. 99

SOURCE 6

66 Professor Bauer looked after our children. He was a dedicated paediatrician but he found time one night to sit with me for long hours at the bedside, while Nicholas, our eldest son, tossed with fever. Towards morning Nicky lay peacefully sleeping. Professor Bauer hesitated before leaving the house and then asked me quietly if I still wished for him to attend my family. I was tired; he had to explain ... he was a Jew. 'I am no longer a German citizen,' he explained. One thing he felt I should know. He had received threatening letters bidding him to keep his hands off Aryan children ... I called at his flat some weeks later, to find that he had gone to Holland. 99

SOURCE 8

66 Autumn 1939. Herr Neisse was not only our occasional gardener, but also our Block Warden, the Party representative in our immediate neighbourhood. Besides pruning trees, mowing lawns and sweeping up leaves, he collected Party subscriptions, sold emblems for the newly launched Winter Help campaign – postcards, pamphlets, any odd or end which might help to swell the Party coffers. He was also supposed to send reports on the behaviour of his flock to Party Headquarters, so that careful record might be kept of just who failed to hang out their flag and when, or just how much and how willingly so and so had contributed to the Cause. 99

SOURCE 9

Winter 1939–40. On market days I always had to bestir myself very early indeed, the reason being that I had not lived long enough in Berlin to have my Quellen – my sources of supply as they were called; and as soon as food rationing was introduced, everything that was not on the ration cards disappeared like magic from every shop counter and out of every shop window. Unless you were known to some shopkeeper, therefore, some wholesaler or better still farmer, and were able to come to a deal … The rationing system in Berlin was chaotic … The children and I would travel all over Berlin on the look-out for a shop or a market stall where we could buy our wares a few pfennigs cheaper.

SOURCE 10

Summer 1941. It had been little use pretending that the British accounts of those raids, recited for us the following day on Radio Beromünster – 'Strong forces of RAF bombers attacked selected military targets in the Berlin area, light installations, aero engine factories etc.' – were nearer to the truth than the German reports, which recorded the targets hit as being exclusively morgues, churches or children's hospitals. The damage actually caused, according to market hearsay, had proved barely exciting enough to justify the bus fare for a family outing of a Sunday afternoon, but the significance of the raids lay in the indisputable fact that, night after night, those 'air pirates' gave the lie to the official word that the war was as good as won.

SOURCE 11

Autumn 1943. There was no moon, and there were three air raids in the three nights that I was in Berlin. The bombs fell indiscriminately on Nazis and anti-Nazis, on women and children and works of art, on dogs and pet canaries. New and more ravaging bombs – blockbusters and incendiaries, and phosphorus bombs which burst and glowed green and emptied themselves down the walls and along the streets in flaming rivers of unquenchable flame, seeping down cellar stairs, and sealing the exits to the air-raid shelters. Carl [a neighbour and close friend who had helped hide Jews and was arrested by the Gestapo] had an air-raid trench dug between our two gardens before he was arrested, but he had not had time to cover the tin roof with earth, so every night his mother and I sat together in that trench, listening to the shrapnel splinters bouncing off the roof like vicious hailstones. Carl's mother wore a huge steel helmet during the raids – she looked like a ghost robin, but she would not leave Berlin because she did not wish to be far from her son.

SOURCE 12

Autumn 1944. There's hardly a Nazi to be seen these days. Most of the voluntary offerings for the last Winter Help clothing collection consisted of brown uniforms. The rats are leaving the sinking ship and your enemies have been reduced to old men and schoolboys.

SOURCE 13

Winter 1945. When I reached the Gedächtnisplatz [in Berlin] I was surrounded by a frozen sea of shattered ruins. I had never seen bombing like it before. In the Budapesterstrasse house after house was an empty shell, not one single building had survived. The rubble had been neatly stacked to the gaping windows of the first floors. The centre of Berlin. Capital of Hitler's mighty empire which, he had boasted, would last a thousand years, and I was alone in a silent ghost town.

■ TASK

Imagine you are with Christabel Bielenberg among the ruins of the once great city.

What would you say about how the disaster happened? Write your own account of the rise and fall of Germany under the Nazis, from the enthusiasm of the election victories of 1932 to the bitter defeat of 1945. In your account include your own assessment of:

1. How the Nazis came to power
2. What they attempted to do once they were in power
3. Whether they achieved their objectives
4. What led to the fall of the Nazi regime.

Glossary

anti-semitism hatred of Jews

Aryan Nazi term for a non-Jewish German, for someone of supposedly 'pure' Germanic stock. Correctly used, the term Aryan means a member of the peoples who speak an Indo-European language

censorship examination by authority (e.g. state) of books, newspapers, plays, broadcasts, films, etc. and the suppression of anything considered irreligious, obscene or against the state. Under the Kaiser, censorship had been strict; the Weimar government was liberal, allowing artists free expression; the Nazis censored every aspect of German life on a scale never known before

Chancellor in Germany, the chief minister in the government

constitution the rules by which a state is governed

demobilise to disband troops, particularly after a war

dictatorship one-party state, governed by an absolute ruler; the opposite of a democracy, where the people choose the government and opposing views are tolerated

elite a select, privileged group

euthanasia the bringing about of death to relieve suffering. The Nazis secretly carried out a policy of compulsory 'euthanasia', by cruel and inhuman methods, to kill mentally and physically handicapped people

Führer leader; the title adopted by Adolf Hitler

genocide deliberate extermination of a whole race or nation

Gleichschaltung co-ordination. The Nazis used the word for their policy of controlling all organisations, at every level of society

hyperinflation rapidly accelerating inflation where prices rise ten- or even a hundred-fold in a single month

Kaiser the German emperor

Lebensraum living space. The 'need' of the German people for living space was Hitler's justification for his conquest of other countries

plebiscite a vote by all the people on an important issue: for example, a change to the constitution

Putsch sudden armed uprising, a political revolt

Reich the German empire

Reichstag the German Parliament

reparations compensation for war damage demanded by the Allied powers after Germany's defeat in the First World War

SA Abbreviation for *Sturm-Abteilung*, Stormtroopers, the force of thugs set up by Hitler in 1921 to intimidate his political opponents

SS Abbreviation for *Schutz-Staffel*, 'protection squad'. Originally the private bodyguard for Hitler and other Nazi leaders, the SS later became the main instrument of terror in Nazi Germany

totalitarian a state in which every aspect of people's lives is controlled and monitored by those in power

Volk people; in particular, the German people

Wall Street Crash In 1929, share prices fell disastrously on the New York stock exchange (known as Wall Street from its location). It was followed by worldwide economic collapse and the Depression of the 1930s

Acknowledgements

The authors and publishers would like to thank Christabel Bielenberg and Transworld Publishers Ltd for permission to reproduce extracts from *The Past is Myself*; and Scholastic Ltd for permission to reproduce extracts from *A Boy in your Situation* By Charles Hannam.

Thanks are due to the following for permission to reproduce copyright photographs:

p.6 *t* Ullstein, *b* Süddeutscher Verlag Bilderdienst; **p.7** AKG Photo; **p.8** Robert Hunt Library; **p.9** *t* Bildarchiv Preussischer Kulturbesitz, *b* Hulton Getty; **p.11** Ullstein; **p.12** *t* Ullstein - ADN - Bildarchiv, *b* Ullstein; **p.13** *t & b* Bildarchiv Preussischer Kulturbesitz; **p.14** Bildarchiv Preussischer Kulturbesitz; **p.15** *t* Ullstein, *b* Bundesarchiv Koblenz; **p.18** *t* Mary Evans Picture Library, *c* Daily Herald/Newsgroup Newspapers, *b* Ullstein; **p.19** *t* Landesbildstelle Berlin, *bl* Imperial War Museum, London, *br* Bildarchiv Preussischer Kulturbesitz; **p.20** *t* Bildarchiv Preussischer Kulturbesitz, *b* Ullstein; **p.22** Süddeutscher Verlag Bilderdienst; **p.25** *t* Hulton Getty, *b* Süddeutscher Verlag Bilderdienst; **p.26** Evening Standard/Solo; **p.28** Staatliche Museen zu Berlin, Preussischer Kulturbesitz Nationalgalerie, © DACS 1997 (Photo: Bildarchiv Preussischer Kulturbesitz/J.P. Anders); **p.29** *t* Galerie der Stadt Stuttgart, © DACS 1997 (Photo: Bildarchiv Preussischer Kulturbesitz), *b* AKG Photo; **p.30** AKG/Hilbich; **p.31** *t* Ullstein - Bodo Niemann, *b* AKG Photo; **p.33** Ullstein; **p.36** *l* Bildarchiv Preussischer Kulturbesitz (Photo: Heinrich Hoffmann), *c & r* Süddeutscher Verlag Bilderdienst; **p.37** *t* Süddeutscher Verlag Bilderdienst, *b* Ullstein; **p.41** *t* Ullstein, *b* Süddeutscher Verlag Bilderdienst; **p.42** Bildarchiv Preussischer Kulturbesitz (Photo: H. Hoffmann); **p.43** Bildarchiv Preussischer Kulturbesitz; **p.45** *t* Bildarchiv Preussischer Kulturbesitz, *b* Ullstein; **p.47** *t* Süddeutscher Verlag Bilderdienst, *b* Ullstein; **p.48** *t* Ullstein, *b* Bildarchiv Preussischer Kulturbesitz; **p.49** AKG Photo; **p. 50** Popperfoto; **p. 52** *l* Bildarchiv Preussischer Kulturbesitz, *tr* Ullstein; **p.53** Bildarchiv Preussischer Kulturbesitz; **p.61** Archiv Gerstenberg; **p.62** Süddeutscher Verlag Bilderdienst; **p.63** Ullstein; **p.66** *b* Süddeutscher Verlag Bilderdienst; **p.71** Bildarchiv Preussischer Kulturbesitz; **p.73** London Evening Standard/Solo; **p.75** *t* AKG Photo, *b* U.S. Army Center of Military History, Washington D.C./AKG Photo; **p.76** AKG Photo; **p.80** Telegraph Colour Library; **p.89** *t* Bundesarchiv Koblenz, *b* Süddeutscher Verlag Bilderdienst; **p.90** *t* © Rudolf Meffert/Stern/Picture Press/SOA, *b* Süddeutscher Verlag Bilderdienst; **p.95** *t* Spaarnestad Fotoarchief/NFGC, *bl* Süddeutscher Verlag Bilderdienst, *br* Bundesarchiv Koblenz; **p.96** Archiv Gerstenberg; **p.97** Süddeutscher Verlag Bilderdienst; **p.100** *l* from 'Aktion T4' by H. von Gotz aly (Edition Hentrick, Berlin, 1987), *r* Süddeutscher Verlag Bilderdienst; **p.101** *l* from 'Rasse, Blut und Gene' by Weingart, Krol & Bayertz (Suhrkamp 1988), *r* photo: BFI Stills, Posters and Designs; **p.103** *t* Robert Hunt Library, *c* AKG Photo, *bl* Weimar Archive, *br* Süddeutscher Verlag Bilderdienst; **p.104** Bundesarchiv Koblenz; **p.105** Staatarchiv Bremen; **p.106** Sue Roberts; **p.107** Rijksinstituut voor Oorlogsdocumentatie, Amsterdam; **p.110** Süddeutscher Verlag Bilderdienst; **p.112** AKG Photo; **p.113** AKG photo; **p.114** *t* Bildarchiv Preussischer Kulturbesitz/Sanden, *b* Hulton Getty; **p.115** *t* Archiv Gerstenberg, *b* Bildarchiv Preussischer Kulturbesitz; **p.116** *t* AKG Photo, *bl* Archiv Gerstenberg, *br* Bauhaus-Archiv Berlin (photo: Reinhard Friedrich, Berlin); **p.117** *tl* AKG Photo, *tr* The University of Iowa Museum of Art, Purchase, Mark Ranney Memorial Fund, 1946.1, © DACS 1997, *bl* Ullstein, *br* Süddeutscher Verlag Bilderdienst; **p.118** Robert Hunt Library; **p.119** Ullstein - amw Pressedienst GmbH; **p.120** *b* AKG Photo; **p.121** *tl* Bayerische Staatsbibliothek, Munich/Heinrich Hoffmann, *tr* Bildarchiv Preussischer Kulturbesitz, *b* Weimar Archive; **p.123** *t* Bundesarchiv Koblenz, *b* Robert Hunt Library; **p.124** *t* Institut für Stadtgeschichte, Frankfurt am Main, *b* AKG Photo; **p.126** Weimar Archive; **p.127** Bildarchiv Preussischer Kulturbesitz/Hanns Hubmann; **p.132** *tl* Bildarchiv Preussischer Kulturbesitz/Wolff & Tritschler, *tr* Bildarchiv Preussischer Kulturbesitz, *cl* Bildarchiv Preussischer Kulturbesitz/Carl Weinrother, *cr & bl* Süddeutscher Verlag Bilderdienst, *br* Bildarchiv Preussischer Kulturbesitz/A. Grimm; **p.133** *tl & tr* Bundesarchiv Koblenz, *b* Weimar Archive; **p.134** Bildarchiv Preussischer Kulturbesitz/A. Grimm; **p.136** *t* Ullstein, *b* AKG Photo; **p.137** Archiv Gerstenberg; **p.139** Süddeutscher Verlag Bilderdienst; **p.142** Ullstein; **p.143** *t & b* Imperial War Museum, London; **p.145** Imperial War Museum, London; **p.146** *t, bl, bc* AKG Photo, *br* Bundesarchiv Koblenz; **p.147** *tl* Bundesarchiv Koblenz, *tc* Weimar Archive, *tr* Archiv Gerstenberg, *b* U.S. Army Center of Military History, Washington D.C./AKG Photo; **p.148** AKG Photo; **p.149** Archiv Gerstenberg; **p.150** © Rudolf Meffert/Stern/Picture Press/SOA; **p.151** *t* Süddeutscher Verlag Bilderdienst, *b* Ullstein; **p.152** Süddeutscher Verlag Bilderdienst; **p.153** AKG Photo; **p.155** Ullstein; **p.156** Robert Hunt Library; **p.158** *l* Imperial War Museum, London, *c* Robert Hunt Library, Imperial War Museum, London; **p.159** *tl* Rijksinstituut voor Oorlogsdocumentatie, Amsterdam, *tr* Weimar Archive, *b* Bildarchiv Preussischer Kulturbesitz; **p.160** Photo reproduced by kind permission of Christabel Bielenberg.

Every effort has been made to contact copyright holders, and the publishers apologise for any omissions which they will be pleased to rectify at the earliest opportunity.

Index